Brillia
Baby Names

Geoff and Laura King

Prentice Hall LIFE

If life is what you make it, then making it better starts here.

What we learn today can change our lives tomorrow. It can change our goals or change our minds; open up new opportunities or simply inspire us to make a difference. That's why we have created a new breed of books that do more to help you make more of *your* life.

Whether you want more confidence or less stress, a new skill or a different perspective, we've designed *Prentice Hall Life* books to help you to make a change for the better. Together with our authors we share a commitment to bring you the brightest ideas and the best ways to manage your life, work and wealth.

In these pages we hope you'll find the ideas you need for the life you want. Go on, help yourself.

It's what you make it.

* * *

Brilliant Baby Names

How to choose a name that you and your child will love for life

Geoff and Laura King

Pearson Education Limited
Edinburgh Gate
Harlow
Essex CM20 2JE
England

First published 2007

ISBN 978-0-273-71503-0

Commissioning Editor: Emma Shackleton
Project Editor: Cheryl Lanyon
Copy Editor: Cheryl Lanyon
Designer: Kathryn Gammon
Illustrations: Chris Long
Cover Design: R&D&Co
Production Controller: Franco Forgione

Printed and bound by Graificas Estella, Spain

The Publisher's policy is to use paper manufactured from sustainable forests.

Dedication

This book is dedicated to our three children, whose laughter gives us such joy.

Contents

Introduction

A name is often the first gift you give your child and it can affect their life chances rather more than most people realize. But how do you find a stress-free and enjoyable way to choose a name that you and your child will love for life?

Brilliant Baby Names shows you just how to do that. Whether you are seeking advice about how to choose a name, looking for inspiration or you want to find out the meaning of the names you have in mind, you will find what you're looking for.

There are many pitfalls to be avoided when choosing a name and the choices available to you will vary according to your surname – something that struck us both forcibly as we contemplated our married name of King and the arrival of our first son. What were we to call him? Wayne, Joe, Finn, Luke?

Names taken on marriage can also present pitfalls for the terminologically unwary, as happened to a childhood friend of ours, Cherry Ayres who, finding herself pregnant at 18, persuaded the father to do the honourable thing and found herself Cherry Perry. But, whatever name you have, this book will help make the process of choosing a name for your baby an enjoyable experience.

The book contains over 14,000 names and encompasses the traditional, the modern and the frankly striking. It lists names in common use and a large number of the more exotic, including those from many different countries and cultures. It also has advice on avoiding the common mistakes when choosing names, and it looks at recent scientific studies into the effects (both good and bad) that a name can have on a child's progress in life. Some of these studies suggest that particular names can improve a child's prospects in such areas as their future career, and even their attractiveness to the opposite sex. But which names have which effects? Again, this book gives you all the answers.

Along the way, you will discover why a court in Sweden banned the name Albin but allowed Metallica, and how Californian grandparents have taken to changing *their own* names on the birth of their first grandchild. You will see which names help a child get into university and what a name can reveal about the parents who chose it.

Brilliant Baby Names will help you pick a name that both you and your child will love for life. So, read on – because there are things in this book you will find both amusing and enthralling...

Beginners' guide to pitfalls

How **not** to fall out with your partner

Some parents naming their first child are taken aback by the acrimony it causes between them. The reason for it is that names touch on much deeper and more powerful emotions than most of us realize; and many parents were simply not expecting to encounter such feelings on the subject. For example, Richard might sound like a handsome name to you, but may have been the name of your partner's worst enemy in childhood – meaning they are likely to be emotionally hardwired against it.

When asked how *not* to fall out over a name, most family psychologists give the same first response. They point to the value of keeping tuned in to each other during disagreements; of staying on the same emotional wavelength when arguing. (In fact, most psychologists point to the ability to do this as one of the classic differences between an average marriage and a good one.)

What this means is quashing any urge to ridicule or put down your partner's choice of name, and not putting up a wall to them either. In the end, the only name you can choose is one you're both happy with. There have been cases of parents making secret visits to the registrar's office to secure their own choice of name. That certainly sorts out the naming problem; what it does to the relationship is likely to be less positive!

Often in marriage problems are caused not so much by the two partners as by the family baggage each brings to the relationship, and this applies to the choice of baby names, too.

Keep the family at bay

No doubt you are blessed by fate's allocation of parents-in-law, but spare a thought for those less fortunate. They are most likely to discover the dangers of sharing ideas for baby names with relatives before the baby is born. The problem is that members of extended families often have strong feelings about the name, and may well feel they have a 'right' or 'duty' to take a hand in the naming process. This is exactly the type of 'help' you can do without – and naming the baby after your father-in-law's first wife would be undiplomatic anyway! It's best,

'Being pregnant is an occupational hazard of being a wife.'

Queen Victoria, reigned 1837–1901, queen, and other of nine.

therefore, to keep the name between you and your partner and not present it until the baby is actually born. When that happens, your relatives will immediately be more interested in the baby itself and you will have neatly skirted the naming problem.

If all else fails

The author Leslie Dunkling has done a great deal of research into names. He advises the following:

> 'Some couples are still arguing nine months after the birth and are almost at the divorcing stage. I advise each partner to give the names on their list a mark from 1 to 20. That way, she gives her favourite 20, the one she dislikes most 1, and he does the same. In the end they probably end up with one name both gave 12 to which, when they really think about it, is a good compromise.'

Beware the 'stored name phenomenon'

Leslie Dunkling again:

> 'Some girls of 12 or 13 have already decided what they are going to call their children; it's known as the stored name phenomenon. In America, there was a popular TV programme involving three heroes, Joshua, Jason and Jeremy, and seven years later when their fans started to have kids, these names appeared in great numbers. But the idea that parents copy royalty is a myth. You don't hear of many babies being christened Zara, Princess Anne's rather whimsical choice.'

Don't go over the top

Michael and Karolina Tomaro of Gøteborg, Sweden, are particular experts on this subject. They wanted to name their child Metallica. A child's name needs to be approved in Sweden and so the naming authorities objected on the grounds that it was the name of a rock group. (And also, presumably, on the grounds that it's silly.)

The case eventually went to court and Sweden now has a Metallica Tomaro. That said, the court's decision is not always in favour of the parents and previous names rejected by the authorities include: 'Brfxxccxxmnpcccclllmmnprxvclmnckssqlbb11116', which apparently is pronounced Albin.

Similar laws exist in Brazil, where one father was banned from naming his son Saddam Hussein. Nine years later, he was prevented from calling another one Osama bin Laden.

Don't try too hard to impress

Stephen J. Dubner, co-author of *Freakonomics*, says,

> 'Parents, probably much more than they care to admit, are sending a signal with the name they give their child – a signal to their family and friends about how hip or traditional or culturally aware they are. With parents, you see it most plainly when they tell a stranger the baby's name and wait expectantly for a positive reaction. There's nothing so sad as the sight of a new mom telling the grocer her baby's name is Atticus, then becoming crestfallen at the blank stare she receives.'

There's perhaps another, less obvious, danger in choosing to name your child after figures from history or literature. In the 1940s, a Venezuelan father with Communist sympathies named his three sons Vladimir, Illich and Lenin (Venezuela has more liberal naming laws than Brazil). Young Illich grew up to become the international left-wing terrorist nicknamed Carlos the Jackal.

Tips for success

Choose a name that's harmonious

The rules for finding a harmonious first name are actually quite simple. If your surname starts with a vowel, avoid a first name that ends with one. Car*a* *A*rron, for example, or Catrion*a* *U*nwin. Names like this just don't slip off the tongue easily — and it's the vowels that cause the problem.

The same problem occurs when the last letter of the first name is the same as the first letter of the last name. Names such as Chery*l* *L*anyon and Davi*d* *D*unn.

Finally, it's best to avoid a similar effect when whole syllable sounds are repeated: names such as Ron*an* M*oran*, and Edw*ard* Woodw*ard*. An easy test is to imagine a person of that name telephoning you for the first time. Would you understand their name if they spoke quickly? (One of the authors of this book has the relatively simple name of Geoff King, but people on the phone often think they are talking to Jack Keen.) The reason for this is that people hearing a name for the first time will often hear what sounds familiar to them.

Common or unusual?

Whether you choose a common name or a more unusual one depends in part on your surname. If you have a common or plain surname it's often good to choose a first name with a little flair: Calandra or Aphrodite, for example. But if you do, make sure you choose a traditional spelling: no Kalandras or Afrodites. (More about why this can be a problem in the next section.)

Professor Helen Petrie, a professor of psychology and naming expert at York University, points out,

> 'People with an unusual name say, without exception, that it was a hassle, particularly when they were growing up. They were teased at school, sometimes even by their teachers. Although, as adults, they usually say their name is distinctive and makes them stand out from a crowd.'

Actress Gwyneth Paltrow said exactly this about her first name, which may explain why she called her own child Apple. (See other celebrities' choice of baby names in the Namesakes section on page 218.) As Laura Wattenberg, a researcher in this field, puts it, 'Parents are eager to stand out, but kids are still perfectly happy to fit in.'

On the other hand, a long or unusual surname will often sound better with a straightforward first name: John MacDiarmid, for example. It will also reduce the chances of your child going through life having to spell *both* their names over and over again.

Stress – of the syllable kind

The issues with syllables boil down to two areas: how many syllables are in each name, and which syllable is emphasized in each name? Every name has at least one stressed syllable. For example, *George*, Ac*cal*ia or Den*ise*.

So here are the golden rules:

- It's best to have different numbers of syllables in each name: Joe Quilter sounds better than Joseph Quilter.
- Look at where the syllable stresses fall. The best combination is usually to have stress on the first syllable of each name. (There can be variations on this depending on the sex of your child, and these are discussed in some detail later.)
- If your surname has just one syllable, a first name with two or more syllables will probably sound best — especially for a girl.

The key point about syllables is that once you are aware of their dangers you won't fall into their trap.

Consider the meaning

Some people take a surprising amount of interest in the meanings of their names and your child may turn out to be one of them. Should your child discover the true meaning of his name to be 'untrustworthy tearaway who will never make anything of himself', you will have stored up another problem for his teenage years.

Like father, like son?

In Britain, Canada, South Africa, Australia and New Zealand (but not the USA) during the last hundred years, the practice of naming a child after the parent has pretty much died away. Before that, it was common and, at times, all but compulsory, to do so. For example, in 1377, 35 per cent of English males were called John. From that time on, the name's popularity declined, happily saving us from a challenging range of identity issues.

There are, however, two problems with naming a child after a parent that are still with us today. One is simply the confusion that arises concerning post and personal information (credit cards are a particular problem in this regard). The other issue is that research suggests naming a child after a parent is unlikely to be in the child's best interests.

The research, published in the *Journal of Social Psychology*, used the California Psychology Inventory (CPI). The CPI is a set of 434 true/false questions that are designed to reveal the characters of 'normal' people; in other words, people who do not have psychiatric or clinical conditions. It's something of a gold standard amongst psychologists and, as a result, is used internationally. It found that men with Junior after their name scored considerably lower than the general population on a significant number of the indices.

The conclusion drawn by the authors of the report is that the child's sense of their own identity will suffer if they are named after someone else. It's better to see the child as their own person, and one way to do that is to give them their own name.

A similar trend to be aware of is the desire to name a child after a special place or event, such as where the child was conceived. And anyway, your boss may have called his children Travelodge M4 Westbound and Runners-up League Division Two 1996 for any number of reasons!

The surname of just under 1 per cent of Americans is Smith. That's approximately 2.3 million people.

Having avoided the pitfall of using your own name, you should next avoid the dangers of your parents' and grandparents' names. Arthur, Bertha and Munroe were all fine in their day but can sound dated to modern ears — unless they are experiencing a revival, of course, which does happen.

Often the neatest solution is to use family names as middle names.

Secret messages

Names can convey a surprising amount of information unwittingly. David Hargreaves of Leicester University has conducted research into the impact of names. He finds,

> 'There are several things you can tell from a name. Usually sex, often age – for example, if you're called Susan or Janet you're quite likely to have been born in the 1950s. Names like Wayne and Jason will be associated with lower socio-economic groups, Alexander and Charles with the higher ones. Naming someone is an important decision because of all these associations.'

And finally...

... Just a last comment on the fascinating world of names. Perhaps unsurprisingly, California is making a unique contribution in this sphere.

A growing trend in the state – God knows why – is for grandparents to take on a new name for themselves at the birth of their first grandchild. Some of the new names being chosen are a little unusual, and recent examples include:

Bul-bul
Chickie
Vovo
Noona
Dappy
Vov
Zeide
Bobe
Busia
Jaja
Bubbe
Zayde
Abue
Mem-mee
Poobah

Helen Petrie has conducted extensive studies of names. Her view is that, 'These sorts of names originate in America. Any nation that can call a product "I Feel Like Chicken Tonight" clearly doesn't understand the naming tradition.'

A little psychology

'What's in a name? That which we call a rose
By any other name would smell as sweet.'

William Shakespeare, 1564–1615, playwright. From *Romeo and Juliet*.

When Shakespeare wrote the lines above, he no doubt sensed that we are all shaped by the name we carry, but it wasn't until the 1960s that academics first tried to measure the degree to which this effect occurs. Since then, a series of academic studies has found a whole spectrum of correlations between a child's name and their path in life. Many of the correlations are quite strong and this section summarizes the main findings from all the key studies. The aim of it is not to corral you into choosing from a narrow set of names. Rather, it is to set you up with a summary of all that is known about names, so that you can go ahead and confidently choose a name based on your own personality, preferences and outlook on life; which is exactly as it should be.

Prospects at school

David Figlio is an economics professor at Florida University. Over the years he has shown a remarkable interest in the effect a name has on a person's progress in life. He was also the first person to look for a link between a child's name and their educational achievement, and one of his earliest pieces of research suggested there is indeed a link.

Figlio started his study by inviting his students to draw up a list of names that they perceived to be of lower social status in the USA. Once they had agreed on their list, the professor then studied the exam grades of 55,000 children and compared their results to their names. However, the professor didn't compare the 55,000 children as a group. The twist to his research was to compare the children with lower-status names with *their own siblings* whose names were of a higher status. This allowed him to strip away the socio-economic factors that might otherwise skew the result. What he found was that children whose names were of lower socio-economic status than their siblings, and children with unusually spelled names – Jackquelyn, for example, or Magik (yes, there is one) – scored on average 3–5 per cent less in exams.

This, of course, begs the question, 'why?' Professor Figlio thought the most likely explanation was that teachers were subconsciously judging the children by their names. As he said,

> 'In ways we are only beginning to understand, children with different names but the exact same upbringing grow up to have remarkably different life outcomes. If you want to give your child a name that connotes low status, then you need to be aware of the consequences.'

The professor next decided to take his research a little further. Rather than just look at how a name might affect exam grades, he decided to look at whether a name might affect the actual subjects studied by the child.

To do this, he chose 1000 pairs of sisters from a range of backgrounds across America. This time he asked the students to define how feminine they thought the sisters' names were. So, for example, the students classed names such as Anna, Emma and Elizabeth as very feminine, while a name such as Alex was not. What he found was that the girls with the non-feminine names were twice as likely to study maths or science after 16 than their sisters with the more feminine names. (Sixteen is the age at which most American schoolchildren are able to choose which subjects they study.) He believed the implication of his study was that we are all somewhat typecast by our names. In his words, 'On average, people treat Isabellas differently to Alexes.'

Another academic, Professor Samuel Gray Garwood, has reached a similar view. He says,

> 'Often the kind of behaviour we expect from other people is the kind of behaviour we get. Name expectations are bound to have some influence on the way a teacher interacts with a student named Richard or Roderick.' [In the USA, Richard is considered a high-status name, and Roderick a lower one.]

To test his views, Professor Garwood used his own lecture hall. He would put up several names on the board as an exercise and ask his students to assign grades to them arbitrarily. The results were that, 'Davids and Karens almost always get high marks, while Huberts and Mabels get low ones from students who deny that they are prejudiced by names at all.'

A similar test was carried out in California. In that study, teachers were asked to mark four essays supposedly written by Michael, David, Karen and Lisa. They were then asked to mark four other essays, of the same standard, this time written by Elmer, Hubert, Bertha and Adelle.

Michael and David were ahead of Elmer and Hubert by a wide margin. Karen and Lisa also did a fair bit better than Bertha and Adelle; an outcome that implies the socio-economic effect of a name is more pronounced for boys. But when the names in this study were changed it became apparent that it's not just class and gender stereotypes that affect a child's exam marks. Those with unique or unusual-sounding names – the Jackquelyns and Magiks – do worse in standardized tests than siblings with more conventional names. Psychologists call this type of social bias a 'halo effect', which means we judge a range of aspects of a person's character on the basis of a single piece of information, in this case their name. A rather extreme example of this is Mao Zedong, the Chinese leader, who chose Big Beard Wang as his barber.

So what names do teachers like?

It happens that there was a discussion on a British national teachers' website on just this subject which, unfortunately for the teachers involved, found its way off the website and into the pages of the national press. Most of the teachers' discussions were about classroom behaviour and some mentioned the names of children they thought would be trouble. From this somewhat unscientific source, it seems the average British teacher thinks there is a 75 per cent chance that a child called Bobbie-Jo, Ryan, Jordan or Kristopher will be disruptive in class. Conversely, they think the best-behaved children are those called Kate, Imran, Daniel or Lucy. Politicians and sociologists could no doubt have a lengthy debate about what is going on here. Is it the name itself?; or the prejudices of the teachers becoming a self-fulfilling prophesy?; or simply that conventional parents give their children conventional names?

What is certain is that the effect exists.

The cultural connotations of a name may also have a bearing on how a child's work is marked in school. To date, there have been two key studies into this. The first of these looked at the names and academic achievements of 3065 South African children. Two-thirds of these children had traditional South African names. The other third had English names. The 3065 were chosen so that all the children came from similar socio-economic backgrounds.

Once the group was chosen, the actual study was relatively easy. All that was needed was to plot the children's exam results against the origin of their name. What became apparent was that the third with the English names did significantly better than the other two-thirds in all subjects. Clearly, it could be the name that is causing this or it could be that the parents who give their children English names are the parents more likely to value a western education.

A similar study, which took place in 1999, was funded by the *Washington Post*, Harvard University and the Kaiser Family Foundation. It also aimed to discover how a member of an ethnic group might be influenced by having either an ethnic or a non-ethnic name. This time the group chosen for the study were Hispanic Americans in the USA.

The study had a wonderful simplicity to it. The researchers simply interviewed Hispanic Americans about how integrated they felt into American society, and at the end they asked them for their name.

The results showed a significant correlation between whether a Hispanic American had taken an English name and how integrated they felt into American culture. The authors concluded their report with the following observation,

> 'In many instances, the magnitude of these effects are as strong, or stronger, than that of other more well-studied measures of immigrant status and ethnic identification like generation, ethnic nationality, and religion.'

The issue here is the same as with the South African survey. Either the name, or the attitude of those giving the name, is at play, but which one is actually the cause, and which one the effect?

How names affect a child's popularity

The first modern academic to really study this area was J. McDavid in the mid 1960s. In what was at the time a most original piece of research, he set out to look for a possible link between how popular a child was at primary school and what name they had. His findings, documented in the journal *Child Development*, found a link.

Intriguingly, what he also found was that other groups – such as children from different schools – came to the same conclusions about a child based on their name. It may be that we all have similar prejudices about particular names, or it may be that the name connotations we learn in our early school days are hardwired into us for life.

> Niger has the highest birth rate of any country.
> Sweden has the second lowest birth rate of any country.
> Vatican City has the lowest birth rate of any country.

The next researchers in this field were Busse and Seraydarian with their 'Psychology in the Schools' report in 1979. They looked into the same area – the relationship between the desirability of a child's first name and how popular the child was with their peers. This time they involved over 1500 children in their study.

Their research also concluded that there was a connection between a child's name and that child's popularity. What was new about this study was that it looked, for the first time, at how the two sexes viewed names. They found that a girl's popularity was significantly related to the desirability of her first name. The same effect existed with boys, but was much more muted. As if to emphasize this difference between the sexes, they found that the people most likely to judge a boy by his name were, in fact, girls.

Therefore, in 1995, Bell and Karlin used the California Psychological Inventory (CPI; see page 18) as the basis for their study of 1476 students. Among those students, the four most common male names were James, Michael, Jeffrey and Scott. The four least common were Carl, Rodney, Harold and Darrell. For the girls, the most common were Christine, Jennifer, Laura and Michelle. Rose, Joanne, Grace and Alice were the least common. When compared against the CPI, they found that those students with the most common names were associated with twice as many favourable traits as those with the least common names. This study, however, hit the same problem as the previous ones. Is it just that the families with the more conventional attitudes – who give the more conventional names – are also the more favourably viewed families? Or could it be the actual names they choose to give their children that cause the perception?

Professor Albert Mehrabian of UCLA is a prominent psychologist in several areas, one of which is the influence of names and labels. His first study tried to assess the degree to which a name can impart impressions of popularity, success or kindness. What he found was that the more traditional a person's name, the higher that person is perceived to be in terms of popularity, success and kindness. So that, for example, while the name Breeze was only given 16 per cent by his testers, the name Christopher got 100 per cent. The Professor himself firmly believes it is the name, not the parental background, that is the cause of these differences. He concluded, 'A name is part of an impression package. Parents who make up bizarre names for their children are ignorant, arrogant or just foolish.'

One set of parents who may not have read the Professor's report were the parents of the pair of London-born twins, Kate and Duplicate; and the Iowa parents of Bing and Bang certainly didn't read it!

Professor Andrew Colman is a psychologist at the University of Leicester who has focused his research on the preferences of Australians and Britons regarding names. His surveys consistently find that traditional first names are the most popular. He says,

> 'Whereas familiar surnames like Smith and Jones and unusual surnames like Nall or Codling were universally disliked, and people preferred intermediate surnames like Burton, the opposite was true for first names. The most common ones, like James and Elizabeth or David and Mary, were very popular.'

Until, that is, the name becomes dated. The Professor goes on to say,

> 'What happens when they become over-popular, though, is what we call the "preference feedback mechanism", which works like a central-heating thermostat. As millions of people start giving their baby the same name it self-regulates and begins to be less popular through over-exposure.'

This retreat from over-exposure is the biggest single driver in parents searching for new names for their offspring, and it is this factor which is most responsible for the Jackquelyns and Magiks. One London school found itself in the ironic situation of having two children in the same classroom named Unique!

But can a name make you sexy?

Some academics certainly think so. Researchers at the Massachusetts Institute of Technology set out to investigate the sex appeal of names and came up with a novel experiment. They set up a website on which they posted 24 pictures of young people and then asked visitors to the site to

'Somewhere on this globe, every ten seconds, there is a woman giving birth to a child. She must be found and stopped.'

Sam Levenson, 1911–1980, humorist.

rate the attractiveness of each picture. Once the responses had settled into an established order, a clear hierarchy could be seen among the 24.

At that point, the researchers changed the names underneath the pictures and waited for a new hierarchy to emerge. When they compared the results they found that, on average, a name makes a six per cent difference in terms of attractiveness to the opposite sex. The study was then replicated by Manchester Metropolitan University and they also found a six per cent difference.

In each case, the six per cent figure is an average that hides the extremes. So, for example, both studies found the effect only just showed when the pictures of men were rated, but, when the pictures of females were displayed, the disparities between the ratings were much bigger. (The lowest scores in both studies were for men who had gender-ambiguous names, such as Hilary and Francis.)

So what makes a name sexy?

The answer seems to be that, for men, the shorter the name, the more appealing it sounds. Therefore, names such as Matt and John are always popular with girls. For women, the opposite holds true. The longer and more flowing the name, the more appealing she becomes; and even more so if her name is long on vowel sounds – Ariadne and Calypso, for example, are always rated as sexy.

But there are other factors, too, in what makes a name sexy, and in 2004 the linguist Amy Perfors undertook a test that helped uncover them. Her test had many similarities to those conducted by the two universities in that she used her 'Hot or Not?' website to post pictures of males and females and asked visitors to the site to rate their attractiveness.

She then posted the same photos on different dates and with different names. This time, however, she focused not so much on the names themselves, but on the vowel patterns within the names. What became apparent was the following: the most attractive male names have an emphasis on the 'front vowel': the first 'a' in Adam, for example, or the 'i' in Clinton. It's different for girls. The sexiest names for them nearly always have the main stress on a middle vowel, for instance on the 'i' in Elizabeth or Clarinda.

Girlie girls and manly men

This leads on to the question of which names are perceived to be the most masculine and which the most feminine? To save you conducting your own survey in the busy months leading up to the birth of your offspring, two psychologists, Carol Johnson (University of Sussex) and Helen Petrie (York University), put the question to 225 of their students.

Of the common boys' names in Britain, the most masculine were thought to be, in rank order:

John
David
Richard
Peter
Mark
James
Paul
Michael
Matthew
Edward

The most feminine of the common girls' names were rated as:
Sophie
Elizabeth
Emily
Lucy
Rose
Emma
Katherine
Mary
Diane
Victoria

Interestingly, while the list of the most masculine names follows the rules for the sexiest boys' names, the most feminine girls' names don't comply to the rules for the sexiest girls' names – the majority have the stress on the first syllable and not many of them are particularly long and flowing. So it seems there's a difference between being feminine and being sexy!

The conclusion seems to be that if you choose the right name for your child it will make them more attractive to the opposite sex when they become a teenager. Although how they will use this attribute when they reach this stage is harder to control!

Twins are much more likely to have names beginning with the same letter than separately born children are.

Gender-neutral names

The last 60 years have seen a significant rise in the use of gender-neutral names. Whatever you attribute this to – and people have come up with a number of ideas – there are three characteristics of gender-neutral names that really stand out.

The first is that parents in all the English-speaking countries are a lot more adventurous when choosing names for daughters. They are much more likely to give daughters names that were traditionally male than to give sons girls' names. An androgynous, or gender-neutral, name almost always means a male name for a girl, hardly ever the other way round.

The second factor is that studies continually show that girls have far fewer problems with taking a male or androgynous name. By contrast, a large majority of boys are strongly against having anything other than a distinctly masculine name. All of this means that, while the pool of gender-neutral names is increasing, the increase is nearly all due to the colonization of male names by females. Julian is one of the few clear-cut instances of it happening in reverse.

The third characteristic is that, while the popularity of boys' names changes at a steady and fairly predictable rate, girls' names are a great deal more fluid. They change much more quickly and abruptly.

There are more people called Chang in China than the total population of Germany.

The right name for the job

But why are modern parents so open to giving gender-neutral names to their daughters? The most popular theory is that it might help those girls with their careers. It may be that parents perceive this on a subconscious level. Certainly, studies have implied that professors are more likely to give higher grades to students they think are male, and some employers have been shown to favour CVs of candidates they thought were male. In such cases, being called Ashley or Cameron is an advantage for a girl (as long as she doesn't mind working for a sexist employer).

One study on this subject was published in the 'Journal of Social Psychology' in 2000. It set out to explore a possible link between the name you are given and your success at work. What the researchers found was that the more masculine a man's name, the more successful that man would be in an occupation seen as traditionally male: the military, for example, or construction. On the other hand, the more feminine a girl's name, the more successful she would be at a traditionally feminine occupation: nursing or interior design, for instance.

Does your face fit?

But it's not just the gender of your name that affects your career. Other factors play a part, too. It was for this reason that the psychologists Copley and Brownlow decided on a study of names, faces and fictitious job adverts.

Specifically, the study set out to investigate how 'name warmth' and facial maturity affected job applications. To do this, the participants were given fabricated CVs and asked to rate the candidates' suitability for a range of jobs. The pictures on the CVs were either baby-faced or mature-faced, and either male or female. And the name of the applicant was either 'cold' or 'warm', as determined by pre-testing.

The study revealed that having a warm name did improve that candidate's chances of being chosen for a job requiring warmth, but those same candidates were deemed less suitable for a job requiring competence. Furthermore, those with warm names were judged as more sincere, but less powerful, than those with cold names. Name warmth also modified the perceptions of power and coldness that are typical when looking at mature-faced people. Mature-faced applicants with warm names were judged as less powerful and more suited to a job requiring warmth than mature-faced applicants with cold names. Similarly, mature-faced female applicants with warm names were perceived as more sincere than their cold-named counterparts.

Aaron versus Zebedee

Some researchers into the effects of names study what they call 'alphabetism'. This is a theory which claims that those with names near the front of the alphabet have an advantage in life. The theory certainly works with regard to ballot papers (which are invariably laid out in alphabetical order) because it has long been noted in elections that candidates with surnames near the beginning of the alphabet do slightly better than expected. Pam Woodall, a researcher at the *Economist*, has found the same effect for job applicants. They're often interviewed in alphabetical order, which gives an advantage to those with names near the beginning of the alphabet. The main trouble with alphabetism is that it tends to apply to surnames, which you can't do much about!

It seems that if you want a particular job, you benefit from having a name that is attractive, familiar and perceived as suitable for the job. Employers construe an attractive name as having attractive qualities.

Names, emotions and politics

If you have any thoughts about your child becoming a politician, it's worth bearing in mind that studies suggest politicians are some of the least happy people in society.

Possibly, though, the influence of the name you choose on their election prospects, and indeed on many aspects of human affairs, goes rather deeper than you might think. Certainly, that's the conclusion of Professor G. Smith, who has a keen interest in this subject. The specific area of names he studies is called phonetic symbolism.

Phonetic symbolism is the study of the emotional effect of sounds, and is an area that has been much debated by psychologists. However, the very nature of the subject means that devising accurate scientific tests is difficult. How do you measure emotion statistically? The professor's insight was to realize that elections provide an unusually clear and measurable case in which the emotional effect of a candidate's name can be analysed. Voters undoubtedly prefer to vote on the basis of issues or party loyalty, but these factors are known before the vote takes place and their effect can be allowed for. When these factors are taken out, the professor believes that fairly accurate predictions of election results can be made based on selected phonetic features in the candidates' names.

Nicknames

Much less research has been done on the effects of nicknames than on proper names. That said, Ray Crozier of Cardiff University has studied the area and he focused his attention on the differences in attitude to nicknames that exist between the genders.

What he found was that boys assign far more nicknames than girls and base those nicknames almost entirely on physical traits. Nicknames given by girls are almost always based on character or a sexual connotation – a factor that may well explain why his study reported a much greater dislike of nicknames among girls than boys.

Crozier's interviews with the children on this subject then probed deeper and it became apparent that it's not the children who come out the worse for nicknames – it's the teachers, by a very wide margin.

Crozier found that nearly all teachers suffer from a derogatory nickname, and most were unaware of it. He also found that nearly all teachers' nicknames referred to a physical attribute of the teacher, a factor that implies it's the boys doing the naming. The only silver lining was that nicknames for teachers seem to be particularly witty and apt. In fact, as regards nicknames, just one group in society comes out worse than teachers. It's politicians again!

Intriguing research by Ed Spivey Jr suggests not only that politicians are likely to have nicknames, but the more corrupt they are, the more likely they are to have a nickname, with Tricky Dicky (Richard Nixon) being the best example.

But why might people subconsciously 'know' which politicians are the most suspect? Doubtless, the answer lies in people's collective intuition, but the phenomenon does tie in with other knowledge about nicknames: that is, that when a person is described by their formal name they are judged to be more moral than when they are described by their nickname. Generally, the use of a nickname reduces perceptions of their success and morality, but makes the subject seem more popular and more cheerful.

Does length matter?

To find out more about this question, we need to turn once more to Professor Mehrabian because one of his other studies looked at just this area. It searched for a correlation between the length of a name and how that person is perceived in terms of success, morality, warmth and cheerfulness. (For this study he excluded nicknames lest they skew the results.)

For male names he found that the longer the name, the more people assumed the man had a high social position, and the more they assumed he was moral and successful. By contrast, shorter names implied greater popularity, more warmth and also a more masculine character. Quite simply, shorter names make men more sexy.

For women, he found that the shorter the name, the warmer people believed her to be. Think of the difference between Liz and Elizabeth. Other studies have shown that women are much more likely than men to use a shortened version of their name. What these women might not know is that women are perceived as more sexually attractive the longer and more flowing their name is.

Does your name affect how you see yourself?

One academic with a particular interest in this is Professor Samuel Gray Garwood. (We first met him putting up names in his lecture hall and asking his students to randomly assign grades based on them.) Garwood says his interest in the subject was sparked by his dislike of both his names, Samuel and Gray, and it was that which persuaded him to examine how a name can affect a person's view of themselves. To do this he chose 24 boys whose names had been described as 'desirable' by teachers; and 23 whose names were described as 'undesirable' by those same teachers.

Those with the 'undesirable' names – the Rodericks and Maurices in this instance – were also those with the lowest self-esteem. The boys with the 'desirable' names – the Richards and Jonathans in this instance – had significantly higher self-esteem. Not just that, they also had higher aspirations for future life and were doing better in school tests. Once again this research begs the question, which is the cause and which is the effect?

In another study, Joubert asked 73 females and 47 males, all young adults, how much they liked their first name. The study found that females who were first-born liked their name more than subsequent children liked theirs. It also found that only children had a greater liking for their name than children with siblings. Finally, it found that girls who liked their names tended to be less lonely.

This correlates neatly with Bell's 1984 study in which 924 students filled out a questionnaire designed to assess loneliness. Once it was completed, other students were asked to rate the names of those who filled in the survey in terms of whether those names were seen as desirable. What they found was that the more desirable the name, the less lonely the person was.

A bad name – a bad deal

In 2000, Dr Luke Birmingham was a senior lecturer in forensic psychiatry at Ravenswood House Medium Secure Unit, Hampshire. He decided to look at how people with mental health problems were treated and whether their name affected the treatment they received.

For his study he chose two names commonly seen as attractive – Matthew and Fiona – and two considered unattractive – Wayne and Tracey. He then prepared a case file of a fictitious incident in which a 20-year-old had punched a train conductor and was being held in police custody showing clear signs of a mental-health disorder. Four hundred and sixty consultant psychiatrists were given this fictitious case and asked for their psychological opinion. The four names were distributed randomly in the otherwise identical files.

Thirty-seven per cent of the Waynes received a diagnosis of drug or alcohol abuse as against just 19 per cent of the more middle-class-sounding Matthews. The Matthews were more likely to receive the more sympathetic diagnosis, from the courts' point of view, of schizophrenia.

The women were more likely to be diagnosed with personality disorders than the men, but the class of their name didn't seem to be a factor.

Dr Birmingham summed up his study by saying,

> 'One might hypothesize from the results that Matthew is seen as someone who is suffering from an illness. He is more vulnerable and more in need of intervention. Wayne was more likely to be negatively perceived, which suggests that he was someone who was more troublesome and difficult and brought trouble on himself. Women were more likely to be diagnosed with a personality disorder suggesting they were being more obstructive.'

A study at a New Jersey psychiatric clinic uncovered the same trend. Over the years they found that men with unusual first names were over-represented among their patients. They also found a similar trend for women, but it was less marked.

Do or D.I.E

During the 1980s and '90s, an area of psychology developed which examined the links between the immune system and the mind – psychoneuroimmunology, to give it its proper name. One study that emerged from this was published in 1999. It looked at Californian death certificates from 1969 and 1995, and the researchers compared 2287 men with negative-sounding initials, such as D.I.E. and P.I.G., with 1200 with positive-sounding initials, such as A.C.E. and V.I.P. They found that those with positive initials lived an average of seven years longer.

Another output of this happy branch of psychology found that Bens are the safest drivers, and Ians are the most likely to crash.

Freud on names

As befits an icon of psychology, Sigmund Freud was not quiet on the subject of names. He noted, for example, that the Austrian upper classes were more likely to mispronounce his name than any other group in society. He concluded this was to keep people of his class 'in their place'. He also noted in his writing that, among primitive peoples, a person's name was considered to be one of their most important possessions. And it was partly because of this that he believed that western society tended to undervalue the importance of a name. Freud certainly didn't, though; he devised methods by which his patients could forget about names with which they had unpleasant associations.

A free choice

What would the two sexes like to be called if they had their own way? The consensus among researchers seems to be that men naturally gravitate towards names that suggest action (Kurt, Flint or Lance); women towards ones that suggest glamour (Callista, Saffron and Lucienne).

So what, then, is in a name? The answer would seem to be 'rather

'There are only two things a child will share willingly: communicable diseases and his mother's age.'

Dr Benjamin Spock, 1903–88, author.

more than we first thought'. But no doubt Shakespeare, all those years ago, already knew that. And you now know most of what is currently known about the effects of names. That knowledge means you can read on and chose a name with confidence, knowing your choice will be right for you, and right for your child. Good luck in your search and have fun!

Final notes

When you have chosen the name, may we ask you to look at the website which accompanies this book? Each month, the funniest of the readers' stories about babies and toddlers are published and we would love to hear your stories too. Everything you need to know about these stories can be found at www.brilliant-baby-names.com

Using the names lists

The names lists in this book are alphabetical. Each entry gives the language of origin; a guide to the most common pronunciation/s (**bold** shows emphasis); meaning/s, connotations and associations; and, at the end in *italic* text, various different spellings, short forms and nicknames.

A–Z of Girls' names

Aaliyah (Ah-**lee**-ya) (American) rising. *Aliya*

Aba (**Ab**-a) (Ghanaian) a child born on Thursday. *Abiah*

Abarranne (Ab-are-**an**) (Basque) parent of a multitude.

Abayomi (Ab-a-**yoh**-mee) (Nigerian) happiness.

Abegaila (Ab-ee-**gail**-a) Hawaiian version of Abigail, meaning source of joy.

Abelia (A-**bee**-lee-a) (Hebrew) the female version of Abel, meaning breath or vapour. *Abela, Abele*

Abellona (Ab-ell-**own**-a) (Danish) a female version of Apollo, the Greek god of the sun.

Abiah (Ab-**bee**-a) (Hebrew) God is my father.

Abigail (**Ab**-ee-gail) (Hebrew) source of joy. Wife of King David in the Bible. *Abbey, Abbie, Abby, Abegail, Gale, Gayle*

Abiona (Ah-**bee**-oh-na) (Nigerian) born on a journey.

Abra (**Ab**-ra) (Hebrew) mother of nations.

Abrianna (Abe-ree-**an**-a) (Italian) a form of Abra, meaning mother of nations. *Abryanna, Abryannah*

Abrielle (Ab-ree-**el**) French form of Abra, meaning mother of nations.

Acacia (A-**kay**-sha) (Greek) from the name of a genus of trees and shrubs of about 1300 species; name of the tree from which the Ark of the Covenant was made. Also has connotations of immortality. *Cacia, Casey, Kassy*

Acadia (Ak-**aid**-ee-a) (French) a collective name for the French colonies in North America that stretched from Quebec to Philadelphia in the seventeenth century.

Acaija (Ak-**eye**-ja) (Greek) joy.

Acantha (A-**can**-tha) (Greek) thorny or spiny. *Akantha*

Accalia (Ak-**ail**-ee-a) (Latin) the foster mother of Romulus and Remus, the legendary twin founders of Rome. *Accalya*

Aceline (**Ace**-a-leen) (French) of noble blood.

Achava (Ach-**ah**-va) (Hebrew) frendship.

Ada (**Aid**-a) (German) prosperous and joyful.

Adaani (Ahd-**dah**-nee) (Nigerian) father's girl.

Adabelle (Ad-a-**bell**) derived from Ada and Belle, which respectively mean joyful and beautiful. *Ada, Belle*

Adah (**Aid**-a) (Hebrew) ornament, in the sense of one who gives lustre to others. A figure in the Old Testament. *Ada, Aydah*

Adalia (Ad-**day**-lee-a) (Hebrew) God is my protector.

Adalina (Ad-a-**leen**-a) Hawaiian form of Adelaide, meaning kind lady of noble birth.

Adamina (Ad-a-**meen**-a) (Hebrew) made from the red earth. Feminine version of Adam.

Adanna (Ad-**an**-a) (Nigerian) father's girl.

Adara (Ad-**are**-a) (Hebrew) daughter born in the sixth month. (Greek) beautiful. *Adarah, Adarra*

Adela (A-**day**-la/A-**dell**-a) (Greek) noble. *Adalie, Adelaide, Adelina, Adeline, Della*

Adelaide (**Add**-a-laid) (German) kind lady of noble birth. *Ada, Ady, Adalade*

Adelinda (Add-a-**lin**-da) (German) noble serpent.

Adeline (**Ad**-a-leen) (German) kind lady of noble birth. *Adaline, Adline*

Adelita (Ad-el-**ee**-ta) (Spanish) form of Adela.

Adeliza (Ad-ell-**ee**-za) (English) a combination of Adelaide and Liza.

Adelka (Ad-**el**-ka) another German form of Adelaide.

Adèle/Adelle (Ad-**ell**) (Old French) noble. The name of William the Conqueror's youngest daughter. Saint Adèle was founder of a convent which she ran with great compassion. Her saint's day is 24 December. *Ada, Addy*

Adelpha (A-**dell**-fa) (Greek) sisterly and the friend of mankind. *Adelfe, Adelphe*

Adena (Ad-**een**-a) (Greek) accepted. *Ada, Adenna, Adina, Adynna, Deena, Dena*

Adila (Ad-**ee**-la) (Arabic) just and fair.

Adina (Ad-**ee**-na) (Hebrew) voluptuous and mature. Has connotations of fertility. *Adeen, Deena, Dena*

Adisa (Ad-**ee**-sa) (Spanish) friendly. *Adesa*

Adline (Ad-**leen**) (French) diminutive form of Adèle or Adeline.

Adonia (A-**don**-ya) (Greek) reborn. The name of the Greek goddess of the harvest and resurrection. *Adona*

Adoncia (Ad-**don**-see-a) (Spanish) sweet.

Adora (Ad-**or**-a) (Latin) adored and loved. *Dora, Dori*

Adorinda (Ad-or-**in**-da) (English) a combination of Dora and Linda, names that respectively mean given and pretty.

Adra (**Ad**-ra) (Greek) beautiful.

Adria (**Ad**-ree-a) (English) dark or black. The feminine version of Adrian. Also linked to the Adriatic sea. *Adriane, Adrianna, Adrienne*

Adva (**Ad**-va) (Hebrew) little wave.

Aegle (**Egg**-luh) (Greek) goddess of radiant good health in mythology. *Aigle*

Aemilia (Em-**ee**-lee-a) (Latin) the femine version Aemelius, meaning rival.

Aeronwenn (Eye-**ron**-wen) (Welsh) one meaning is white or pale berries, which has holy connotations. Another derives from *aeron*, meaning slaughter.

Aeryn (**Ar**-in) (Irish) a symbol of peace.
Aethyl (**Eth**-el) (English) short form for longer names containing Aethyl, which is the Anglo-Saxon for noble, such as Aethylflaed.
Aethra (**Eeth**-ra) (Greek) in Greek mythology, the mother of Theseus. *Ethra*
Afia (Af-**ee**-a) English version of the West African name Afua, which means born on a Friday.
Africa (**Af**-rick-a) (American) named after the continent.
Afton (**Af**-tun) (English) thought to be linked to the River Afton in Ayrshire, Scotland. Also referred to in poetry, such as Bobby Brown's *Sweet Afton*.
Agalia (Ag-**gay**-lee-a) (Greek) splendid and happy.
Agape (Ag-**ah**-pay) (Greek) translates directly as love.
Agasha (Ag-**ash**-a) (Greek) a form of Agatha, meaning good and honourable.
Agate (**Ag**-ate) (Old French) the name of a gemstone. *Agatte*
Agatha (**Ag**-a-tha) (Greek) good and honourable. *Agathe*
Agathangelos (Ag-ath-**an**-jel-os) (Greek) compound name composed of *agathos* meaning good, and *angelos* meaning angel.
Agave (Ag-**ah**-vee) (Greek) noble. The daughter of Cadmus, legendary founder of Thebes, and the goddess Harmonia. (English) the name of a plant native to Mexico and the southwest of the USA.
Aggie (**Ag**-ee) (English) short form of Agatha (good and honourable), or Agnes (pure and holy).
Aghna (**Own**-a) (Irish) chaste and holy.
Agnes (**Ag**-ness) (Greek) pure and holy. Saint Agnes was martyred in AD 303 and is the patron saint of engaged couples. She is often pictured with a lamb, and her saint's day is 21 January. *Ines, Inez, Nessie, Neysa, Nina, Ninete*
Agrona (Ag-**roe**-na) (Celtic) the goddess of war in Celtic mythology.
Ahava (A-**ha**-va) (Hebrew) beloved.
Aiblin (Ab-**leen**) (Irish) bright and shining.
Aibhilin (Eye-**leen**) (Irish) little bird.
Aïda (Eye-**ee**-da) (Arabic) reward. Used by Verdi in his famous opera *Aïda*, in which it is the name of an Ethiopian princess.
Ailaina (Al-**ain**-a) (Scottish) rock.
Aileen (**Ail**-een) Scottish version of the English name Eileen, which means bird. *Aleen, Alleen*
Ailish (Eye-**leesh**) Irish version of the English name Alice, which means noble.
Ailsa (**Ail**-sa) (Scottish) derived from the Scottish island Ailsa Craig.
Aimee (**Aim**-ee) (French) beloved. *Aime, Aimey, Aimme, Amy*
Aine (**Awn**-ya) (Irish) radiance. In Irish folklore Aine is the queen of the fairies.
Aingeal (**Ang**-el) (Irish) angel.
Aintre (**Ain**-truh) (Irish) from the joyful estate. *Aintree, Aintrey*

Aisha (**Eye**-sha) (Arabic) alive. The name of one of Mohammed's wives. *Aeesha, Aiesha, Ayeisha, Ayisa*
Aisling (**Ash**-ling) (Gaelic) dream or vision. *Aislinn*
Aithne (**Eth**-nuh) (Irish) small fire. Also a feminine version of Aidan.
Akela (Ak-**el**-la) (German) noble.
Akiva (Ak-**ee**-va) (Hebrew) shelter.
Alaia (Al-**eye**-a) (Arabic) virtuous.
Alaine (A-**lain**) (Gaelic) rock. Feminine version of Alan. *Alaina, Alainah, Alanah, Alanna, Alannah*
Alala (A-**lah**-la) (Greek) the name of the Greek goddess of war, sister to Ares, the god of war. Also the war cry of Alexander the Great's soldiers.
Alamea (Al-a-**mee**-a) (Hawaiian) ripe and verdant.
Alana (**Al**-a-na) (Hawaiian) floating. (Celtic) feminine form of Alan, which means handsome. *Alahna, Alahnah, Alaina, Alainah, Alanna, Alannah*
Alba (**Al**-ba) (Latin) white. (Spanish) dawn.
Alberta (Al-**bert**-a) (English) the name of a Canadian state and the feminine form of Albert.
Albertina (Al-bert-**ee**-na) (English) a combination Albert and Tina. *Albertyna*
Albina (Al-**been**-a) (Italian) little white one.
Alcina (Al-**see**-na) (Greek) sorceress. *Alsena*
Aldara (Al-**dar**-a) (Greek) winged gift.
Aldona (**Al**-don-a) English form of the Spanish name Aldonza, which means sweet. *Aldonah, Aldone*
Aldreda (Al-**dray**-da) (Old English) wise counsellor.
Aleah (Al-**ee**-a) (Arabic) honourable. *Alea*
Aleela (Al-**ee**-la) (African) crying girl.
Aleen (**Al**-een) (Dutch) bright light.
Alegria (Al-egg-**ree**-a) (Spanish) joy.
Alema (Al-**emm**-a) (Hawaiian) soul.
Alessandra (Al-ess-**and**-ra) (Greek) she who defends. A feminine version of Alexander.
Alessia (Al-**ess**-ee-a) (English) a form of Alicia (see Alice), which means noble. *Alisia*
Alethea (Al-**ee**-thee-a) (Greek) truth.
Aletta (Al-**ett**-a) (Greek) carefree.
Alexa (Al-**ex**-a) (Greek) short for Alexandra. *Alexavia, Alexia, Alexina, Alexis*
Alexandra (Al-ex-**and**-ra/Al-ex-**ahn**-dra) (Greek) a feminine form of Alexander (defender of mankind).
Alfonsina (Al-fon-**seen**-a) (Italian) feminine form of Alfonsus (see Alphonsus).
Alfreda (Al-**freed**-a) (English) feminine form of Alfred, which means elf counsel.
Alhena (Al-**heen**-a) (Arabic) ring.
Alice (**Al**-iss) (English) noble. Saint Alice was a nun who experienced visions and ecstacies. Her saint's day is 15 June. *Alicia, Alison, Alix, Alyce, Ellisa, Elsie, Ilsa*

Alida (Al-**eye**-da) (Latin) the winged one.
Alienor (**Al**-ee-nor) (German) foreign. *Ali, Aly*
Alima (Al-**ee**-ma) (Arabic) skilled in dancing and music. *Alimah*
Alina (Al-**eye**-na) (Russian) noble and lightsome. *Alinna, Allina*
Alisa (Al-**iss**-a) (Hebrew) happiness. Also a derivative of Elizabeth.
Alisha (Al-**ee**-sha) An alternative spelling of Alisa, meaning happiness.
Alison (**Al**-iss-on) (Old English) the light of the sun. Also a diminutive of Alice. *Alisen, Allison, Alyson*
Aliwera (**Al**-ee-vee-ra) (German) a compound of *ali* meaning foreign, and *wera* meaning true. *Ali, Aly*
Alissa (Al-**iss**-a) (English) also spelled Alyssa, both names being derived from the alyssum flower.
Aliza (Al-**eez**-a) (Hebrew) full of joy.
Alka (**Al**-ka) (Polish) noble and bright.
Allegra (Al-**egg**-ra) (Italian) full of life: in the masculine form, *allegro*, a term most commonly found in musical script.
Allena (Al-**ain**-a/**Al**-en-a) (English) bird. *Aline, Eileen*
Allie (**Al**-ee) (English) short form of Alison, which means noble.
Allora (Al-**ore**-a) (Australian) the aboriginal for the place of the swamp. Also a town in Queensland, Australia.
Alma (**Al**-ma) (English) derived from the Latin word for soul.
Almeda (Al-**meed**-a/Al-**maid**-a) (Latin) determined to succeed.
Almedha (Al-**med**-a) (Welsh) shapely.
Almena (Al-**men**-a) (English) constant protector. Originally a feminine derivative of William.
Almira (Al-**mee**-ra) (English) derived from the Arabic *almiri*, meaning exalted one. *Almirah*
Alodie (**Al**-oh-dee) (Old English) prosperous.
Alona (Al-**own**-a) (Hebrew) oak tree.
Alondra (A-**lonn**-dra) English form of the Spanish name Alejandra, a version of Alexandra.
Alouette (Al-oo-**et**) (French) skylark.
Aloysia (A-low-**ish**-a) (German) the feminine form of the Latin name Aloysius, meaning famous warrior. *Lois*
Alphonsine (Al-fon-**seen**) (Spanish) feminine form of Alfonso (see Alphonso), which means ready and noble. *Alfonsine*
Althea (**Al**-thee-a) (Greek) to heal. A figure in Greek mythology. When her son was born she was given a firebrand and told her son would live as long as the fire lasted. After 20 years, she destroyed it in a fit of pique, so killing the boy.
Altheda (Al-**thay**-da) (Greek) flower-like.
Aluna (Al-**oo**-na) (Kenyan) coming here.
Alvada (Al-**vah**-da) (Spanish) pure and white.

Alverna (Al-**vern**-a) (English) honest friend.
Alvernise (Al-ver-**neece**) (English) honest friend. *Alvernice*
Alvina (Al-**vee**-na) (Old English) counsellor of the elves.
Alvira (Al-**vee**-ra) (Latin) the fair one. *Alvirra*
Alvita (Al-**vee**-ta) (Latin) vivacious, full of life.
Amalina (**Am**-a-lee-na) (German) industrious and striving. *Amalie*
Amana (Am-**ahn**-a) (Hebrew) loyal.
Amanda (Am-**an**-da) (Latin) fit to be loved. *Amandah*
Amandeep (**Am**-an-deep) (Hindi) light of peace.
Amara (Am-**ah**-ra) (Greek) immortal. *Amarra*
Amaranth (**Am**-er-anth) (Greek) unfading flower.
Amaris (Am-a-**rees**) (Hebrew) covenant of God. *Amares*
Amber (**Am**-ber) (English) the honey-brown colour; and the fossilized resin of coniferous trees, used to make jewellery.
Amberlee (**Am**-ber-lee) (American) a combination of Amber and Lee (one who lives in a clearing in a wood).
Amberlyn (**Am**-ber-lin) (American) combination of Amber and Lynn (pretty). *Amberlinn*
Ambrosine (**Am**-broze-een) (Greek) divine and immortal. The feminine form of Ambrose. *Ambrocine*
Amelia (Am-**ee**-lee-a) (Old German) hard-working. A character in Shakespeare's *Othello* who rather fits the description. *Ameliah, Amilia*
Amera (Am-**ee**-ra) (Arabic) royal, noble.
Amethyst (**Am**-a-thist) (Greek) named after the violet-coloured gemstone.
Amiela (Am-ee-**el**-a) (Hebrew) of God's people.
Amina (Am-**ee**-na) (Arabic) honest and truthful.
Amity (**Am**-it-ee) (Latin) friendship.
Amor (Am-**or**) (Spanish) loved.
Amorita (Am-or-**ee**-ta) (Latin) little beloved one. *Amora*
Amorelle (Am-or-**el**) (French) one who loves passionately. *Amorel, Amorell*
Amy (**Aim**-ee) (French) beloved. *Aime, Aimee, Aimme, Amey, Ami, Amie, Ayme*
Ananda (An-**an**-da) (Sanskrit) joy. Ananda was cousin to Buddha.
Anabelle (**An**-a-bell) (Latin) lovable. *Anabel, Annabell, Annabelle*
Anala (An-**ah**-la) (Hindi) full of fire.
Analise (**An**-a-**lee**-sa) (Scandinavian) gracious and consecrated by God. *Analeese, Analese*
Anastasia (An-a-**stay**-see-a/An-a-**stah**-zee-a) (Greek) resurrection or awakening. Following the murder of the Russian royal family in 1918, stories circulated for years afterwards that the Princess Anastasia had survived. Also the name of a fourth-century saint. *Anastasiya*

Analy (**An**-a-lee) (American) full of grace.
Anatola (An-a-**tole**-a) (Greek) from the east.
Ancelin (**On**-sa-lin) (French) the feminine form of Lancelot.
Ancillia (An-**sill**-ee-a) (Latin) hand maiden.
Andela (An-**dell**-a) (Czech) angel.
Andrea (**An**-dree-a) (Latin) feminine version of Andrew. *Andreah, Andreena*
Andreanne (An-dree-**an**) (Latin) womanly. *Andrenna, Andrianna, Andrina*
Andromeda (An-**drom**-eh-da) (Greek) she who is fit to rule over men. A mythological beauty who was chained to a rock, but was rescued by the hero Perseus.
Anemone (An-**em**-own-ee) (Greek) the woodland wild flower. In Greek mythology, Anemone was a beautiful nymph who was turned into the first anemone flower.
Aneura (An-**eye**-ra) (Welsh) golden. The feminine form of Aneurin.
Angela (**An**-jell-a) (Greek) messenger of God.
Angelica (An-**jell**-ick-a) (Latin) messenger of God. Also the mother of King Arthur's illegitimate son. Also a plant name. *Anjelica*
Angelina (An-jell-**ee**-na) (Latin) angelic. *Angelia*
Angeline (An-jell-**een**) (American) angelic.
Angevin (**On**-je-vin) (French) from the province of Anjou in France. The Angevin dynasty ruled large swathes of Europe in the Middle Ages, including Britain (except Scotland), from 1154 to 1485.
Angharad (Ang-**ha**-red) (Welsh) free from shame, much loved.
Aniela (An-**eel**-a) Polish form of Angela.
Anisah (An-**ee**-sa) (Arabic) friendly. *Anisa*
Anita (An-**ee**-ta) (Spanish) a pet form of Anna, meaning graceful and merciful. Also a version of the Hebrew name Hannah, which means grace, or favoured by God.
Ann (**An**) (Hebrew) graceful and merciful. Originally derived from Hannah. Saint Ann was the mother of Mary and thus the grandmother of Jesus. Saint's day: 26 July. *Anabel, Anita, Anna, Annabella, Anne, Annette*
Anna (**An**-a) (Hebrew) graceful and merciful. Originally a derivative of Hannah. *Ana, Anne*
Annalynn (**An**-a-lin) (American) a combination of Anna and Lynn (meaning pretty). *Analine*
Annemarie (An-ma-**ree**) (American) a combination of Anne and Marie, the French form of Mary, meaning bitter. *Annamaria*
Annette (An-**et**) (Hebrew) graceful and merciful. *Nettie*

Annika (**An**-ik-a) (Scandinavian) outgoing and giving.
Annissa (An-**iss**-a) (Greek) outgoing and giving.
Annora (An-**or**-a) (Irish) honour.
Anona (An-**oh**-na) (Latin) of the harvest.
Anselma (An-**sell**-ma) the feminine form of Anselm (divine protector).
Ansley (**An**-zlee) (English) happy in the clearing.
Anthea (**An**-thee-a) (Greek) flowery.
Antigone (An-**tig**-on-ee) (Greek) impulsive and defiant.
Antoinette (Ant-wa-**net**/On-twa-**net**) French feminine form of Anthony, meaning praiseworthy and priceless. Forever associated with Queen Marie Antoinette who was guillotined in the French Revolution. *Nettie*
Antonia (Ant-**own**-ee-a) (Latin) praiseworthy. Feminine form of Anthony. *Antonella*
Aoibheann (Eve-**ann**) (Irish) beautiful and with a fair nature.
Aoife (**Eef**-a) (Irish) mythical name of a warrior princess.
Aphra (**Aff**-ra) (Hebrew) dust.
Aphrodite (Aff-ro-**die**-tee) (Greek) named after the Greek goddess of love who had unparalleled beauty.
Apollonia (A-poll-**own**-ee-a) (Greek) a feminine version of Apollo, who was the Greek sun god. The name has strong associations with music and poetry.
Apona (Ap-**own**-a) (Native American) a type of butterfly.
April (**Ape**-ril) (Latin) from April, the first month in the pre-Christian calendar, and the beginning of spring.
Apple (**Ap**-ull) (English) yes, it simply means apple, from the name of the well-known fruit!
Arabelle (**A**-ra-bell) (Latin) beautiful. Also has connotations of one who can be entreated. *Arabele, Arabella*
Arachne (A-**rack**-nee) (Greek) a mythological maiden who was turned into a spider.
Arcadia (Are-**kade**-ee-a) (Greek) name of a mountainous region of Greece. Arcadia also has connotations of a perfect land.
Arcelia (Are-**sell**-ee-a) (Spanish) treasured.
Ardelle (Are-**dell**) (Latin) warm and enthusiastic.
Arelie (**A**-rell-ee) (Latin) golden girl.
Aretha (A-**ree**-tha) (English) derived from the Greek word *arete* meaning virtuous. *Aritha*
Arethusa (A-reth-**ooze**-a) (Greek) waterer. In Greek mythology, Arethusa was the name of a water nymph who was changed into a fountain by the goddess Artemis.
Aretta (A-**rett**-a) (Greek) virtuous.
Argenta (Are-**jent**-a) (Latin) silver one.
Aria (**Ah**-ree-a) (Latin) beautiful melody.

Ariadne (A-ree-**ad**-nee) (Greek) helper. In Greek mythology, daughter of King Minos of Crete. She helped the hero Theseus find his way out of the Labyrinth by giving him a ball of thread to mark his way. Today, the term Ariadne's thread means a route out of difficult problems.
Ariana (A-ree-**ah**-na/A-ree-**an**-a) (Latin) derived from Aria, meaning beautiful melody. Also a derivative of Arian (born under the sign of Aries).
Arianda (A-ree-**an**-da) (Greek) helper. From the same root word as Ariadne. *Ariane, Arianne*
Aricia (A-**ree**-see-a) (Greek) princess of the royal blood.
Arielle (**A**-ree-ell) the feminine form of the Hebrew gender-neutral name Ariel, which means lion of God.
Ariene (A-**ree**-en) (Welsh) silver. *Arianne, Arienne*
Arina (**A**-ree-na) English form of the Russian Irina (see Irene), which means peace.
Arista (A-**riss**-ta) (Greek) the best. Also a star in the constellation of Virgo.
Arlea (**Are**-lee-a) (Greek) heavenly.
Arleana (Are-lee-**an**-a) American form of Arlene.
Arlene (**Are**-leen) (Irish) pledge, or promise.
Arlette (Are-**let**) (German) eagle.
Arlinda (Are-**lin**-da) (Albanian) the feminine form of Arlind, which means gold.
Armina (Are-**meen**-a) (German) warrior maid. Also the feminine form of Herman (soldier). *Erma*
Arnalda (Are-**nal**-da) (German) strong as an eagle. Also the feminine form of Arnold. *Arna*
Artemis (**Are**-tem-iss) (Greek) huntress. The name of a Greek goddess associated with virginity, hunting and help for women in childbirth. So difficult was her birth that as soon as she was born she helped her own mother deliver her twin brother.
Arthlese (Arth-**leece**) (Irish) wealthy. *Athlice*
Aruna (A-**roon**-a) (Hindi) a short form of Arundhati, the Hindu goddess of the night.
Arwen (**Are**-wen) (English) noble maiden. Name of a female character in J. R. R. Tolkien's book *The Lord of the Rings*.
Asenath (A-**see**-nath) (Egyptian) the Biblical name of Joseph's Egyptian wife.
Asha (**Ash**-a) (Hindi) hope. *Ashah*
Ashanti (A-**shan**-tee) (African-American) the name of a tribe from west Africa, from where vast numbers of slaves were taken. *Anshante*
Ashlie (**Ash**-lee) the female form of the gender-neutral name Ashley, which means clearing of the ash trees.
Ashling (**Ash**-ling) English form of the Irish name Aisling, which means dream or vision.

Asia (**Aish**-a) named after the continent. Also a short form of the Polish name Joasia, which means God is gracious.
Aspasia (Ass-**pay**-see-a) (Greek) witty.
Assumpta (Ass-**ump**-ta) (Irish) based on the Christian festival, the Assumption, which celebrates when the Virgin Mary was transported to heaven. The date of the festival is 15 August.
Asthore (Ass-**toor**) (Irish) loved one.
Astra (**Ass**-tra) (Greek) star.
Astrid (**Ast**-rid) (Norse) divinely beautiful. The most popular girl's name in Norway.
Atalanta (At-a-**lan**-ta) (Greek) joyful. In Greek mythology, Atalanta was an exceptional athlete who challenged suitors to races for her hand in marriage. She was eventually tricked into accepting one of them.
Atara (At-**are**-a) (Hebrew) feminine form of Atarah, which means crown. The biblical name of the wife of Jerahmeel.
Athalia (Ath-**ale**-ee-a) (German) noble.
Athanasia (Ath-an-**ace**-ee-a) (Greek) immortal.
Athelean (**Ath**-uh-leen) (Old English) noble.
Athene (A-**thee**-nee) (Greek) immortal and wise. The Greek goddess of wisdom, arts and crafts. The city of Athens is named after her. *Athena*
Aubree (**Awe**-bree) (English) the feminine form of the gender-neutral name Aubrey, which means elf power.
Augusta (Awe-**gust**-a) (Latin) the feminine form of Augustus, which means majestic and revered.
Aura (**Awe**-ra) (Latin) an intangible atmosphere that surrounds a person.
Aurease (**Awe**-reece) (Latin) golden.
Aurelia (Awe-**ree**-lee-a) (Italian) the feminine form of Aurelius, which means golden.
Aurnia (**Or**-nee-a) (Irish) golden lady.
Aurora (Awe-**raw**-ra) (Italian) in Roman mythology, the goddess of dawn.
Autra (**Awe**-tra) (Latin) gold.
Autumn (**Awe**-tum) (English) from the name of the season.
Ava (**Aive**-a) (Latin) bird. Also the Greek form of Eve.
Avalina (Av-a-**leen**-a) (English) a variant of the Old English name Avaline, meaning little bird.
Avalon (**Av**-a-lon) (Celtic) isle of apples. The legendary resting place of King Arthur and Queen Guinevere. *Avilon*
Averill (**Aiv**-rill/**Av**-rill) (English) slayer of the boar.
Aviana (Av-ee-**an**-a) (Latin) fresh.
Avianca (Av-ee-**an**-ka) (Latin) fresh.
Aviva (Av-**ee**-va) (Hebrew) the feminine form of the boy's name Aviv, which means spring.
Avoca (Av-**oke**-a) (Irish) sweet valley. Also a place name in County Wicklow, Ireland.

Avril (**Av**-rill) (French) born in the month of April.
Axelle (Ax-**ell**) French feminine form of Axel, which means father of peace.
Aya (**A**-ya) (Japanese) a popular Japanese name meaning colourful.
Ayla (**Eye**-a) (Hebrew) oak tree.
Aylwen (**Ail**-wen) (Welsh) fair brow.
Ayshea (**Eye**-sha) (Arabic) flourishing. One of the wives of Mohammed. *Aysheah*
Azalea (Az-**ail**-ee-a) from the flower name, itself derived from the Greek word *azaleos*, which means dry.
Azarni (Az-**are**-nee) (Japanese) thistle flower.
Azura (A-**zoor**-a/A-**zyoor**-a) (English) derived from the name of the clear blue colour azure. The original source of this word may be the Persian word for blue sky. *Assura*

B

Baba (**Ba**-ba) (African) born on a Thursday.
Babette (Bab-**ette**) (French) my God is my oath.
Balbina (Bal-**bee**-na) (Latin) stammerer.
Bambi (**Bam**-bee) (Italian) a short form of *bambino*, the Italian for child.
Barbara (**Bar**-ba-ra) (Greek) foreign or barbarian. One of the four key virgin saints in the Catholic church.
Bathsheba (Bath-**shee**-ba) (Hebrew) beautiful daughter of Sheba.
Beata (Bee-**ah**-ta) (Latin) blessed. *Beatha*
Beatrice (**Bee**-a-triss) (Latin) she who is blessed. Also a fourth-century saint. *Beatrise, Beatrix*
Bebhinn (Bev-**een**) (Irish) fair lady.
Becca (**Beck**-a) (English) a shortened form of Rebecca, meaning to join together.
Bedelia (Bed-**ee**-lee-a) (Old English) strength.
Begonia (Bee-**go**-nee-a) (English) from the name of the popular houseplant.
Belia (**Bee**-lee-a) (Spanish) beautiful. *Belicia*
Belina (Bell-**ee**-na) (French) a goddess.
Belita (Bell-**ee**-ta) (Spanish) little beauty. *Belleita*
Bella (**Bell**-a) (Italian) beautiful.

Belladonna (Bell-a-**don**-a) (Italian) beautiful woman.
Bellarosa (Bell-a-**rose**-a) (Italian) beautiful rose. *Bellarose*
Belle (**Bell**) (French) beautiful. Also a nickname for Annabel, Arabella, Belinda, Isabel and Isabella.
Bellona (Bell-**own**-a) (Latin) warlike. The name of the Roman goddess of war.
Benedicta (Ben-a-**dick**-ta) (Latin) blessed. The feminine form of Benedict. *Benita, Benedetta*
Benilda (Ben-**ill**-da) (Latin) benign and of good intentions.
Berdine (**Ber**-dyne) (Old German) glorious maiden.
Berenice (Ber-**neece**/Ber-a-**nee**-ka) (Greek) bringer of victory. *Bernice*
Bernadette (Burn-a-**det**) (French) the feminine form of Bernard, which means brave as a bear. The Virgin Mary appeared to Bernadette at Lourdes and she became a saint. *Bernadine, Berneen, Nadette*
Bernia (**Burn**-ee-a) (Old English) maiden of battle.
Bernina (Burn-**ee**-na) (French) the name of a particular mountain range in the Alps.
Berry (**Beh**-ree) (English) berry. Also used as a nickname for Berenice and Bernadette.
Berta (**Bert**-a) (Old English) a bright or famous pledge. Also the feminine form of Gilbert.
Bertha (**Berth**-a) (Old English) famous. *Berthe*
Berthilda (**Berth**-ill-a) (Old English) shining warrior maid.
Berwyn (**Ber**-win) (Welsh) fair-haired friend, or bright friend. *Berwin, Berwynn*
Beryan (**Ber**-yan) (Gaelic) the name of a Cornish saint.
Beryl (**Beh**-rull) (Sanskrit) precious pale-green stone.
Bess (**Bess**) (English) consecrated to God. A short form of Elizabeth. *Bessie, Bessy*
Beth (**Beth**) (Hebrew) from the house of God.
Bethan (**Beth**-an) (Gaelic) life force. (Hebrew) a short form of Elizabeth.
Bethany (**Beth**-an-ee) (Hebrew) from the house of figs. Also the town in which Lazarus was raised from the dead.
Bethesda (Beth-**es**-da) (Hebrew) from the house of mercy. Also a place mentioned in the Bible.
Bethia (**Bee**-thee-a) (Hebrew) daughter of God.
Betrys (**Bet**-riss) Welsh form of the Italian name Beatrice, which means she who is blessed.
Betsey (**Bet**-see) (English) a form of Elizabeth. *Betsy*
Bettina (**Bet**-ee-na) (Italian) a short form of Benedetta, which means blessed.
Betty (**Bet**-ee) (English) a common pet name for Elizabeth.

Beverly (**Bev**-er-lee) (English) from the clearing of the beaver. Often used as a boy's name in Europe. *Bev, Beverlee, Beverley*
Bianca (Bee-**an**-ka) (Italian) white or bleached. Features in two of Shakespeare's plays: *Othello* and *The Taming of the Shrew*. *Biancha, Biancia*
Bibi (**Bee**-bee) (Arabic) lady.
Bibiane (Bib-ee-**ah**-na) (Italian) a form of Viviane, which means alive.
Bidane (Bee-**dane**) (Basque) way.
Biddy (**Bid**-ee) (Irish) strong and spirited. The name of an ancient Celtic goddess. Also a short form of Bridget.
Bienvenida (Bee-en-ven-**ee**-da) (Spanish) welcome.
Bijou (Bee-**zhoo**) (French) small jewel.
Bindy (**Bin**-dee) (English) a short form of the German name Belinda, which means, er, serpent!
Birdie (**Bird**-ee) (English) little bird.
Birgitta (**Beer**-git-a) (Scandanavian) a form of Birgit, which means exalted one.
Birkita (Ber-**kee**-ta) (Celtic) strong.
Bisera (**Biss**-air-a) (Bulgarian) name derived from the Slavic word *biser*, which means pearl.
Bitsie (**Bit**-see) (American) small.
Bitta (**Bit**-a) Scandinavian form of the Irish name Bridget.
Blaithin (Blaw-**heen**) (Irish) little flower. *Blatheen*
Blanca (**Blank**-a) (Spanish) white or bleached.
Blanche (**Blaansh**) (Norman) white or bleached.
Blanchefleur (**Blaansh**-flur) (Norman) white flower. Also a name from Arthurian legend.
Blanda (**Bland**-a) (Latin) cherished.
Blathnaid (**Blaw**-nid) (Irish) from the flowers.
Bliss (**Bliss**) (English) joyful.
Blodwen (**Blod**-win) (Welsh) white flower or blessed flower.
Blondelle (Blond-**ell**) (French) the little blond one.
Blossom (**Bloss**-um) (English) named after flower blossom.
Bluebell (**Bloo**-bell) (American) a flower. A name that was popular in the nineteenth century, but much less so today. *Bluebelle*
Bly (**Blye**) (Native American) tall. *Blye*
Bodil (**Bo**-dill) (Scandinavian) battle maiden.
Bogdana (**Bog**-duh-na) (Bulgarian) gift from god. *Bogna*
Bona (**Bon**-a) (Latin) good.
Bonduca (Bon-**doo**-ca) (Celtic) a form of Boudicca, who was Queen of the Iceni in eastern England in the first century AD. *Boudica, Boudicea*
Bonfilia (Bon-**fil**-ee-a) (Italian) good daughter.
Bonita (Bon-**ee**-ta) (Spanish) pretty. *Bonitta*
Bonnie (**Bon**-ee) (Scottish) pretty and good. *Bonny*

Boronia (Bo-**roe**-nia) (English) derived from a species of plant of that name.
Borislava (Bo-riss-**lah**-va) (Russian) feminine form of Borislav, which means battle glory.
Bracha (**Bra**-ka) (Hebrew) a blessing.
Branca (**Bran**-ka) (Czech) glory.
Brandy (**Bran**-dee) (English) named from the drink and also a feminine form of Brandon. *Brandee, Brandie*
Branislava (Bran-iss-**lah**-va) (Czech) feminine form of Branislav, which means glorious protector.
Branwen (**Bran**-win) (Welsh) means both beautiful and holy raven. In Arthurian legend, the name of the daughter of Llyr. *Branwin, Branwyn*
Breana (**Bree**-an-a) (English) feminine form of Brian. *Breyana*
Breann (**Bran**) (Irish) a form of Breana.
Breck (**Breck**) (Irish) freckled.
Bree (Bree) (Gaelic) strong and spirited. The name of an ancient Celtic goddess. Sometimes a short form of Bridget and Brianna, but also a name in its own right. *Brid*
Breeda (**Bree**-da) (Irish) strength.
Breena (**Bree**-na) (Irish) glowing.
Brenda (**Bren**-da) (Old German) flaming sword. (Irish) glowing.
Brenda Lee (**Bren**-da-**lee)** (American) a combination of Brenda and Lee.
Brendette (Bren-**det**) (French) small and royal.
Brenna (**Bren**-a) Irish form of Brenda.
Bretta (**Bret**-a) (Celtic) from Britain.
Briallen (Bree-**al**-en) (Welsh) primrose.
Brianna (Bree-**an**-a) (Celtic) noble and honourable. A feminine form of Brian. *Bryanna, Bryanta*
Brianne (**Bree**-an) (Irish) strong.
Bridget (**Brid**-jit) (Irish) strong and virtuous. Originally a Celtic goddess of healing, but the name now has strong Christian connotations, thanks to a series of Saint Bridgets. *Brigid*
Bridley (**Brid**-lee) (Irish) wise. *Brid, Bridlee, Bridly*
Brie (**Bree**) (French) from the town famous for its cheese.
Brielle (Bree-**el**) (English) a short form of Gabrielle, which is the feminine form of Gabriel.
Brighid (**Breed**) (Irish) full of force. *Brigh*
Brigitte (Bri-**zheet**) French form of Bridget, meaning strong and virtuous.
Brina (**Bree**-na) (Celtic) protector.
Brinlee (**Brin**-lee) (American) sweetheart.
Briony (**Bry**-an-ee) (English) a vine-like plant. Also means to grow and swell. *Brionee, Brioney*
Britney (**Brit**-nee) (English) little Britain. *Brittany*
Britt (**Brit**) (Swedish) a form of the Irish name Brighid. *Brit, Britte*
Brona (**Bro**-na) (Irish) sorrowful. *Bronach*
Bronnen (**Bron**-en) (Cornish) from the rushes.

Bronislava (Bron-iss-**lah**-va) (Czech) the feminine form of Bronislav, which means glorious protector.

Bronwyn (**Bron**-win) (Welsh) white-breasted. A figure from Welsh legend who was married to an Irish king. Unhappy with the marriage, she sent a message via a bird to her brother, who sent a fleet to rescue her. *Bronwinn*

Brunetta (Broo-**net**-a) (French) brown-haired.

Bruna (**Broo**-na) (German) brown-haired. The feminine form of Bruno. *Bruella, Brunella*

Brunhilde (**Broon**-hill-da) (German) warrior maiden. The name of a warrior queen in Germanic legend.

Bryher (**Briar**) (Cornish) the name of one of the Scilly Isles, off the coast of Cornwall.

Bryn/Brynn (**Brin**) (Welsh) hopeful. *Brynna*

Buffy (**Buf**-ee) (English) a pet form of Elizabeth. *Buffee, Buffie*

Bunny (**Bun**-ee) (English) pet form of Berenice/Bernice, meaning bringer of victory. *Bunnie*

Burgundy (**Ber**-gun-dee) (English) derived from the name of the wine, which was named after a region in France. Also the deep-red colour associated with the wine.

Buttercup (**But**-er-cup) (English) named after the wild yellow flower.

C

Cachet (Ka-**shay**) (French) desirable.

Cadence (**Kay**-dense) (Latin) graceful and rhythmic melody.

Cady (**Kay**-dee) (English) a short form of Cadence and an alternative form of Katie. *Cadee, Cadi, Cadie*

Caecilia (Ses-**ee**-lia) (Latin) feminine form of Caecilius, which means blind.

Caelyn (**Kay**-lin) (American) loved forever.

Cailín (Col-**een**) (Irish) slender girl. *Cainwen, Colleen*

Cairine (Ca-**ree**-na) a derivative of the Greek Catherine, meaning pure, but also used as an independent name.

Cairistiona (Ca-riss-**stee**-na) Scottish form of Christiona, which means follower of Christ.

Caitlin (Cat-**leen**) (Irish) pure one. *Cait*

Caja (**Kye**-a) (Cornish) a daisy-like flower. *Caya*

Cala (**Ca**-la) (Arabic) castle.

Calandra (Ca-**lan**-dra) (Greek) lark. *Kalandra*

Calantha (Ca-**lan**-tha) (Greek) beautiful and blossoming. *Kalantha*

Caledonia (Ca-led-**oh**-nee-a) (Latin) girl from Scotland.

Calida (Ca-**lee**-da) (Latin) warm and loving. *Calyda, Kalida, Kalyda*

Calinda (Ca-**lin**-da) (American) a combination of Cal (short for many names beginning Cal-) and Linda, meaning pretty.
Calista (Ca-**liss**-ta) (Greek) most beautiful of women. *Kalista*
Calla (**Cal**-a) (Greek) beautiful. (English) name of the cala lily flower. *Cala, Kala*
Callidora (Cal-ee-**door**-a) (Greek) one given the gift of beauty. *Callie, Cally, Kallidora*
Calligenia (Cal-ee-**jen**-ee-a) (Greek) born beautiful.
Calliope (Cal-**eye**-oh-pee) (Greek) beautiful poetry. *Caliopa, Caliope, Kaliopa, Kalliope*
Callison (**Ca**-liss-un) (American) a combination of Cal (short for many names beginning Cal–) and Alison, meaning light of the sun.
Callisto (Ca-**liss**-toe) (Greek) in Greek mythology, the daughter of the King of Arcadia. *Callie, Cally, Kalisto*
Callula (Ca-**loo**-la) (Greek) beautiful little one. *Cally, Kallula, Kally*
Caltha (**Cal**-tha) (Latin) little flower.
Calvina (Cal-**vee**-na) (Italian) feminine form of Calvin/o, meaning little bald one.
Calypso (Ca-**lip**-so) (Greek) concealer. In Greek mythology, a beautiful nymph who held Odysseus captive on his return from Troy. *Kalypso*
Camarin (**Cam**-rin) (Native American) protector. *Camarinne*
Cameo (**Cam**-ee-o (Italian) small picture.
Camellia (Cam-**ee**-lee-a) (English) a flower name.
Camilla (Ca-**mill**-a) (Latin) temple servant. Originally it was a generic name for beautiful young girls who helped in religious ceremonies during the early Christian period. Her saint's day is 14 July. *Camelia, Camille*
Camira (**Cam**-ee-ra) (Australian) an Aboriginal word meaning of the wind.
Candice (**Can**-dace) (Latin) daughter of the wind. *Candase, Candace*
Candida (Can-**dee**-da) (Latin) white and pure.
Candra (**Can**-dra) (Latin) luminescent.
Candy (**Can**-dee) (English) sweet one. Also a nickname for Candace and Candida. *Candee*
Cantara (Can-**ta**-ra) (Arabic) small bridge. *Cantarah*
Caoilainn (Kay-**leen**) (Irish) fair and slender.
Caoimhe (**Kwee**-va) (Irish) gentle and graceful.
Caplice (**Cap**-leece) (American) spontaneous.
Capri (**Cap**-ree) (English) from the Italian island of the same name.
Caprice (Ca-**preece**) (Italian) on a whim.
Capucine (Cap-oo-**chine**) (French) derived from the French for the nasturtium flower.

Cara (**Ca**-ra) (Italian) dear friend, darling. (Irish) friend.
Caramia (Ca-ra-**mee**-a) (Italian) derived from the Italian phrase *cara mia* meaning my beloved.
Cardinia (Card-**in**-ee-a) (Australian) the Aboriginal word for dawn.
Carina (Ca-**ree**-na) (Italian) the Italian derivation means darling. (Scandinavian) from the root word for the keel of a ship, so implying steadiness and guidance. (Australia) the Aboriginal word for bride. *Karina*
Carinthia (Ca-**rin**-thea) (German) named after the beautiful region of southern Austria that borders the Adriatic sea. *Karinthia*
Carissa (Ca-**riss**-a) (Greek) refined. *Carrie, Carry, Karissa*
Carita (Ca-**ree**-ta) (Italian) charity.
Carla (**Car**-la) (French) a feminine version of Carl, meaning free man.
Carleigh (**Car**-lee) (Old English) freeholder. *Carley, Carly*
Carlene (**Car**-leen) (English) a feminine version of Carl, which means free man. *Carlenne*
Carlissa (Car-**liss**-a) (Italian) a feminine version of Carl, meaning free man.
Carlotta (Car-**lot**-a) (Old English) a free person. A feminine form of Carl, which means a free man.
Carly (**Car**-lee) (American) a feminine version of Carl, meaning free man. *Carlee, Carlie*
Carmel (**Car**-mel) (Hebrew) the literal translation is fertile field or vineyard, but the name also appears in the Bible as Mount Carmel, the place where Elijah proved God to be greater than the pagan gods. Her saint's day is 16 July. *Carmela, Carmelita, Carmella, Karmel*
Carmen (**Car**-men) (Spanish) a form of Carmel, but with dancing connotations because of Bizet's opera of the same name. *Karmen*
Carnation (Car-**nay**-shun) (English) named after the flower. These names were at their most popular in the Victorian period.
Carol (**Ca**-rol) (German) woman. Also a derivation of Caroline. The fourth of November is the feast of Saint Carol. *Carla, Carole, Carolyn*
Carolina (Ca-rol-**ee**-na/Car-ol-**ine**-a) (Spanish) small and womanly.
Caroline (**Ca**-roe-line) (German) womanly.
Carolyn (**Ca**-roe-lin) (American) a combination of Carol, meaning woman, and Lynn, meaning pretty.
Caron (**Ca**-ron) (Welsh) a name meaning love in Welsh.
Carreen (Ca-**reen**) (English) a character in Margaret Mitchell's famous book, *Gone With the Wind*.
Caresse (Ca-**ress**) (French) touched by love. *Caressa*
Carrie (**Ca**-ree) (English) a pet form of Caroline. *Carry*

Carrigan (**Ca**-ree-gan) (Irish) name derived from the Irish word *carraig*, which means rock.
Carys (**Ca**-riss) (Welsh) derived from the Welsh *caru*, meaning love. *Caris*
Casilda (Ca-**sill**-da) (Spanish) the name of an eleventh-century saint.
Casilde (Ca-**sill**-duh) (Latin) of the home.
Cass (**Cass**) (English) short form of Cassandra, meaning entangler of men. *Cassie*
Cassandra (Cass-**and**-ra/Cass-**ahn**-dra) (Greek) entangler of men. A figure in Greek mythology who was given the gift of seeing the future, but the curse that no one would believe her prophecies. Thought to be an original Greek derivation of Alexandra. Saint's day: 11 October. *Kassandra*
Cassia (**Cass**-ee-a) (Greek) cinnamon.
Castalia (Cass-**tay**-lee-a) (Greek) fountain. A figure from Greek mythology, Castalia was a beautiful nymph who was transformed into the fountain at Delphi by the sun god Apollo. Thereafter, it was said that those who then drank from the fountain would gain the gift of poetry. *Kastalia*
Catalina (Ca-ta-**lee**-na) Spanish form of Catherine, meaning pure. Also used as a name in its own right.
Catalonia (Ca-ta-**lon**-ya/ Ca-ta-**low**-nee-a) (Spanish) a region of Spain, from which the name is derived.
Catarina (Cat-a-**ree**-na) Portuguese form of Catherine, meaning pure. Also used as a name in its own right.
Catherine (**Cath**-er-in) (Greek) pure. Catherine became a saint after a vision in which the Virgin Mary asked her to make a medal. The design is oval and brass and is known as the miraculous medal. Saint's day: 25 November. She is the patron saint of medals. *Kate, Kateri, Kathleen, Kathryn, Katrina, Kay, Kit, Kitty, Trina*
Cathleen (**Cath**-leen) (Irish) pure, virginal. *Cathlene*
Cathryn (**Cath**-rin) (English) form of Catherine, which means pure. *Catalina, Caterina, Kate, Kateri, Katherine, Kathryn, Katrina, Kay, Kit, Kitty, Trina*
Cathy (**Cath**-ee) (English) pet form of Cathryn. *Cathee, Cathie*
Catina (Ca-**teen**-a) (English) a shortened form of the Portuguese name Catarina, meaning pure.
Catline (Cat-**leen**) (Irish) a form of Caitlin, meaning pure one.
Catrice (Cat-**rice**) Greek form of Catherine (pure). *Katrice*
Catriona (Cat-**roe**-na/Cat-**ree**-oh-na) Gaelic form of Catherine, which means pure. The English variant spelling is Catrina.
Cayla (**Cay**-la) (Hebrew) unblemished. *Caylia*
Cayleigh (**Cay**-lee) (Irish) a gathering together for a dance. *Caylee, Caylie*

Cayley (**Cay**-lee) (American) joyful.
Cecilia (Sess-**ee**-lee-a) (Latin) unseeing. Saint Cecilia was a third-century saint who is remembered on 22 November. Cecilia's parents wed her to a pagan nobleman. Eager to convert her new husband, she told him about the angel that always escorted her. He wanted to see the angel, too, so he asked for his soul to be purified by baptism. The next time she prayed, her husband saw the angel place a crown on both their heads. *Cecil, Cecile, Cecily, Cicely, Ceil, Sheila.*
Cecily (**Sess**-ill-ee) (Irish) the blind one. *Cecilie*
Ceinwyn (**Kine**-win) (Welsh) beautiful jewel.
Celandia (Sel-**and**-ee-a) (Greek) the swallow. *Kelandia*
Celandine (**Sell**-and-ine) (Greek) yellow flower. *Kelandine*
Celena (Sel-**ee**-na) (Greek) goddess of the moon. *Celina, Celine, Seleene, Selina*
Celeste (Sel-**est**) (Latin) heavenly. *Celestia, Celestin, Celestine*
Celestina (**Sel**-ess-**tee**-na) (English) blended form of Celeste (meaning heavenly) and Tina (a short form of names ending -tina).
Celestyn (**Sel**-ess-tin) (Polish) heavenly.
Cera (**See**-ra) (French) colourful.
Cerdwin (**Serd**-win) (Celtic) the Celtic mother goddess.
Ceren (**Ke**-ren) (Turkish) young gazelle. (Gaelic) star.
Ceres (**Seer**-ees) (Latin) the name of the Roman goddess of fertility and the harvest.
Ceridwen (Ker-**rid**-wen) (Welsh) fair and a poet. The goddess of poetry in Welsh legend. *Ceridwin*
Cerise (Se-**reece**) (French) originally the meaning was cherry, the furit. It now more commonly refers to the cherry-red colour.
Cerys (**Kair**-iss) (Welsh) love. *Ceris*
Chalette (Sha-**let**-a) (Spanish) rose.
Chalice (**Chal**-iss) (English) a name derived from chalice, meaning cup.
Chaline (**Sha**-lyn) (American) one who smiles.
Challie (**Sha**-lee) (American) charismatic.
Champagne (Sham-**pain**) (French) champagne. Meaning both the bubbly drink and the region of northeast France where it is made.
Chanah (**Cha**-na) (Hebrew) grace.
Chandra (**Chan**-dra) (Sanskrit) shining moon.
Chanel (Sha-**nel**) (French) derived from the fashion house founded by Coco Chanel.
Chanelle (Sha-**nel**) (French) a relatively new name based on the name of the fashion house Chanel.
Chania (**Chan**-ee-a) (Hebrew) camp.
Chanina (Cha-**nee**-na) (Hebrew) grace.
Chanise (Sha-**neece**) (American) adored.

Chantal (Shon-**tal**) (French) from a rocky area. Saint Chantal's husband was killed in a hunting accident. Over time she learned to forgive the man who shot him, to such an extent that she even became godmother to his child. Saint Chantal's feast day is 18 August. *Chantale, Chantelle*
Chardonnay (**Shar**-don-nay) (French) place name of a small town near the city of Macon, France, in the heart of the wine region. The word chardonnay was accepted formally into the English language in the early part of the twentieth century, with the meaning of white burgundy wine.
Charis (**Cha**-riss) (Greek) the original meaning was grace, but over time it has been extended to include charity as well. First used as a given name in the seventeenth century. *Carisma, Chareesse, Charisa, Charise, Charisma, Charissa, Charisse, Charysse, Kara, Karis, Karisma, Karisse, Sherisa*
Charita (Cha-**ree**-ta) (Hindi) good. Now often used as a variation on the name Charity. *Cherita, Sharita*
Charity (**Cha**-rit-ee) a name based on the word charity. Spectacularly popular amoungst the Puritans.
Charla (**Shar**-la) (American) a feminine form of Charles, meaning free man.
Charlaine (**Shar**-lane) German) freeholder. *Charlana, Sharlaine, Sharlene, Sharline*
Charlee (**Char**-lee) (American) womanly and full-grown. Also a feminine form of Charles.
Charlene (**Shar**-leen) (French) free person. A feminine form of Charles. *Charleen, Charline*
Charlotte (**Shar**-lot) (French) free person. A feminine form of Charles.
Charmaine (Shar-**main**) (Latin) song of charm. *Charmain*
Charnelle (Shar-**nel**) (American) sparkling.
Charo (**Char**-oh) (Spanish) pet form of Rosario, which means rosary.
Chasina (Cha-**see**-na) Hebrew) strong.
Chastity (**Chass**-tit-ee) (Latin) chaste.
Chava (**Cha**-va) (Hebrew) full of life.
Chelentha (Che-**len**-tha) (American) one who smiles.
Chelle (**Shell**) (French) a short form of Michelle, the French feminine form of Michael.
Chelsea (**Chel**-see) (Old English) chalk landing place or island. Now associated with areas of London and New York.
Chemdiah (**Shem**-dee-a) (Hebrew) God is my hope.
Chenille (Shen-**eel**) (American) soft.
Cher (**Shair**) (French) dear. In the case of the American singer it is short for Cherilyn.
Cherice (Sher-**eece**) (French) cherry and the cherry-red colour, cerise. Also means held dear. *Cherise*
Cherelle (Sher-**el**) (French) dear.

Cherette (Sher-**et**) (French) dear.
Cherie (Sher-**ee**) (English) a variant of the French name meaning dear. *Cheri*
Cherilynn (**Sher**-il-in) (American) a combination of Cheryl and Lynn.
Cherinne (**Sher**-in) (American) happy.
Cherry (**Cher**-ee) (English) named after the fruit.
Cheryl (**Cher**-ul/**Sher**-ul) (American) a combination of Cherry and Beryl. *Sheryl*
Chesna (**Shez**-na) (Slavonic) peaceful.
Cheyenne (**Shy**-anne) (Native American) named after the North American tribe. Also the name of Marlon Brando's daughter.
Chiara (Kee-**ah**-ra) (Italian) clear.
Chickie (**Chick**-ee) (English) derived from the Spanish name Chiquita, meaning little one.
Chika (**Chee**-ka) (Japanese) wisdom.
Chikako (Chik-**ak**-o) (Japanese) child of wisdom.
Chiquita (Chik-**ee**-ta) (Spanish) little one.
Chirtsey (**Churt**-sea) (Scottish) a pet form of Christine, which means follower of Christ. *Chirtsee, Chirtsie*
Chita (**Chee**-ta) (Spanish) a short form of Conchita, which means conception.
Chloe (**Klo**-ee) (Greek) young green roots. The name appears both in the Bible and in Greek mythology. *Cloe*
Chloris (**Klo**-riss) (Greek) derived from the name of the Greek goddess of vegetation. *Khloris*
Chrissy (**Criss**-ee) (English) bearing Christ. Derived from Christopher. *Chrissie, Krissy*
Christa (**Criss**-ta) (German) a short form of Christina, meaning anointed.
Christabelle (**Criss**-ta-bell) (American) a combination of Christine, meaning follower of Christ, and Belle, meaning beautiful. *Christobel*
Christal (**Criss**-tull) (English) clear as ice. *Crystal, Krystal*
Christalin (**Cris**-ta-lin) (American) combination of Christa (anointed) and Lynn (pretty). *Christalyn*
Christen (**Cris**-ten) the English form of the German name Kristen (which means follower of Christ).
Christine (**Criss**-teen) (English) anointed one. A feminine version of Christian. *Christian, Christiana, Christianne, Christina, Kirsten, Kristin, Nina, Tina*
Christmas (**Criss**-mass) (English) born at Christmas.
Chruse (**Croos**-uh) (Greek) the golden one.
Chrysilla (**Criss**-ill-a) (Greek) golden-haired.
Chrysanthemum (Criss-**an**-tha-mum) (Greek) named after the flower.
Chula (**Choo**-la) (Hebrew) musical.
Ciannait (Kee-**ahn**-a) (Irish) ancient wisdom.
Ciara (**Kee**-ra) (Celtic) dark or black. A feminine form of Ciaran.

Ciera (**Kear**-a) English variant of the Spanish name Sierra, which means mountain range. *Cieara*
Cilla (**Sill**-a) (Italian) originally from a Roman family name, but now more often a short form of Priscilla. Also a name in its own right.
Cinderella (Sin-der-**ell**-a) (French) little cinder girl. Often shortened to Cindy.
Cindy (**Sin**-dee) (French) little cinder girl. Also a short form of Cinderella, Cynthia and Lucinda. *Sindy*
Ciona (See-**oh**-na) (American) steadfast.
Cipriana (Sip-ree-**an**-a) (Italian) cautious.
Circe (**Ser**-see) (Greek) witch-goddess, seductive. The name of a figure in Greek mythology who was a great seductress.
Ciri (**See**-ree) (Latin) regal.
Cirine (Ke-**reen**) (Irish) exalted. *Sirine*
Cissy (**Siss**-ee) (English) a pet form of Frances, which means girl from France.
Claiborne (**Clay**-born) (Old English) born of the earth.
Clair/Claire (**Clair**) (Latin) clear and bright.
Clara (**Clah**-ra) (Latin) clear and bright.
Clarabelle (**Clah**-ra-**bel**) (English) a combination of Clara (clear) and Belle (beautiful). *Clarabel*
Claramay (**Clah**-ra-**may**) (English) bright pearl.
Claramond (**Clah**-ra-mond) (German) bright protector.
Clare (**Clair**) (Latin) derived from the Latin *clarus* which means bright. Also a place name in Ireland and an aristocratic family name (the two are connected). The eleventh of August is the feast day of the medieval Saint Clare. Towards the end of her life she was too frail to attend Mass, but God displayed it to her on her wall and she became the patron saint of television! *Claire, Clairette, Clara, Claretta, Clarice, Clarissa, Clarita*
Clarice (Cla-**reece**) (Latin) little brilliant one. *Clarise*
Clarinda (Cla-**rin**-da) (English) elaborated form of Clare, meaning clear and bright.
Clarissa (Cla-**riss**-a) a form of Clarice, meaning little brilliant one.
Clarissant (Cla-**riss**-ant) in Arthurian legend, the name of a female character in Chrétien de Troyes' *Perceval, the story of the Grail.*
Clarity (**Cla**-rit-ee) (English) clear.
Claudia (**Claw**-dee-a) (French) little lame one. Female form of Claud/e. Named after the Roman god of the lame. Saint Claud died in the early 700s, but when his tomb was opened 400 years later, the body was found to be uncorrupted. His burial place then became a destination for pilgrims and miraculous cures occurred there. Saint's day: 6 June. *Claudette, Claudine*
Claudie (**Claw**-dee) (English) pet form of the name Claudette (see Claudia).

Clea (**Clee**-a) (Greek) glory.
Cleanthe (Clee-**an**-tha) (Greek) glory flower.
Clemence (**Clem**-ence) (French) the feminine form of Clemens (see Klemens), which means clement and merciful. Saint's day: 23 November. *Clementina, Clementine, Clemmy*
Cleo (**Clee**-o) (Greek) short form of Cleopatra, which means her father's glory or renown. The most famous Cleopatra was Queen of Eygpt and the lover of both Julius Caesar and Mark Antony. She nearly became Empress of Rome but, following military defeat and on hearing of Mark Antony's death, she took her own life.
Cleva (**Clay**-va) (English) one who lives on a hill.
Cliantha (Clee-**an**-tha) (Greek) flower.
Clio (**Clee**-o) (Greek) one of the nine Muses of Greek mythology. Clio was historian to the gods.
Clodagh (**Cloe**-da) (Irish) from the Irish word for muddy – *cladach*. (Greek) flourishing. *Cloeda, Cloda*
Cloreen (**Clor**-een) (American) happy. *Cloreene*
Cloressa (Clore-**ess**-a) (American) consoling.
Clorinda (Clore-**in**-da) (Latin) happy.
Clover (**Clove**-er) (English) from the flower name.
Clydette (Cly-**det**) (American) feminine form of Clyde.
Clytie (**Cly**-tee) (Greek) splendid.
Coco (**Co**-co) diminutive form of the Spanish name Socorro. Also the root word for chocolate.
Colanda (Co-**lan**-da) African-American version of Yolanda.
Colette (Col-**et**) (French) triumph of the people. Also a derivative of Nicolette (see Nicola). Saint Colette's feast day is 6 March. *Collette*
Colisa (Col-**iss**-a) (English) delightful.
Colleen (Col-**een**) based on the Irish word for girl.
Columbine (**Col**-um-bine) (Spanish) dove. The feast of Saint Columba is 23 November. *Columba, Columbia, Columbina*
Comfort (**Cum**-fort) from the English verb to comfort.
Concordia (Con-**cor**-dia) (Latin) the name of the Roman goddess of peace and harmony.
Condoleezza (Con-doe-**lee**-za) (American) the name derives from the musical term *con dolcezza* which means to play with sweetness.
Conlee (**Con**-lee) (American) a form of Connelly, meaning dark. *Conly*
Constance (**Con**-stance) (English) steady and firm. Saint Constantine was a king who, when his wife died, became a monk. His feast day is 11 March. *Consantia, Constanza*
Consuela (Con-**sway**-la) (Spanish) consolation.

Contessa (Con-**tess**-a) (Italian) pretty. Also Italian for Countess. *Contesa*
Cora (**Core**-a) (Greek) maiden.
Coral (**Co**-ral) (English) coral.
Corazon (Co-ra-**zon**) (Spanish) heart.
Cordelia (Cor-**dee**-lee-a) (Latin) from the heart. (Irish) harmony. Most famously used by Shakespeare as the name of one of King Lear's daughters. Of his three daughters, she had the kindest heart. *Delia*
Cori (**Core**-ee) (Irish) one who cares.
Corinna (Cor-**in**-a) (Greek) maiden. *Korinda*
Corinne (**Co**-rin) French version of the Irish name Cory, which means from the hollow.
Corinthia (Cor-**in**-thee-a) (Greek) woman from the town of Corinth. *Korinthia*
Corissa (Cor-**iss**-a) (Greek) kind-hearted. *Korissa*
Cormella (Cor-**mell**-a) (Italian) fiery.
Cornelia (Cor-**nee**-lee-a) (Latin) practical. Her saint's day is 16 September.
Corona (Cor-**own**-a) (Spanish) crown or halo.
Corrianna (Co-ree-**an**-a) (American) playful.
Corrinda (Cor-**in**-da) (French) feminine, girly.
Cory (**Core**-ee) (Irish) means from the hollow.
Cosette (Co-**zette**) (French) warm.
Cosima (**Coss**-ee-ma) name based on the Greek word for universal order. *Kosima*
Cotton (**Cot**-on) (English) named after the plant.
Cournette (Cor-**net**) (American) a feminized version of coronet.
Crescent (**Cres**-sent) (French) named from the shape of the quarter moon. (Greek) a short form of Cressida, meaning strong and golden.
Cressida (**Cress**-id-a) (Greek) strong and golden. A character from Shakespeare's *Troilus and Cressida*. *Cressa, Cressie*
Cristin (**Criss**-tin) (Irish) dedicated. *Crystyn*
Cristina (Criss-**tee**-na) Greek form of Christina. *Crista*
Crystal (**Criss**-tull) (Greek) originally from a Greek word meaning ice, the name now carries connotations of purity and transparency. *Crystalle, Krystal*
Cullen (**Cull**-en) (Irish) attractive.
Cursten (**Kers**-ten) American form of Kirsten which is the Scandinavian version of Christine, meaning anointed one.
Cyan (**Sy**-an) (Greek) light blue. Also a nymph from Greek mythology. Nymphs are female spirits associated with nature.
Cybil (**Sib**-ill) (Greek) prophetess. *Sybil*
Cynthia (**Sin**-thee-a) (Greek) named after Mount Cynthus. In Greek mythology, Artemis, goddess of hunting, was born on this mountain.

D

Dabria (**Dab**-ree-a) (Latin) the name of an angel.
Dacia (**Day**-see-a) (Greek) a woman from Dacia, an ancient European country that approximates to modern Romania.
Daffodil (**Daf**-o-dil) (English) from the name of the flower. This name was originally derived from its Greek name, asphodel.
Dafnee (**Daf**-nee) American form of Daphne, a nymph in Greek mythology.
Dagna (**Dag**-na) (Scandinavian) new day.
Dahlia (**Day**-lee-a) (English) from the flower, which is named after the Swedish botanist, Dahl.
Daireena (Da-**reen**-a) (Irish) fruitful.
Daisy (**Day**-zee) (Old English) from the flower. In Old English it was called day's eye because the yellow centre looked like the sun.
Daiya (**Die**-ya) (Polish) gift.
Dalia (**Dah**-lee-a/**Day**-lee-a) (Hebrew) flowering branch. *Dalya*
Dalice (**Da**-liss) (American) able. *Dallise*
Damalis (Da-**mal**-iss) (Greek) calf. *Damalys*
Damara (Da-**mar**-a) (Greek) gentle girl.
Damaris (Da-**mar**-iss) (Greek) a woman converted to Christianity by Saint Paul.
Dame (**Da**-muh) (German) lady.
Damhnait (**Dav**-nit) (Irish) little fawn. *Damh* is the Irish for fawn
Damia (**Day**-mee-a) (Greek) to tame. A feminine form of Damian and Damon.
Damiana (Day-mee-**ah**-na) (Greek) tame. A feminine form of Damian and Damon. *Damiane*
Damita (Da-**mee**-ta) (Spanish) princess or noble lady.
Damosel (**Dam**-sell) (English) damsel or young, unmarried woman.
Dana (**Dah**-na) (Irish) brave and poetic. Name of the Celtic mother goddess in pre-Christian Ireland. The Irish winner of the Eurovision Song Contest in 1970.
Danae (**Dan**-nay) (Greek) bright and pure.
Danala (Dan-**ah**-la) (English) happy. *Danalla*
Danelle (Dan-**el**) (American) a combination of Dan and Elle.
Daniah (**Dah**-nee-ah) (Hebrew) God's judgement.
Danica (Dan-**ee**-ka) (Slavic) morning star.
Danielle (Dan-**yell**) (French) female form of Daniel, which means God is my judge. The feast day of Saint Daniel is 16 February. *Danialla, Daniella, Danya, Danylla*
Danita (Da-**nee**-ta) (English) a pet form of Daniella (see Danielle).
Danna (**Dan**-a) (American) cheerful. *Dana*

Danu (Dan-**oo**) (Welsh) the mother of the gods in Celtic mythology.
Danuta (Dan-**oo**-ta) (Polish) little dear one.
Daphne (**Daf**-nee) (Greek) in Greek mythology she was a nymph chased by the god Apollo. Rather than lose her virginity, she changed herself into the first laurel tree. *Dafnee*
Daralis (Da-**ral**-iss) (Hebrew/English) cherished wisdom. *Daralice*
Darcelle (**Dar-sell**) (American) secretive.
Darcie (**Dar**-see) (French) an old Norman family name (D'Arcy). *Darcy*
Daria (**Da**-ree-a) (Greek) luxurious.
Darian (**Da**-ree-an) (Old English) valuable.
Darielle (Da-ree-**el**) (French) wealthy.
Darlee (**Dar**-lee) (English) darling. *Darlie*
Darlene (**Dar**-leen) (English) derived from the Old French word for little darling.
Darrelle (Da-**rel**) (French) beloved one. The feminine form of Darrell (see Darryl).
Darri (**Da**-ree) (Australian) Aboriginal for track or path. *Darrie*
Darshana (**Dar**-sha-na) (Hindi) named after a Hindu philosophical term meaning looking at.
Darshelle (Dar-**shell**) (African-American) confident.
Dasha (**Dash**-a) (Greek) a gift of God.
Dasheena (Dash-**ee**-na) (African-American) bright and flashy.
Dashelle (Dash-**ell**) (African-American) striking.
Datiah (**Dat**-ee-ah) (Hebrew) obeying God's law. *Datia*
Daureen (**Door**-een) (American) darling.
Davan (**Da**-van) (Irish) the adored one. Also a feminine form of David, which means beloved.
Daveena (Da-**vee**-na) (English) variation on the Hebrew name Davina.
Davida (Da-**vee**-da) Scottish feminine version of David, meaning beloved
Davina (Da-**vee**-na) (Hebrew) cherished one. A feminine form of David, meaning beloved.
Dawn (**Dawn**) (English) daybreak. *Dawna*
Dayana (Day-**ah**-na) (Hebrew) derived from the Hebrew word *daya* meaning bird. *Dayanna*
Dea (**Dee**-a) based on the Latin word for goddess.
Deana (Dee-**an**-a) (Latin) the divine one. Also a feminine form of Dean. *Deanna*
Deanna (Dee-**an**-a) (English) lover of the sea. *Deanne*
Dearbhail (Da-**rool**) (Irish) of destiny.
Debbie (**Deb**-ee) (English) derived from the Hebrew word for a bee. An industrious woman. Also short for Deborah. *Debby*

Deborah (**Deb**-or-a) (Hebrew) based on the word for bee. Deborah was the only female ruler of Israel. She guided the divided Israelites and delivered them from the oppression of the Chanaanites. *Debra, Debrah*

Dee (**Dee**) (Celtic) based on the Celtic word for river and goddess (in Celtic mythology the two were closely related).

Deesha (**Dee**-sha) (American) dancing.

Deianira (**Dee**-a-**neer**-a) (Greek) the wife of the Greek hero (and later demi-god) Heracles (Hercules).

Deirdre (**Dear**-dra/**Dear**-dree) (Irish) sorrowful wanderer. The name of a character from Irish folklore.

Deitra (**Dee**-it-ra) English variation on the Irish name Deirdre.

Dejana (De-**yah**-na) (Serbian) feminine form of Deja, meaning to take action.

Delaine (De-**lain**) (American) Elaine with the D- prefix.

Delana (De-**lan**-a) (German) noble protector. *Delanna*

Delbin (**Del**-bin) (Greek) a flower name.

Delfina (Del-**fee**-na) (Greek) dolphin. *Delphina*

Delanah (De-**lan**-a) (American) wise. *Delanna*

Delannah (Italian) (De-**lan**-a) soft as wool.

Delia (**Dee**-lee-a) (Greek) a woman from the island of Delos. Also another name for Artemis, the Greek goddess of hunting. *Cordelia, Deliah, Della*

Delicia (De-**liss**-ee-a) (Latin) delight. *Delisia*

Delilah (De-**lye**-la) (Hebrew) delightful night. In the Bible, she tricked Samson into divulging the secret of his strength. *Delila*

Delinda (De-**lin**-da) (English) a form of the German name Adelinda, which means noble serpent. *Dalinda*

Delise (De-**leece**) (American) Elise with the D- prefix. *Delice*

Della (**Del**-a) (English) a woman from the island of Delos. Also a diminutive of Adèle and Adelaide.

Dellana (De-**lan**-a) (Irish) the female form of Delaney, which means descended from the challenger.

Delma (**Del**-ma) (Irish) short form of Fidelma, which means forever good.

Delon (**Del**-on) (American) musical.

Delora (De-**lore**-a) (English) a variant of the Spanish name Dolores, which means sorrow.

Delores (De-**lore**-ez) (English) a variant of the name Dolores, meaning sorrow.

Delphia (**Del**-fee-a) (Greek) brotherly. Also means from the city of Philadelphia. *Delfia*

Delphine (Del-**feen**) (Latin) female from Delphi. Delphi was famous in the ancient world for its oracle, and therefore the name has connotations of one who foretells the future. *Delfine*

Deltrese (Del-**treece**) (African-American) jubilant. *Deltrece*

Delwyn (**Del**-win) (English) proud friend.
Delyth (**Del**-eth) (Welsh) the name is derived from the Welsh word *del*, which means pretty.
Demeter (De-**mee**-ter) (Greek) Earth Mother. Greek goddess of harvests and fertility.
Demi (De-**mee**) (French) half. (Greek) a diminutive of Demeter, the goddess of harvests and fertility.
Dena (**Den**-a) (English) a variant of the Hebrew name Dinah, which means revenged.
Deneen (De-**neen**) (American) a form of the Hebrew name meaning absolved.
Denetria (De-**nee**-tree-a) (Greek) given by God.
Denise (De-**neez**) (French) feminine version of Denis. Denis is based on the name of the Greek god Dionysus who was god of wine, revels and excess. Saint Denis was the first bishop of France and patron saint of the country. His feast day is 9 October.
Denisha (**Den**-ish-a) (American) a feminine form of Denis.
Deolinda (Dee-o-**lin**-da) (Latin) beautiful goddess.
Dericka (**Der**-ik-a) (German) ruler of the people.
Derora (De-**roar**-ra) (Hebrew) flowing stream.
Derrona (Duh-**roe**-na) (American) natural.
Dervla (**Derv**-la) (Irish) based on the Gaelic *deirbhile* which means daughter of a poet.
Desdemona (Dez-de-**moan**-a) (Greek) ill-fated. A character in Shakespeare's play *Othello*, who was indeed ill-fated.
Desire (Dee-**zire**) (English) desire.
Desirée (De-**zeer**-ray) (French) French word for desired girl.
Destiny (**Dess**-tin-ee) (Latin) fate or destiny.
Destry (**Dess**-tree) (American) blessed by destiny.
Devina/Devinda (Dev-**ee**-na/Dev-**in**-da) (Celtic) poet. Also a feminine form of Devlin, meaning brave and fiery.
Dew (**Dyoo**) (English) dew.
Dextra (**Dex**-tra) (Latin) right-handed, skilled with the hands.
Dia (**Dee**-a) (Greek) like a goddess. Sometimes used as a name for Hera, who was queen of the Greek gods.
Diana (Die-**an**-a) (Latin) this is the Roman name for the Greek deity called Artemis. She was the goddess associated with hunting, virginity and help for women in childbirth.
Diane (Die-**an**) (French) the French form of Diana.
Diantha (Dee-**an**-tha) (Greek) divine flower of Zeus. *Dianthia*
Diarah (Die-**ah**-ra) (American) pretty. *Diara*
Dicia (**Diss**-ee-a) (American) carefree spirit.

Dido (**Die**-doe) (Phoenician) bold. The legendary founder of Carthage, in what is now northern Africa.
Dielle (Dee-**el**) (Latin) one who worships God.
Dilys (**Dil**-iss) (Welsh) genuine and true.
Dinah (**Die**-nah) (Hebrew) revenged. A biblical figure who exacted revenge for being raped. *Dina*
Diona (Dee-**oh**-na) (Greek) divine girl. *Dyona*
Dionne (**Dee**-on) (Greek) in Greek mythology, the mother of Aphrodite, goddess of beauty and love. *Dyonne*
Divina (Div-**ee**-na) (Italian) divine. *Divine*
Dixie (**Dix**-ee) (American) southern girl. Originally a Scandinavian word for sprite.
Diya (**Dee**-ya) (Arabic) happiness. *Diyah*
Diza (**Dee**-za) (Hebrew) joy. *Disa*
Dolores (Dol-**or**-ez) (Spanish) sorrowful woman.
Dominica (Do-mi-**nee**-ka) (Latin) the female form of Dominic, which means follower of God.
Dominique (Do-mi-**neek**) (French) the French female form of Dominic.
Domino (**Dom**-in-o) (French) masked. From the masks worn at a masquerade.
Donata (Don-**ah**-ta) (Italian) celebrated gift.
Donatela (Don-a-**tell**-a) (Italian) celebrated gift. *Donatella*
Donelle (Don-**el**) French form of Donna, meaning lady.
Donna (**Don**-a) (Italian) lady. Saint's day: 17 April. *Dona, Donata, Donatilla*
Dora (**Dor**-a) (Greek) gift. A shortened form of either Theodora or Dorothy (both meaning gift of God).
Dorcas (**Dor**-cass) (Greek) doe or gazelle. English Bibles usually translate the name Tabitha as Dorcas.
Doreen (**Door**-een) (Irish) gift. The Irish version of Dora, meaning gift.
Dorianne (**Dor**-ee-an) (Greek) gift. *Dorianna*
Doris (**Dor**-iss) (Greek) feminine version of Theodore, meaning gift of God. In Greek mythology, she was the wife of Nereus and mother of the sea nymphs.
Dorothy (**Dor**-oth-ee) (Greek) gift from God. An extremely popular name at the beginning of the the twentieth century. *Dorothea*
Dorte (**Door**-ta) Danish form of Dorothy and Dorothea.
Dory (**Door**-ee) (English) pet form of Dora, meaning gift.
Dosia (Do-**see**-a) (Latin) a nickname for Theodosia, which means God-given.
Dot (**Dot**) (English) nickname for Dorothy, meaning gift from God. *Dottie, Dotty*
Dreena (**Dree**-na) (American) cautious.
Druella (Droo-**ell**-a) (Old German) vision of the elves.

Drusillia (Droo-**sill**-ee-a) (Greek) soft eyes. Drusilla is the Latinized version. The name of the wife of the Roman governor of Jerusalem, who was converted to Christianity by Saint Paul.
Duana (**Dwayne**-a) (Celtic) song.
Dubhnait (**Dav**-nit) (Irish) little dark one. *Davneth*
Duena (Dyoo-**en**-a) (Spanish) chaperone.
Dulcibella (Dul-si-**bell**-a) (Italian) sweet and beautiful.
Dulcie (**Dul**-see) (Latin) sweet. *Dulce, Dulcea*
Dusana (Doo-**san**-a) (Czech) spirit, or soul. *Dusa, Dusanka, Dusicka, Duska*
Dwynwen (**Dwin**-wen) (Welsh) fair and holy. The Welsh patron saint of lovers who, rather inappropriately, turned her suitor into ice. Often shortened to Dwyn.
Dyan (**Die**-an) (Italian) the divine one. Diana, the goddess of hunting in Roman mythology. *Dyanne*
Dyani (Die-**an**-ee) (Native American) deer.
Dylana (**Dil**-an-a) (Sanskrit) meditation.
Dympna (**Dymf**-na) anglicized form of the Irish name *Damhnait*, which means little fawn.
Dyna (**Die**-na) (Greek) powerful. *Dinah*
Dyonne (Dee-**on**) (American) marvellous. *Dyone*

Eabha (**Ee**-a-va) the Irish form of Eve, which means life.
Eadaoin (**Aid**-een) (Irish) derived from the Irish word *etain* meaning face. The English variation is spelled Aideen.
Eadburga (**Ed**-burga) (Anglo-Saxon) from the rich fortress.
Ealasaid (**Yal**-a-sat) (Gaelic) Scottish Gaelic form of Elizabeth. Another Scottish variation is Ealisaid.
Eamhair (**Ee**-mer) Scottish form of the Irish name Eimer, which means ready.
Earlean (**Er**-leen) (English) the feminine form of Earl. *Earlene, Earline*
Eartha (**Erth**-a) (Old English) from the earth.
Easter (**East**-er) (English) named after the Christian festival, and a pagan English festival of the fertility goddess Eoesta.
Eavan (**Ee**-van) (Irish) beautiful. *Eav*
Ebba (**Eb**-a) (Old English) fortress.
Eberta (E-**bur**-ta) (Old German) bright and brilliant.
Ebony (**Eb**-on-ee) (Greek) the name of the dark hardwood.
Ebrel (**Eb**-rel) (Cornish) born in April. This was the first month of the pre-Christian Roman and Celtic calendars.

Echo (**Ek**-o) (Greek) in Greek mythology, a beautiful nymph who annoyed the queen of the gods with her constant chatter. As punishment she was cursed so that she could only speak when spoken to, and then only repeat the endings of words.

Edaena (**Ed**-ee-na) (Old English) blessed.

Edalene (**Ed**-a-lean) (Old English) blessed.

Edana (Ee-**dah**-na) (Irish) little fiery one.

Edda (**Ed**-a) (Old English) rich. *Eda*

Edena (Ed-**ee**-na) (Hawaiian) renewal or rejuvenation.

Edeva (Ed-**ee**-va) (Old English) a rich gift.

Edina (Ed-**ee**-na) (English) prosperous friend. Also the feminine form of Edwin, which means the same.

Edith (**Ee**-dith) (English) prosperous friend. Saint's day: 11 October. *Eadie, Eda, Edythe*

Edna (**Ed**-na) (Hebrew) rejuvenation. (Irish) kernel. Also a short form of Edwina,a feminine form of Edwin, which means prosperous friend.

Edia (Ee-**dee**-a) (Hebrew) mighty.

Edwardina (Ed-war-**dee**-na) (English) prosperous guardian. A female form of Edward, meaning the same.

Edwina (Ed-**wee**-na) (Old English) prosperous friend. A feminine form of Edwin. Saint's day: 12 October. *Edna*

Eerin (**Ee**-rin) (Australian) Aboriginal for a small, grey owl.

Efia (**Eff**-ee-a) (Ghanaian) born on Tuesday. *Effie, Effy*

Eglantine (**Egg**-lan-teen) (French) French name for the briar-rose. *Eglantyne*

Eibhlin (**Eve**-lin) an Irish form of Evelyn and pronounced the same way.

Eiddwen (**Ith**-wen) (Welsh) beloved fair one. *Eiddwyn*

Eileen (**Eye**-leen) Irish form of Helen, meaning bright. *Eileena*

Eilis (**Ee**-liss) Irish form of Elizabeth, meaning oath of God.

Eilwen (**Iyl**-win – sounds like 'I'll win') (Welsh) fair of brow. *Eilwyn*

Eirian (**Eye**-ree-an) (Welsh) silver.

Eirianne (**Ee**-ree-an) French form of Eirian, meaning silver.

Eirwen (**Eye**-er-win) (Welsh) white as snow. One variation is Eira which is the Welsh word for snow. *Eirwyn*

Eithne (**Eth**-ne) (Irish) little fire. Also a figure from Irish mythology.

Ekala (**Ee**-kah-la) (Australian) an Aboriginal word for lake.

Ekata (Ee-**kah**-ta) (Sanskrit) unity.

Ela (**El**-a) (Old English) elfin. Also a diminutive for Eleanor, Elizabeth, Ellen and Helen.

Elaine (El-**laine**) French form of Helen (which is Hélène, but 'h' is not pronounced in French so it sounds like Elaine).

Elana (Ee-**lah**-na) (Hebrew) tree.
Elanora (**Ee**-la-**no**-ra) (Australian) the Aboriginal word for a home by the sea.
Elberta (El-**bert**-a) (Latin) noble and illustrious. Also the feminine form of Albert, meaning noble knight. *Elbertina, Elbertine*
Eldora (El-**dor**-a) (Spanish) golden.
Eleanor (**El**-an-or) (German) foreign. Eleanor of Aquitaine was probably the most remarkable woman of the Middle Ages. She was wife to one King of England (Henry II) and mother to two others (Richard the Lionheart and King John). She also experienced many remarkable adventures along the way. *Elinor, Leanore, Lee, Lenora, Lenore, Leora*
Electra (El-**ek**-tra) (Greek) radiant. In Greek mythology, she avenged the death of her father by killing her own mother after she took another lover.
Elena (El-**lee**-na) (Greek) light.
Eleri (**El**-er-ee) (Welsh) the name of a river.
Elexus (El-**ex**-us) Greek form of the Latin name Alexis, which is short for Alexandra, meaning defender of mankind. *Elex, Elexis, Lex, Lexus*
Elfin (**El**-fin) (Old English) elf-like. *Elvin*
Elfreda (El-**free**-da) (Italian) ready and noble. A feminine form of Alphonse (see Alphonso).
Eliana (El-e-**ah**-na) (Hebrew) literally, God has answered me. *Elianna*
Elida (Ee-**lye**-da) (Latin) the little winged one. *Elyda*
Elina (El-**ee**-na) Finnish form of Helen, meaning bright.
Eliora (E-lee-**or**-a) (Hebrew) a feminine form of Elior, which means God is my light.
Elise (**El**-eez) French shortened form of Elisabeth (see Elizabeth), meaning oath of God.
Elisha (El-**ee**-sha) (Hebrew) God is my salvation.
Elissa (El-**iss**-a) (Greek) consecrated to God.
Eliza (El-**ize**-a) (Hebrew) a shortened version of Elizabeth. *Elisa*
Elizabeth/Elisabeth (Hebrew) oath of God. The mother of John the Baptist, and confidante of the Virgin Mary. There are three different saints named Elizabeth, each of whom has a different feast day: 4 January, 4 July and 17 November. *Bess, Bette, Betty, Elisa, Lisa, Liz*
Elkana (El-**ka**-na) (Hebrew) literally, God is jealous.
Elke/Elkie (**El**-ka/**El**-kee) German forms of Alice, meaning noble.
Ella (**El**-a) (German) foreign. The same root as the word Welsh, which means foreign in Anglo-Saxon.
Ellamay (**El**-a-**may**) (American) a combination of Ella (foreign) and May (the month).
Elle (**El**) (French) she.

Ellen (**El**-en) Welsh form of Helen. The name of one of the legendary King Arthur's daughters.
Ellendea (El-**len**-dee-a) (Greek) God's light.
Ellice (**El**-iss) (Greek) Jehovah is God. Also the feminine form of Elias.
Ellie (**El**-ee) (English) short form of both Ellen and Eleanor. *Elly*
Elma (**El**-ma) (Greek) pleasant and fair.
Elmas (**El**-mas) (Armenian) diamond. *Elmaz*
Elmira (El-**mee**-ra) (English) noble.
Elodie (**El**-oh-dee) (French) wealthy and prosperous. The Spanish version is Elodia.
Eloise (El-oo-**eez**) (French) originally derived from the Old German Heloise. Now most commonly a derivation of Louise.
Elrica (El-**rye**-ka) (German) the ruler of all. *Ulrika*
Elsa (**El**-sa) German short form of Elisabeth, which means oath of God.
Elspeth (**Else**-peth) Scottish version of Elizabeth. Often shortened to Elsie.
Eluned (**El**-oo-ned) (Welsh) object of adoration.
Elva (**El**-va) (Old English) of the elves.
Elvina (El-**vee**-na) (Old English) friend of the elves. *Elvyna*
Elvira (El-**vee**-ra) (Spanish) ancient name for Granada, in Spain.
Elysia (El-**ee**-see-a) (Greek) ideal happiness. (Latin) blissful.
Elyssa (El-**iss**-a) (Latin) consecrated to God.
Elzira (El-**zeer**-a) Portuguese form of Elizabeth.
Ember (**Em**-ber) (English) smouldering remains of a fire.
Emelda (Em-**ell**-da) (English) a floret, or small flower.
Emelia (Em-**ee**-lee-a) (English) ambitious and industrious. A form of Amelia.
Emerald (**Em**-er-ald) named after the green gemstone.
Emily (**Em**-ill-ee) (Latin) eager. Saint's day: 24 December. *Amelia, Emeline, Emilia, Emiliana, Emma*
Emina (Em-**ee**-na) (Latin) a noble or lofty maiden.
Emma (**Em**-a) (German) entire.
Emmaline (**Em**-a-leen) (German) entire. In Arthurian legend Emmaline was a blind princess whose sight was restored by Merlin.
Emuna (Em-**oo**-na) (Arabic) faith.
Emmylou (**Em**-ee-**loo**) (American) a combination of Emily and Louise.
Ena (**En**-a) (English) anglicized version of the Irish name *Eithne*, which means little fire.
Endora (En-**dore**-a) (Hebrew) fountain.
Engracia (En-**gra**-see-a) (Spanish) graceful.
Enid (**Ee**-nid/**En**-id) (Welsh) soul. In Arthurian legend, the name of the wife of Sir Geraint.

Engelberta (En-gel-**bert**-a) (Old German) bright angel.
Enola (Ee-**no**-la) (American) a short form of Magnolia, named after the flowering tree.
Enore (Ee-**nor**-ra) (Greek) light. *Enora*
Enya (**En**-ya) (Irish) means little flame. Related to Eithne and Ena. *Anya*
Epona (Ee-**poe**-na) a Celtic goddess. She carried soldiers who died in battle to paradise.
Erasma (Ee-**ras**-ma) (Greek) amiable.
Erika (**Eh**-rick-a) Scandinavian form of Erica, the feminine of Eric, meaning king of all. Saint Eric was a King of Sweden. Saint's day: 18 December.
Erlina (Air-**lee**-na) (Celtic) girl from Ireland.
Erlinda (Er-**lin**-da) (Hebrew) lively.
Erline (Er-**leen**-a) (English) noblewoman. The feminine form of Earl, meaning nobleman. *Erlyne*
Erma (**Er**-ma) English form of the German name Irma, which means whole and complete. She was a key character in Sigmund Freud's analysis of dreams.
Ermina (Er-**mee**-na) (Norman) derived from the white fur, ermine.
Ermintrude (**Er**-min-trood) (German) loved by all. *Ermin*
Erna (**Ern**-a) (German) feminine form of Ernest, which means determined.
Ernestine (**Er**-ness-teen) (German) battle to the last, or determined. The short form is Erna or Ernie.
Ersilia (Er-**sill**-ee-a) (Italian) derived from the Latin word *hersilia*, meaning delicate or tender.
Erwina (Er-**wee**-na) (Old German) honourable friend.
Eselde (Es-**sell**-da) (Celtic) a form of Isolde (see Yseult), which means of fair aspect.
Eshe (**Ai**-shay) (Hindi) desire. *Esha*
Esne (**Ez**-nuh) (English) happy.
Esme (**Ez**-mee) (French) held in esteem. Also a feminine form of Edmund, which means successful defender). *Esma*
Esmerelda (Ez-mer-**el**-da) (Spanish) emerald.
Essence (**Ess**-ens) (English) based on the Latin for essential, meaning being.
Essie (**Ess**-ee) often used as a short form of either Estella or Esther.
Estefania (Es-ta-**fann**-ya) (Spanish) garland or crown. A feminine form of Stephen. *Estephania*
Estelle (Ess-**tell**) (Greek) star. *Estella*
Esther (**Ess**-ter) (Hebrew) myrtle. (Persian) the morning star, or Venus. In the Bible, Esther was the Jewish wife of a Persian king. She used her position to avert a massacre of the Jews. *Ester, Edissa, Stella, Estelle, Estella*
Estrella (Ess-**tray**-a) Spanish form of Stella, meaning star.
Etain (**Ee**-ten) (Irish) a female character from Irish mythology.
Etana (Ee-**ta**-na) (Hebrew) strong.

Etaney (**Et**-a-nee) (Hebrew) focused. *Etani*
Eternity (Ee-**turn**-it-ee) (English) everlasting.
Ethel (**Eth**-ull) (German) noble.
Etheldreda (Eth-el-**dray**-da) (English) from the Anglo-Saxon name Aethelthryth, which means noble strength.
Ethelfleda (Eth-el-**flay**-da) (English) from the Anglo-Saxon Aethelflaed, meaning noble beauty.
Ethelinda (Eth-el-**in**-da) (English) from the Anglo-Saxon Aethenlinda, meaning noble serpent.
Ethne (**Eth**-na) (Irish) little fire. *Eithne, Ena, Enya*
Etta (**Et**-a) (English) a short form for a number of longer names ending in -etta, such as Georgetta (see Georgia). Also an Old German term for little. *Ettie, Etty*
Euadne (You-**ad**-nee) (Greek) the name of a female character from Greek mythology.
Eudora (You-**dore**-a) (Greek) a good gift.
Eudosia (You-**doe**-see-a) an English form of the Greek name Eudoxia, which means one who seems well.
Eugenia (You-**jean**-ee-a) (Greek) well-born. Her saint's day is 2 June. *Eugenie, Genie*
Eulalia (You-**lay**-lee-a) (Greek) well-spoken. *Eula, Eulia*
Eulanda (You-**lan**-da) (American) fair.
Eunice (**You**-niss) (Greek) good victory. In the Bible, she is the mother of Timothy, who preached the Scriptures. *Eunyce*
Euphemia (You-**fee**-mee-a) (Greek) one who speaks well of others.
Euphrasia (You-**fray**-see-a) (Greek) delight and joy.
Eurwen (**Your**-wen) (Welsh) fair. *Eurwyn*
Eva (**Ee**-va) German and Italian form of Eve, meaning life. The patron saint of tailors. Saint's day: 24 December. *Eve, Eveline, Evelyn, Evita*
Evadine (Ev-**ad**-ee-na) (Greek) the name of a character from Greek mythology. *Evadyne*
Evadne (Ev-**ad**-nee) (Greek) fortunate.
Evana (Ev-**ah**-na) (Slavic) God is gracious.
Evangeline (E-**van**-jel-een) (Greek) the bearer of good news. *Evangelia, Evangelyne*
Eve (**Eev**) (Hebrew) life. A well-known figure from the Bible. *Eveline, Evellina*
Evette (Ee-**vet**) (French) diminutive of the name Evonne, a feminine form of Yves, meaning little archer. *Yvette*
Evonne (Ee-**von**) (French) feminine form of Yves, meaning little archer. (Greek) the wood of the yew tree. (Archers' bows are traditionally made from yew.) *Yvonne*

F

Fabia (**Fay**-bee-a) (Latin) bean planter. *Fabiana, Fabienne*
Fabrienne (Fab-ree-**en**) (French) little blacksmith.
Fabrizia (Fa-**britz**-ee-a) (Italian) maker of things, or craftswoman.
Faina (**Fie**-na) (Old English) the Anglo-Saxon word for cheerful.
Fairlee (**Fair**-lee) (English) from the yellow meadow.
Faith (**Faith**) (Latin) trust and belief. A Roman widow, Saint Wisdom (or Sofia) had three daughters, Saints Faith, Hope and Charity, who all suffered for Jesus. Faith, aged 12, miraculously survived being scourged and thrown into boiling pitch. Hope (10), and Charity (9), were unharmed when tossed into a furnace. Their feast day is 1 August. *Fay, Fidelia*
Faline (**Fay**-line) (Latin) like a cat.
Fanchone (Fan-**shown**) (French) born of freedom.
Fanny/Fannie (**Fan**-ee) (American) short for Frances, meaning from France.
Fantasia (Fan-**tay**-see-a) (Greek) imaginative.
Farley (**Far**-lee) (English) from the fern clearing. *Farlee, Farlie*
Farrah (**Fa**-ra) (English) full of beauty. *Farah, Farra*
Farren (**Fa**-ren) (Old English) traveller. *Faren*
Fatima (**Fat**-im-a) (Arabic) weaner. The favourite daughter of the prophet Mohammed. *Fatimah*
Fauna (**Fawn**-a) (Latin) she who favours.
Fausta (**Faow**-sta) (Latin) lucky. *Faustina, Faustine*
Fawn (**Fawn**) (French) young deer. *Fawna, Faunee*
Fay (**Fay**) (French) meaning either faith or fairy. Morgan le Fay was half-sister to King Arthur. *Fayina, Fayleen, Faye*
Fayre (**Fair**) (English) with light-coloured hair. *Faire*
Federica (Fed-er-**ee**-ka) Italian feminine form of Federico, or Frederick, which means peaceful ruler.
Fedora (Fe-**dore**-a) (Greek) divine gift.
Feena (**Fee**-na) (Irish) small deer.
Feidhlim (**Fie**-lim) (Irish) ever good. The Irish name Fidelma has the same meaning.
Felda (**Fel**-da) (Old German) of the field.
Felicia (Fe-**lee**-see-a) a feminine form of Felix, and an alternative form of Felicity, both meaning lucky. *Felica, Felice, Felicita*
Felicienne (Fe-liss-ee-**en**) French feminine form of Felicien, or Felix, which means lucky.
Felicity (Fell-**iss**-it-ee) (Latin) lucky or opportune. Saint Felicity is the patron saint of women who want to become pregnant. The seventh of March is her feast day. *Felice, Felicia, Felicita*

Fenella (Fen-**ell**-a) (Irish) a variant form of the name Fionnuala, which means white-shouldered.

Fenna (**Fen**-a) (Irish) fair-haired. *Fena*

Feodora (Fee-o-**dore**-a) (Greek) gift of God.

Fern (**Fern**) (English) fern. *Ferne*

Fernanda (Fer-**nan**-da) (German) born with an adventurous spirit.

Feronia (Fe-**roe**-nee-a) (Latin) the name of a goddess in Roman mythology. *Feronya*

Fiala (**Fee**-a-la) (Czech) violet flower.

Fidelia (Fi-**day**-lee-a) (Latin) a form of Fidelity, meaning true and faithful.

Fidelity (Fid-**ell**-it-ee) (Latin) true and faithful. *Fidelitee*

Fidelma (Fid-**ell**-ma) the Irish feminine form of Feidhlim, which means ever good.

Fifi (**Fee**-fee) (French) a short form of Josephine (the feminine of Joseph, meaning God will add).

Filberta (Fil-**bert**-a) (Spanish) brilliant. *Philberta*

Filia (**Fil**-ee-a) (Greek) friend. *Philia*

Filippa (**Fil**-ip-a) (Italian) a lover of horses. *Fillipa, Philippa*

Findabhair (**Finn**-da-**veer**) (Irish) heroine in Irish mythology. The short form is Finn.

Finesse (Fin-**ess**) (French) elegant and subtle.

Fiona (Fee-**oh**-na) (Scottish) white and fair. *Fi*

Fionnuala (Finn-**oo**-la) (Irish) white-shouldered. In Irish legend, her stepmother had hired a witch to kill Fionnuala and her three brothers, but Fionnuala's purity was such that the witch could not go through with the plan. Instead, the four siblings were turned into white swans. *Finola, Fionola*

Fiorella (Fee-o-**rell**-a) (Italian) a little flower.

Fiorenza (Fee-o-**ren**-za) (Italian) flower.

Finvarra (Fin-**var**-a) (Irish) a place name. *Finbharra*

Flannery (**Flan**-er-ee) (Irish) red-haired. *Flanna*

Flavia (**Flah**-vee-a) (Latin) with golden hair.

Fleur (**Flur**) (French) flower. *Fleurette*

Flo (**Flow**) (American) a short form of Florence, meaning flowering or blossoming.

Flora (**Floor**-a) (Latin) flower. Also a short form of Florence. Saint Flora of Beaulieu did not like her cloistered life in the convent and felt tempted to return home to her family, but she stayed in the order and eventually was rewarded with the gifts of visions and prophecies. Her feast day is 5 October. *Florella, Florelle*

Floramaria (**Flor**-a-ma-**ree**-a) (Italian) flower of Mary. A combination of Flora and Maria.

Florence (**Flor**-ence) (Latin) flowering or blossoming. Florence Nightingale was named after the Italian city. *Floss, Flossie*

Florian (**Flor**-ee-un) (Latin) blossoming.
Florida (**Flor**-id-a) Spanish form of Florence and name of an American state.
Florimel (**Flor**-im-el) (Greek) nectar.
Flower (**Flao**-wer) (English) flower.
Fontaine (Fon-**tayne**) (French) fountain. *Fontana, Fontanna*
Fortuna (For-**tyoon**-a) (Latin) Roman goddess of good luck. *Fortune*
Frances (**France**-iss) (French) from France. Also the feminine version of Francis. Saint's day: 13 November. *Cesca, Fanny, Francesca, Franchette, Francine, Françoise, Fran, Frannie*
Francesca (Fran-**chess**-ca) (Italian) Italian form of Frances, meaning from France.
Francine (**France**-een) French form of Frances, which means from France. *Fransine*
Francisca (Fran-**sis**-ca) Spanish form of Frances, meaning from France.
Frederica (Fred-er-**ee**-ka) (German) peaceful ruler. Also the feminine version of Frederick. Often shortened to Freda. *Fredella, Frederika, Frederike*
Freya (**Fray**-a) (Scandinavian) the Norse goddess of beauty, love and fertility. *Fray, Freja, Frieda*
Fulla (**Full**-a) (German) full.
Fulvia (**Full**-vee-a) (Latin) tawny-haired. The name of Mark Antony's wife. *Fulvya*
Fynballa (Fin-**bal**-a) (Irish) fair.

G

Gabriela (Gab-ree-**el**-a) (Hebrew) God is my strength. See also Gabriel. Gabriel is an angel celebrated on 29 September. *Briel, Gabbi, Gabby, Gabriella, Gabrielle*
Gai (**Gay**) (English) blithe and cheerful.
Gail (**Gale**) (Hebrew) father's joy. Also a short form of Abigail, *abba* being the Hebrew word for daddy. *Abbie, Abby, Gale, Gayle*
Gaia (**Guy**-a) (Greek) Earth Mother, 'life is one'. Symbolizes the fact that all life is related and, to some degree, part of the same being. *Ghia*
Gala (**Gah**-la) (Arabic) gathering for a festival. *Galah*
Galanta (Ga-**lan**-ta) (Greek) snowdrop.
Galatea (Gal-a-**tee**-a) (Greek) milky white. Wife of Pygmalion in Greek mythology.
Galena (Ga-**lee**-na) (Latin) a lead-like metal.
Galiena (**Ga**-lee-na) (Old German) tall girl. *Galienah*
Galilah (Ga-**lil**-a) (Hebrew) the redemption of God.
Ganya (**Gan**-ya) (Hebrew) garden. *Ganyah*
Gardenia (Gar-**den**-ee-a/Gar-**deen**-ee-a) (Latin) the name of a genus of about 250 flowering plants. *Gardenyia*

Garland (**Gar**-land) (French) a crown or wreath of flowers.
Garnet (**Gar**-net) (French) a dark red gemstone.
Gaylene (**Gay**-leen) (Hebrew) father's joy. Also a derivation of Abigail.
Gaynor (**Gay**-ner) (English) fair and beautiful. An anglicized version of Guinevere. *Gaenor, Gayna, Gayner*
Gazelle (Gaz-**el**) (Latin) antelope.
Gebriele (**Geb**-ree-el) (Hebrew) woman of God. Also a female form of Gabriel, meaning God is my strength.
Gedala (**Jed**-a-la) (Australian) the Aboriginal word for day.
Gelesia (Jel-**ee**-see-a) (Greek) laughing like a bubbling spring.
Gemina (Jem-**ee**-na) (Greek) a twin.
Gemma (**Jem**-a) (Italian) based on the Latin word for jewel. Saint Gemma was favoured by mystical experiences, special graces and the stigmata. Her saint's day is 11 April. *Gem, Jem, Jemma*
Gena (**Jen**-a) (Latin) noble and well-born.
Genesia (Jen-**ee**-see-a) (Latin) the newcomer.
Genesis (**Jen**-a-sis) (Hebrew) origin.
Genevieve (**Jen**-a-veev) (French) woman of the people. (Celtic) white wave.
Genette (Jen-**et**) (French) God is gracious. Also the French feminine form of John, meaning favoured by God. *Gen, Gennie, Genny*
Geneva (Jen-**ee**-va) (Latin/Swiss) after the city in Switzerland.
Genji (**Gen**-jee) (Chinese) gold.
Genna (**Jen**-a) (English) fair and soft. Also a form of Guinevere and Genny (see Genette). *Jen, Jenna*
Gennelle (Jen-**el**) (British) a variant of Gina, from Georgina. *Genel, Jenelle*
Gennifer (**Jen**-if-er) (British) fair and soft. Another form of Guinevere. *Gen*
Geona (Jee-**oh**-na) (American) sparkling. *Geonna*
Georgia (**Jor**-ja) (Greek) farmer. Also a feminine form of George. *George, Georgeanna, Georgette, Georgi, Georgiana, Georgina*
Georgina (Jor-**jee**-na) see Georgia.
Geraldine (**Jer**-al-deen) (Old German) spear ruler. Also the feminine form of Gerald.
Geralyn (**Jer**-a-lin) (American) a combination of Geraldine and Lynn (meaning pretty).
Gerda (**Gird**-a) (Scandinavian) enclosure or stronghold.
Germaine (Jer-**mayne**) (French) from Germany. (Old English) cousin.
Gertrude (**Gert**-rood) (Old German) spear maiden.
Geva (**Jee**-va) (Hebrew) from a hill.
Ghera (**Ge**-ra) (Australian) the Aboriginal word for the leaf of a gum tree.
Ghislaine (Giss-**lane**) (French) a pledge. *Ghislayne, Gislayne*

Ghita (**Gee**-ta) (Italian) pearl.
Gianna (Jee-**ah**-na) (Italian) God is gracious. Gia is the short form.
Gigi (**Zhi**-Zhi) (French) girl from the farm. Also the feminine form of George.
Gila (**Guy**-la) (Hebrew) joy.
Gilanah (Jil-**ah**-na) (Hebrew) exultation or joy. *Gilana*
Gilberta (Gil-**bert**-a) (English) the feminine form of Gilbert, which means bright promise.
Gilda (**Gil**-da) (Irish) servant of god.
Gilian (**Jil**-ee-an) (Latin) from a Roman family name. Also the feminine form of Julian, and a derivative of Julia, both meaning fair-skinned. *Gill*
Gillian (**Jil**-ee-an) (Greek) soft-haired. Also a derivation of Julian, meaning fair-skinned. *Gill, Gillie, Gilly*
Gina (**Jee**-na) (Italian) a diminutive of Georgina, the feminine form of George, meaning farmer.
Ginger (**Jin**-jer) (English) one with red hair. Also a diminutive of Virginia, and a spice.
Ginny (**Jin**-ee) (English) virginal maiden. Also a diminutive of Virginia.
Gioffreda (Jof-**fray**-da) (Italian) God's peace.
Giovanna (Jov-**ah**-na) (Italian) the feminine form of Giovanni, which is the Italian version of John.
Giselle (Ji-**zel**) (Old English) shining pledge.
Gita (**Gee**-ta) (Sanskrit) song.
Githa (**Gith**-a) (Anglo-Saxon) a gift.
Giuseppina (Jyoo-sep-**ee**-na) (Italian) the Italian feminine version of Joseph, meaning God will add.
Gladys (**Glad**-iss) (Welsh) delicate flower. *Gladis*
Gleda (**Glay**-da) (Old English) to make happy.
Glenda (**Glen**-da) (Welsh/English) to make happy, or girl from the valley.
Glenna (**Glen**-a) (Celtic) from the valley.
Glennice (**Glen**-iss) (British) a form of Glenda, meaning to make happy, or girl from the valley. *Glennyce*
Glenys (**Glen**-iss) (Welsh) holy, pure. *Glenis*
Gloria (**Glore**-ee-a) (Latin) glory. *Glorianne, Glorielle*
Glynis (**Glin**-iss) (Welsh) holy, pure. *Glenys*
Gobnet (**Gob**-net) (Irish) little smith. *Gobnait*
Godiva (Go-**die**-va) (Old English) God-given. Famous for Lady Godiva, who rode naked around Coventry to challenge her husband's over-possessive nature.
Golda (**Gold**-a) (Old English) gold.
Goldie (**Gold**-ee) (English) golden one. Also a form of Golda.
Gormlaith (**Gorm**-la) (Irish) a female character from Irish mythology. *Gorm* is Irish for illustrious.
Grace (**Grace**) (Latin) grace.

Grainne (**Grahn**-ya) (Irish) a female character from Irish fokelore. *Graidhne, Grania*

Grear (**Greer**) (Scottish) watchful. *Greer*

Gregoria (Greg-**ore**-ee-a) (Greek) watchful and vigilant.

Greta/Gretchen (**Gret**-a/**Gret**-chen) German diminutive form of Margaret, meaning pearl.

Gretna (**Gret**-na) named after the Scottish border town famous for marriages.

Griselda (Griz-**el**-da) (Old German) grey battle heroine.

Griselia (Gri-**see**-lee-a) (Spanish) patient.

Guinevere (**Gwin**-ee-vere) (Welsh) fair and beautiful. She was the wife of King Arthur and, fatefully, the lover of Sir Lancelot.

Gwendolyn (**Gwen**-doe-lin) (Welsh) white and pure. The wife of Merlin. *Gwen, Gwendoline*

Gwyneth (**Gwin**-eth) (Welsh) luck and bliss. *Gwynith*

Gypsy (**Jip**-see) (English) originally meaning either a gypsy or an Egyptian.

Gytha (**Gee**-tha) (Old English) war-like.

Hadara (Ha-**da**-ra) (Hebrew) beautiful ornament.

Hafwen (**Hav**-wen) (Welsh) summer. *Hafwyn*

Haidee (**Hide**-ee) (Greek) modesty. *Haydee, Haydie*

Hala (Ha-**lah**) Arabic word for the aura around the moon. *Halah*

Halcyon (**Hal**-see-on) (Greek) a figure from Greek mythology. Mourning her dead husband, she threw herself into a river but was saved by Aphrodite, the goddess of love. Because of this, Halcyon became the first kingfisher.

Haldana (Hal-**dah**-na) (Norwegian) half Danish.

Halimeda (Ha-lee-**mee**-da) (Greek) lover of the sea.

Halona (Ha-**loe**-na) (Native American) fortunate.

Hanele (**Han**-uh-luh) (Hebrew) full of compassion. *Haneleh*

Hania (**Han**-ee-a) (Hebrew) resting place. *Haniah*

Hannah (**Han**-a) (Hebrew) favoured. In the Bible, Hannah was childess. She prayed to God for a baby and had Samuel, who became a prophet. *Hanna, Hannette*

Hanu (**Han**-oo) (Hawaiian) the breath of the spirit.

Harlinne (**Har**-leen) (English) feminine form of Harley, meaning from the clearing of the army. *Harleen, Harlene*
Harmony (**Har**-mon-ee) (Greek) concord. In Greek mythology, the daughter of Ares (god of war) and Aphrodite (goddess of love). She symbolized the balance between male and female. *Harmonie*
Harriet (**Ha**-ree-et) (Old German) ruler of the home. *Hattie*
Hasana (Ha-**sah**-na) (Swahili) first-born female twin.
Hasna (**Hass**-na) Arabic word for beautiful. *Hasnah*
Hasina (Ha-**see**-na) (Hebrew) strength. *Hasinah*
Hattie (**Hat**-ee) a pet form of Harriet, meaning ruler of the home.
Hayley (**Hay**-lee) (English) from the hay clearing. (Scandinavian) heroine. *Haylee, Haylie*
Hazel (**Hay**-zel) (English) tree name, and a light-brown colour. *Hazelle*
Heather (**Heth**-er) (English) named for the plant. In English folklore, heather is said to protect the wearer from danger.
Heaven (**Hev**-en) (English) heaven. *Haven*
Hebe (**Hee**-bee) (Greek) young. In Greek mythology she personified youth.
Hedda (**Hed**-a) (Greek) warrior. *Heddie, Hedy*
Heidi (**Hide**-ee) (German) Swiss form of Adelaide (kind lady of noble birth).
Helanna (Hel-**lah**-na) (American) a combination of Helen (bright) and Anna (graceful and merciful).
Helen (**Hel**-en) (Greek) bright. Also the root of the Greeks' name for their country – Hellas. In Greek mythology, a beautiful princess whose elopement sparked the Trojan War and whose face 'launched a thousand ships'. Saint Helena was divorced by her husband for someone with better political connections. She is the patron saint of divorcees and difficult marriages. Her saint's day is 18 August. *Helena, Hélène*
Helga (**Hel**-ga) Anglo-Saxon for holly.
Helice (Hel-**eece**) (Greek) spiralling.
Helios (**Hee**-lee-os) (Greek) of the sun.
Helsa (**Hel**-sa) Scandinavian form of Elizabeth.
Henna (**Hen**-a) (English) a form of Henrietta, the French feminine version of Henry, which means home ruler.
Henrietta (Hen-ree-**ett**-a) French feminine form of Henry, which means home ruler. The thirteenth of July is her feast day. *Hally, Harietta, Harriette, Henriette*
Hera (**Hee**-ra) (Greek) lady. Queen of the Greek gods, associated with marriages.
Hermina (Her-**my**-na) (Latin) noble. *Herminia*
Hermione (Her-**my**-on-ee) (Greek) messenger. Also the female form of Hermes, the messenger of the Greek gods. *Hermia*

Hermosa (Her-**mo**-sa) (Spanish) beautiful.
Hesper (**Hess**-per) (Greek) evening star.
Hester (**Hess**-ter) (Origin unclear) Originally a form of Ester, meaning myrtle, but now a name in its own right.
Hestia (**Hess**-tee-a) (Latin) Roman goddess of the hearth and home.
Hetta (**Het**-a) (German) form of Hedda, meaning warrior.
Hibernia (High-**ber**-nee-a) (Latin) from the winter isle. The name the Romans gave to Ireland.
Hilda (**Hill**-da) (German) battle maid. The extended form is Hildegard. Her saint's day is 17 November.
Hildegard (**Hill**-de-gard) see Hilda.
Holly (**Hol**-ee) (Old English) tree name.
Honesty (**On**-ess-tee) (Latin) honesty.
Honey (**Hun**-ee) (English) honey.
Honour/Honoria (**On**-er/On-**or**-ee-a/ Hon-**or**-ee-a) (Latin) honour. *Nora, Norah, Noreen, Norine*
Hope (**Hope**) (English) originally the Old English word for a small valley, but now associated with the sense of hope.
Hortense (Hor-**tense**) (Latin) garden. *Hortencia*
Hosanna (Hoe-**san**-a) (Hebrew) literally, save now. *Hosannah*
Hyacinth (**High**-a-sinth) (Greek) based on the ancient Greek word for botany. Also the name of a flower.
Hyone (High-**oh**-nee) (Greek) dream from the sea.

I

Ianira (**Eye**-a-**near**-a) (Greek) enchantress.
Ianthe (Eye-**an**-tha) (Greek) violet flower.
Ida (**Eye**-da) (German) worker. Also associated with Mount Ida (Crete) where the king of the Greek gods, Zeus, was raised. Saint Ida is patron saint of widows and brides. Saint's day: 4 September.
Idalia (Id-**day**-lia / Id-**ah**-lee-a) (Spanish) of a sunny disposition.
Ide (**Eye**-da) (Irish) thirsty for knowledge.
Idelia (Id-**ee**-lee-a) (Old German) noble.
Idil/Idelle (Eye-**dil**/Eye-**del**) Welsh forms of Ida, meaning worker.
Idylla (Eye-**dill**-a) (Greek) from the Greek word for perfection. *Idilia, Idylia*
Iesha (Eye-**ee**-sha) (Arabic) healthy and vibrant, full of life. *Ieshah*
Ignatia (Ig-**nay**-shee-a) (Latin) the feminine form of Ignatius, meaning fiery and ardent. Her saint's day is 31 July.
Igraine (Ee-**grain**) (Irish) full of grace.
Ilana (**Eye**-la-na) (Hebrew) tree. *Ilaine, Ileana*
Ilene (Il-**ee**-nuh) Irish form of Helen, meaning bright.
Ilima (Eye-**lee**-ma) (Hawaiian) flower of Oahu. Oahu is the third largest of the Hawaiian islands.

Imala (**Eye**-mah-la) (Native American) determined.
Iman (Im-**ahn**) (Arabic) one who has faith. *Imana, Imanah*
Imelda (Im-**el**-da) (Old German) the literal translation is all-out battle.
Imogen (**Im**-oh-jen) (Celtic) daughter. A name invented by Shakespeare for his play *Cymbeline*. Shakespeare chose all his names for a reason and this one appears to be based on the Latin word for picture. *Imogene*
Immaculata (Im-**ak**-you-**la**-ta) (Latin) spotless. The eighth of December is the date on which the Immaculate Conception occurred.
Ina (**Ee**-na) (Latin) motherly.
Inari (In-**are**-ee) (Finnish) from the lake.
India/Indira (**In**-dee-a/In-**deer**-a) (Hindi) of India. The country is named after the River Indus.
Indigo (**In**-dig-o) (Latin) a colour. It is dark blue with a hint of purple.
Inga/Inge (**In**-ga) (Scandinavian) protected by Ing, the goddess of peace. *Inja*
Ingeborg (**Ing**-ga-borg) (Scandinavian) from the castle of Ing.
Ingrid (**In**-grid) (Norse) beautiful and fertile.
Inira (In-**nee**-ra) (Welsh) honourable.
Innocence (**In**-o-sense) (English) innocence.
Inola (In-**ole**-a) (Cherokee) fox.
Iola (Eye-**ole**-a) (Greek) daybreak.
Iolanthe (Eye-o-**lan**-tha) English form of Jolande/Yolande, which means violet flower.
Iona (**Eye**-oh-na) (Scottish) from the Hebridean island famous for its monastery. *Ione*
Ira (**Eye**-ra) (Hebrew) alert. Also a short form of Irina (see Irene).
Ireland (**Ire**-land) (English) Ireland.
Irene (**Eye**-reen) (Greek) peace. Named after the goddess of peace in Greek mythology. Saint Irene was caught with texts of the Scriptures when this was punishable by death. When she refused to offer sacrifice to the pagan gods, she was sent to a brothel. Once there, she remained unmolested, however. Her saint's day is 3 April. *Irena, Irina, Renata, Renée*
Iris (**Eye**-riss) (Greek) named after the flower and the Greek word for rainbow.
Irma (**Er**-ma) (German) whole and complete. Saint's day: 24 December. *Erma, Irmina, Irmine*
Irvette (**Eer**-vet) (Welsh) white river. (Irish) good-looking. *Irvete*
Isa (**Iss**-a) (Spanish) a short form of Isabel, the Spanish form of Elizabeth.
Isabel (**Iz**-a-bell) (Spanish) Spanish version of Elizabeth, with an ending suggesting beauty. Isabella is the Italian version and Isabelle the French. Saint's day: 26 February. *Isobel*
Isadora (Iz-a-**dore**-a) (Greek) gift from Isis, who was a river goddess.

Iseult (Eess-**yoolt**) (Welsh) beautiful. In Arthurian legend, a beautiful Irish princess who fell hopelessly in love with Tristan. Forced apart by resentful parents, they were buried together when they died. Their story has much in common with Shakespeare's *Romeo and Juliet*. *Isolde*
Isha (**Eye**-sha) American form of Aisha. *Ishana*
Isibeal (**Ish**-bel) (Irish) Irish form of Elizabeth.
Isis (**Eye**-sis) (Egyptian) Isis was the Egyptian goddess of fertility and rebirth. Also the name given to the Thames as it passes through Oxford. *Isys*
Ismena (Iss-**mee**-na) (Greek) wisdom.
Ita (**Eye**-ta) (Irish) thirsty.
Italia (It-**al**-ya) (Italian) from Italy.
Ivanna (**Eye**-vah-na) (Slavic) God is gracious. Often shortened to Iva. *Ivana*
Ivy (**Eye**-vee) (English) from the plant. The name was at its most popular in the nineteenth century.

J

Jacinda (Ja-**sin**-da) (Greek) beautiful. *Yacinda*
Jacintha (Ja-**sin**-tha) (Greek) the Greek word for sapphire. *Yacintha*
Jacki (**Jack**-ee) (English) a pet form of Jacqueline. *Jackie, Jacky, Jaclyn*
Jacqueline (**Jack**-a-lin) (French) the feminine form of Jacques, which is a French version of James (disciple of Jesus) and Jacob (which means supplanter). There are many spelling variations of this name.
Jada (**Jay**-dah) (Hebrew) wise.
Jaden (**Jay**-den) (English) an elaborate form of Jade. *Jadyn, Jaiden*
Jaen (**Jah**-en) (Hebrew) ostrich. *Jaene*
Jaelyn (**Jay**-lin) (African-American) ambitious. *Jaelin*
Jaffa (**Jaf**-a) (Hebrew) beautiful.
Jaimica (**High**-mik-a) (Spanish) supplanter. Feminine of James (disciple of Jesus) and Jacob (supplanter).
Jaina (**Jay**-na) (Hindi) of good character.
Jala (**Jay**-la/**Yay**-la) (Arabic) charity. *Jalah*
Jalene (**Jay**-leen) (American) from Jane with the ending -lene. *Jalena*
Jalila (Ja-**lee**-la/Ya-**lee**-la) (Arabic) the feminine form of Jalil, which means exalted and sublime. *Jalilah*

Jalinda (Ja-**lin**-da) (American) a combination of Jay (the bird) and Linda (pretty). *Jaylinda*

Jamari (Ja-**mar**-ree) (French) warrior.

Jamasina (Jam-a-**see**-na) (Hebrew) supplanter. The one who replaces.

Jamila (Ja-**mil**-a) (Ya-**mil**-a) (Arabic) beautiful. *Jameela, Jamyla, Janilah*

Jan (**Jan**) (English) God is gracious. Also a short form for names beginning with Jan, such as Janet and Janice. *Jana*

Janae (**Jan**-nay) (American) giving.

Jancis (**Jan**-sis) (American) a modern name derived from Jane and Frances.

Jane (**Jayne**) (Old French) a feminine form of John, meaning favoured by God. Her saint's day is 4 February. *Janella, Janelle, Janessa*

Janelle (Ja-**nelle**) (American) a modern name derived from Jane and the feminine suffix -elle.

Janet (**Jan**-et) (Scottish) originally the Scottish form of Jane, meaning favoured by God. Sometimes altered to Janie.

Janice (**Jan**-iss) (English) God is gracious. A feminine form of John, meaning favoured by God. *Janelle, Janet, Janiece, Janine*

Janna (**Jan**-a) (Hebrew) flourishing. *Jannah*

Jannali (Jan-**ah**-lee) (Australian) the Aboriginal word for the moon. Also a place in Australia, near Sydney.

Janthina (Jan-**thee**-na) (Greek) a violet-coloured flower.

Jaquenetta (Jak-a-**net**-a) (French) derived from the Hebrew word for supplanter. Also a feminine form of Jacob and James.

Jarah (**Ja**-rah) (Hebrew) honey. *Jara*

Jarmila (Yar-**mil**-a) (Slavonic) one who graces spring.

Jannette (Jan-**et)** (American) lovely.

Jardina (Jar-**deen**-a) (Hebrew) to flow downward. *Jardeena*

Jasmine (**Jaz**-min) the English form of the Persian name Yasmin; the name of the fragrant flower. *Jasmyne, Jazmine,*

Jaye (**Jay**) (Sanskrit) victory. Also the name of a female Buddhist goddess.

Jayel (**Jay**-el) (Hebrew) a form of the biblical name Jael, which means wild she-goat. *Jayle*

Jaylene (**Jay**-leen/ Jay-**leen**) (American) Jay with the ending -lene. *Jaylee, Jayline*

Jaylo (**Jay**-low) (American) combination of Jennifer and Lopez, after the American singer of that name. *J. Lo, Jalo, J-Lo*

Jayne (**Jane**) (Hindi) victorious.

Jean (**Jeen**) Scottish form of Jeanne, which is the French feminine form of John, meaning favoured by God. *Jeane, Jeanie, Jeannetta, Jeannie, Jeannine*

Jelena (Ye-**lee**-na) (Russian) shining light.

Jemima (Jem-**eye**-ma) (Hebrew) dove. In the Bible, the beautiful daughter of Job and the eldest of his ten childen. *Jemine, Jemma*

Jenelle (Je-**nelle**) (German) full of knowledge and understanding.
Jenna (**Jen**-a) Latin form of the English name Jenny, which means white and smooth. Also the short form of Jennifer, Jennica and many other names beginning with Jen-. *Jena*
Jennica (**Jen**-ik-a) (Romanian) God is gracious.
Jennifer (**Jen**-if-er) (Cornish) Cornish version of Guinevere, which means fair and beautiful. Often shortened to Jen, Jenni or Jenny.
Jensine (**Jen**-seen) (Hebrew) God is gracious.
Jera (**Jeh**-ra) (English) from the Old English word *jera*, meaning year.
Jeralyn (**Ye**-ra-lin) (English/Welsh) a combination of Jera and Lyn (meaning pretty). *Jeralin*
Jerarda (Jer-**are**-da) (English) brave spear woman. Feminine form of Gerard.
Jerusha (Jer-**oo**-sha) (Hebrew) the married one. *Jerushah*
Jesca (**Jess**-ca) (Hebrew) God sees. Mentioned in Genesis. *Jescah*
Jessenia (Jes-**sen**-ee-a) (English) a form of Jessica. *Jess, Jessalyn, Jessamyn*
Jessica (**Jess**-ik-a) first use of the name is in Shakespeare's *The Merchant of Venice*, implying he invented it. *Jessika*
Jewel (**Joo**-well) (Old French) the original meaning was plaything, but this has now been eclipsed by the meaning precious stone.
Jezebel (**Jez**-a-bel) (Hebrew) dominant and impure. In the Bible, a persecutor of the Jews, and shameless in her conduct.
Jill (**Jill**) (Italian) from a Roman family name. Also the feminine form of Julian and a derivative of Julia (fair-skinned).
Jillian (**Jill**-ee-an) (English) an elaborated form of Jill. *Jilleen, Jilly*
Jimena (Je-**mee**-na) (English) a variant of the Spanish name Ximena, which means hearkening.
Jinny (**Jin**-ee) (English) a variation of Ginny, which means virginal maiden.
Joakima (Jo-**kee**-ma) (Hebrew) the Lord will judge.
Joan (**Jone**) (English) a form of Jane, a feminine form of John, meaning favoured by God.
Joanna (Jo-**an**-a) (Greek) a feminine version of John, meaning favoured by God. A member of King Herod's household who was healed by Jesus. *Jo, Joannie, Joanne, Johanna*
Joandra (Jo-**an**-dra) (English) an elaborated form of Joanna, meaning favoured by God.
Joaquima (Jo-**kee**-ma/Hwa-**kee**-ma) (Spanish) a feminine form of Joaquim, meaning founded by God.
Jobey (**Jo**-bee) (Hebrew) persecuted. *Joby*
Jocasta (Jo-**cass**-ta) (Greek) adorned with woe. She was the tragic mother of Oedipus who inadvertently became his wife and mother of his children. *Jokasta*

Jocelyn (Joss-a-lin) (German) little Goth. *Joseline*
Joci (Jo-see) (Latin) happy.
Jodie (Jo-dee) an English derivation of the Hebrew Judith, meaning woman of Judea. *Jode, Jody*
Jochebed (Joke-a-bed) (**Yoke**-a-bed) (Hebrew) God is glory. In the Bible, the mother of Aaron and Moses.
Jocosa (Jo-**co**-sa) (English) a medieval form of Joyce, which means lord.
Jodelle (Jo-**del**) (American) Jo, which is short for many names beginning with Jo-, plus the ending -delle.
Joelle (Jo-**el**) French feminine form of Joel, which means the Lord is God.
Joellianna (Jo-el-ee-**ah**-na) (Hebrew) Jehova is God.
Johanna (Jo-**an**-a) (Latin) feminine of Johannes, a form of John (favoured by God). *Joanne, Joane, Johanne, Johnna*
Johanneke (Yo-**han**-ik-a) Dutch form of Johanna, meaning God is gracious.
Jolan (Yo-lan) Hungarian form of the English Yolanda, which means violet flower. A common short form is Jola.
Jolanda (Yo-**lan**-da) Italian form of the English Yolanda, a violet flower.
Jolanta (Yo-**lan**-ta) Polish form of Yolanda, meaning violet flower.
Jolene (Jo-**leen**) (American) a combination of Jo and Marlene. *Joleen*
Jolie (Zho-**lee**) (French) pretty.
Jolienne (Jo-lee-**en**) (French) an elaborated form of Jolie, meaning pretty.
Jolisa (Jol-**ee**-sa) (American) a combination of Jo and Lisa.
Jonella (Jo-**nell**-a) (English) the pet form of Joni, meaning favoured by God.
Joni (Joan-ee) (Hebrew) favoured by God. Also a feminine form of John.
Jonice (Jo-**neece**) (Hebrew) a variant of Joni and of Joan.
Jonina (Jo-**nee**-na) (Hebrew) dove.
Jonita (Jon-**ee**-ta) (English) a modern feminine form of John, meaning favoured by God.
Jonnell (Jon-**el**) (American) quite a popular name in the US, for which there are several variations, including Jenelle, Jinelle, Johnelle, Jonella and Junelle.
Jonquil (Jon-kwil) (English) named after the small, yellow daffodil native to Spain and Portugal. *Jontelle*
Jora (Jore-a) (Hebrew) autumn rain. *Jorah*
Jordana (Jor-**dah**-na) (English) feminine form of the gender-neutral name Jordan, which lterally means flowing down.
Jorie (Jore-ee) (English) a nickname for Marjorie, which means pearl.
Josée (Zho-**zay**) (French) the feminine form of Joseph, which means God will add. This is usually taken to mean 'will add another child' (i.e. after Jesus is born from Joseph's virgin wife).
Josefina (Jo-sef-**ee**-na/Ho-sef-**ee**-na) (Spanish) the feminine form of José, which is a diminutive of Joseph, meaning God will add. *Josaphine, Josephina*

Josephine (**Jo**-zef-een) French feminine version of Joseph, which means God will add. Most famous as the name of the first wife of Napoleon. (She and Napoleon had a very passionate relationship, but both managed to be unfaithful to each other on numerous occasions.) Saints' days: 19 March and 18 September. *Jo*

Josette (Jo-**zet**/**Zho**-zet) (French) a short form of Josephine, meaning God will add.

Josiane (Jo-see-**an**/Zho-zee-**an**) (French) a pet form of Josephine, meaning God will add.

Josie (**Jo**-see) (English) a short form of Josephine, meaning God will add. *Josey*

Joss (**Joss**) (English) nickname for Jocelyn.

Jovana (Yo-**va**-na) (Serbian) the feminine form of Jovan, which means God is gracious.

Jovita (Jo-**veet**-a) (Latin) the joyful one.

Joy (**Joy**) (English) from the emotion, joy. *Joye*

Joyanne (Joy-**an**) (American) a combination of Joy and Anne (meaning graceful and merciful).

Joyce (**Joyce**) (Norman) lord.

Joyleen (Joy-**leen**) (American) a combination of Joy and Helen (bright). *Joylene*

Juana (**Hwa**-na) (Spanish) feminine form of Juan, the Spanish for John, meaning favoured by God.

Juanita (Hwa-**nee**-ta) Spanish diminutive form of Juan, the Spanish for John, meaning favoured by God.

Jucinda (Joo-**sin**-da) (English) derived from the Latin word *jucunda*, meaning happy.

Judith (**Joo**-dith) (Hebrew) woman of Judea. Also related to the Hebrew word for praise. In the Bible, she saved her people from the Assyrians by cutting off the head of their king as he slept. Saint's day: 29 June. *Jude, Judy*

Judy (**Joo**-dee) a short version of Judith, sometimes used as a name in its own right.

Jula (**Jo**-la) (Zimbabwean) depth.

Julia (**Joo**-lee-a) (English) a feminine form of Julian, meaning fair-skinned. *Juliana, Julianne, Julie*

Juliet (**Joo**-lee-et) (English) anglicized version of the Italian Giulietta, which means youthful. Forever famous as one of Shakespeare's 'star-crossed lovers'. *Juliette*

June (**Joon**) (Latin) named after the month, which in turn was named after Juno, the queen of the Roman gods. She has a particular association with marriage.

Justine (**Just**-een) (Latin) just and fair. A feminine form of Justin. Her saint's day is 1 June.

K

Kady (**Kay**-dee) (Irish) first-born child. *Kadie*
Kachina (Ka-**chee**-na) (Native American) dancer.
Kaela (**Kai**-la) (Aramaic) loved. *Kaelah, Kaelea*
Kaisa (**Kai**-sa) (Scandinavian) pure.
Kaitland (**Kate**-land) (Irish) a form of Kaitlin.
Kaitlin (**Kate**-lin) (Irish) pure.
Kalama (Ka-**lah**-ma) (Hawaiian) flaming torch.
Kalere (Ka-**ler**-a) (Swahili) short girl.
Kali (**Kah**-li) (Hindi) the dark one. Named after a Hindu goddess.
Kalida (**Ka**-lid-da) Greek form of the name Calida, meaning warm and loving.
Kalila (Ka-**lye**-la) (Arabic) loved. *Kalilah*
Kalina (Ka-**lye**-na) (Slavic) flower.
Kalinda (Ka-**lin**-da) (Hindi) of the sun.
Kalisa (Ka-**lee**-sa) (American) combination of Kate and Lisa.
Kalista (Ka-**liss**-ta) Greek form of Calista, meaning most beautiful of women. *Kallista*
Kallan (Ka-**lan**) (Slavic) from the river.
Kallie (**Kal**-ee) Greek form of Callie (see Callidora and Callisto).
Kalonice (Ka-lo-**nee**-see) (Greek) beauty's victory.
Kalliope (Ka-lee-**oh**-pee) Greek form of Calliope, meaning beautiful poetry.
Kalyca (Ka-**lee**-sa) (Greek) rose.
Kama (**Kah**-ma) (Sanskrit) love. Named after the Hindu god of love.
Kamari (Ka-**ma**-ri) (Swahili) like the moon.
Kamballa (Kam-**bal**-la) (Australian) young lady.
Kamila/Kamilah (Ka-**mil**-a) (Arabic) whole and complete.
Kanani (Ka-**nan**-i) (Hawaiian) beautiful.
Kana (**Ka**-na) (Welsh) beautiful.
Kandi (**Kan**-dee) (American) candy.
Kandice (**Kan**-diss) (Greek) white. Greek form of Candice.
Kara (**Kah**-ra) Danish form of Katherine, meaning pure.
Kareela (Ka-**ree**-la) (Australian) southern wind.
Karelle (**Ka**-rel) Danish form of Carol, meaning woman.
Karen (**Ka**-ren/**Kah**-ren) Danish form of Katherine, meaning pure.
Karenza (Ka-**ren**-za) (Gaelic) loving.
Kariane (**Ka**-ree-**an**) (American) combination of Kari and Ann (graceful and merciful).
Karida (Ka-**ree**-da) (Arabic) virginal. *Karidah*
Karima (Ka-**ree**-ma) (Arabic) noble. *Karimah*
Karin (**Ka**-rin/**Kah**-rin) Swedish version of Katherine.
Karissa (Ka-**riss**-a) (Greek) dear.

Karmel (**Kar**-mel) (Hebrew) garden. *Carmel*
Karmen (**Kar**-men) (Latin) song. *Carmen*
Karolanne (**Ka**-rol-**an**) (American) a combination of Karol/Carol, meaning woman, and Anne, meaning graceful and merciful. *Karolaine*
Karoline (**Ka**-ro-line) Slavic form of Caroline.
Karolyn (**Ka**-ro-lin) (American) a version of Carol, plus Lyn. *Karolin*
Karyn (**Kar**-in) (American) a version of Karen, from Katherine, meaning pure.
Kassi (**Kass**-ee) (Polish/American) a short form of Kassandra (see Cassandra).
Katarina (Kat-a-**ree**-na) Czech form of Katherine, meaning pure.
Kate/Kathy/Katie (**Kate**/**Kath**-ee/**Kate**-ee) (Greek) short forms of Katherine. Often used in their own right.
Katelyn (**Kate**-lin) (American) a combination of Kate (pure) and Lynn (pretty). *Katelin*
Katherine (**Kath**-er-in) (Greek) pure. *Kathrin, Kathryn, Kitty*
Kathleen (**Kath**-leen) (English) anglicized version of the Irish Caitlin, meaning pure one.
Kathryn (**Kath**-rin) (American) an alternative spelling of Katherine. *Kathrin*
Katina (Ka-**tee**-na) Russian form of Katherine, meaning pure.
Katrina (Ka-**tree**-na) German form of Katherine, meaning pure.
Kaulana (Cow-**la**-na) (Hawaiian) famous.
Kay (**Kay**) (English) key. A recent derivation is Kayla.
Kayle (**Kayl**) (Irish) slender. *Kaylee, Kayleigh*
Kayleen/Kaylene (**Kay**-leen) (Hebrew) much loved.
Keala (Kee-**ya**-la) (Hawaiian) pathway.
Keanna (Kee-**an**-a) (German) bold. (Irish) beautiful. *Keanu*
Keare (**Keer**-a) (Irish) dark-haired.
Keena (**Kee**-na) (Irish) brave. *Keenan*
Keira (**Keer**-a) (Irish) a form of Ciara, meaning small and dark. *Kiara*
Keisha (**Kee**-shah) (African-American) favourite. *Kesha*
Keita (**Kee**-ta) (Scottish) from the woods.
Kenzie (**Ken**-zee) (Scottish) pale-skinned.
Keren (**Ker**-en) (Hebrew) horn (container) of eye paint. One of the daughters of Job.
Ketina (Ket-**een**-a) (Hebrew) girl.
Keziah (Kez-**ee**-a) (Hebrew) a spice, and a daughter of Job in the Bible. *Kezia*
Khalida (Ka-**lye**-da) (Arabic) immortal, forever. *Khalidah*
Kia (**Kee**-a) (African) the beginning of the seasons. (American) a short form of Kiana.
Kiana (Kee-**an**-a) (American) Anna, meaning graceful and merciful, with the prefix Ki-. *Kiannah*

Kiara (Key-**a**-ra) (Irish) small and dark. *Ciara, Keira*

Kiaria (Kee-**ah**-ree-a) (Japanese) blessed by fortune.

Kim (**Kim**) see Kimberley.

Kimberley (**Kim**-ber-lee) named after the South African town and diamond-mining centre. Often shortened to Kim, most famously by Rudyard Kipling in his novel of the same name. *Kimberly*

Kina (**Kee**-na) (Hawaiian) girl from China.

Kineta (Ki-**net**-a) (Greek) full of energy.

Kini (**Kee**-nee) the Hawaiian form of Jean, a feminine form derived from John, meaning favoured by God.

Kiona (Kye-**own**-a) (Native American) from the hills.

Kira (**Keer**-a) (Latin) light.

Kirima (Ki-**ree**-ma) (Innuit) hill.

Kirsten (**Curse**-ten) Scandinavian form of Christine, which means anointed one.

Kirstie (**Curse**-tee) (Scottish) a short, Scottish version of Christine. *Kirsty*

Kitty (**Kit**-ee) (Greek) nickname for Katherine, meaning pure.

Kiyo/Kiyoshi (**Kee**-o/Kee-**osh**-ee) (Japanese) happiness in the family.

Klarissa (Kla-**riss**-a) (German) bright, clear. *Clarissa*

Kolina (Ko-**lee**-na) (Swedish) a form of Katherine, meaning pure. *Kolinya*

Koleyn (**Ko**-lin) (Australian) born in winter.

Kolora (Ko-**lore**-a) (Australian) from the lake.

Kona (**Kone**-a) (Hawaiian) ladylike.

Kora (**Core**-a) (Greek) a form of Cora, meaning maiden.

Kori (**Core**-ee) (American) a form of Cory, an Irish name meaning from the hollow.

Korina (Core-**ee**-na) Greek form of Corinna, meaning maiden.

Kornelia (Cor-**nee**-lee-a) Greek form of Cornelia, meaning practical. Feminine form of Cornelius, meaning the colour of horn.

Kristie (**Kris**-tee) (Scandinavian) a form of Kristina. *Kristy*

Kristina (Kris-**tee**-na) Swedish form of Christina, meaning anointed one. *Krystina*

Krystal (**Kris**-tull) a variation of Crystal, meaning pure, transparent.

Kumari (**Koo**-mar-ee) (Sanskrit) womanly.

Kumberlin (**Kum**-ber-lin) (Australian) sweet.

Kyla (**Kye**-la) a feminine form of Kyle, which means from the land of the cattle.

Kylie (**Kye**-lee) (Australian) from the Aboriginal word for boomerang. (Celtic) a variant of Kyle or Kayley. *Kylee*

Kyra/Kyria (**Kye**-ra/**Kye**-ree-a) (Greek) female ruler.

Kyrene (**Kye**-reen) (Greek) noble.

L

Lace/Lacey (Lace-ee) (Norman) from the town of Lassy in Normandy.
Lachlanina (Lok-la-**nee**-na) (Scottish) from the land of the lochs. The feminine form of Lachlan.
Lacrecia (La-**kree**-see-a) (Latin) a form of Lucretia, meaning rewarded.
Lahela (La-**hey**-la) Hawaiian form of Rachel.
Laina/Laine (Layn-a/**Layn**) (English) feminine form of the gender-neutral name Lane.
Lakendra (La-**ken**-dra) (American) Kendra with the prefix La-.
Lakkari (La-**kar-**ee) (Australian) from the honeysuckle tree.
Lalana (La-la-na) (Sanskrit) womanly.
Lalirra (La-**leer**-a) (Australian) talkative.
Lalita (La-**lee**-ta) (Sanskrit) darling.
Lana (Lah-na) (Latin) wool. (Irish) alluring.
Lanata (La-**nah**-ta) (American) Natalie with the prefix La-.
Landa (Lan-da) (American) a very recent invention that's a combination of Lana and Wanda.
Lantha (Lan-tha) (American) a combination of Lana and Samantha.
Laoise (Lee-sha) (Irish) from the Irish county of Laois.
Lara (Lah-ra) (Russian) a short form of Larissa, who was a key character in the novel *Dr Zhivago*. (Latin) shining. A a river nymph in Roman mythology.
Lareina (La-**rain**-a) (Spanish) the queen. *Lareine, Larena*
Larina (La-**ree**-na) (Greek) seagull.
Larissa (La-**riss**-a) (Greek) from the town of Larissa, the birthplace of the hero Achilles.
Larita (La-**ree**-ta) (American) Rita with the prefix La-
Larmina (Lar-**mee**-na) (Persian) blue sky. *Larminah*
Latara (La-**ta**-ra) (American) Tara with the prefix La-.
Latasha (La-**tash**-a) (American) Tasha with the prefix La–.
Latona (La-**tone**-a) (Latin) in Roman mythology, the mother of the gods Apollo (patron of music) and Artemis (patron of hunting and childbirth).
Latrecia/Latricia (La-**tresh**-a/ La-**trish**-a) (American) Tricia with the prefix La–.
Laura (Lore-a) (Latin) laurel tree and also the feminine of Laurence. *Lara, Laraine, Laureen, Laurel, Lauren, Laurette, Lora, Loretta, Lorraine*
Lauren (Law-ren) a version of the names Laura and Laurie (see gender-neutral names).
Lavender (Lav-in-der) (Latin) named after the fragrant plant with purple-blue flowers.

Laverna (La-**vern**-a) (Latin) the name of the Roman goddess of thieves.
Laverne (La-**vern**) (Latin) verdant as the spring.
Lavina (La-**veen**-a) (Latin) clean and purified.
Lavinia (La-**vin**-ee-a) (Latin) in Roman legend, Lavinia was the wife of Aeneas, founder of Rome, and was therefore the mother of all Romans.
Layla (**Lay**-la) (Arabic) night. *Laila, Leila*
Layne (**Lane**) (English) feminine form of Lane (gender-neutral).
Leah (**Lee**-a) (Hebrew) weary. *Lea*
Leala (**Lee**-a-la) (Old English) loyal wife.
Leanda (Le-**an**-da) (Greek) a figure from Greek mythology who was half lion, half woman.
Leandra (Le-**an**-dra) (American) a combination of Leah (weary) and Sandra (from Alexandra).
Leanna (Lee-**an**-a) (American) a combination of Leah (weary) and Anna (graceful and merciful).
Leannette (Lee-an-**et**) (American) a combination of Leah (weary) and Annette (a form of Anne, which means graceful and merciful).
Leanore (Le-a-**no**-ra) (American) a combination of Leah, which means weary and Nora, which is from Eleanor, meaning foreign.
Lecia (**Less**-ee-a) (Latin) a pet form or nickname for Felicia, which itself means lucky.
Leda (**Lee**-da) (Greek) womanly. In Greek mythology, she was a queen of Sparta who was seduced by the god Zeus, who was disguised as a swan. Afterwards, she laid two eggs from which two sets of twins were born.
Leena (**Lee**-na) from the Sanskrit root for devoted.
Leewan (**Lee**-wan) (Australian) of the wind.
Lei (**Lay**) (Hawaiian) garland of flowers.
Lelia (**Lel**-ee-a) (Arabic) dark beauty. *Layla, Leyla, Leylah*
Lemana (Le-**mah**-na) (Australian) oak tree.
Lena (**Lay**-na) (Latin) temptress. (Scandinavian) hard-working.
Lenita (Le-**nee**-ta) (Latin) gentle.
Lenna (**Len**-a) German form of Helen, meaning bright.
Leona (Lee-**oh**-na) (Latin) lioness. *Lee, Leola, Leonie, Leonita, Leontine*
Leonore (Lee-an-**or**) (American) a combination of Leo (lion) and Nora (from Eleanor).
Leora (Lay-**or**-a) (Hebrew) inner light.
Leticia (Le-**tee**-sha) based on the Latin word for joy. This name has a different spelling in almost every country in which it is used, but this spelling is the most common.
Levana (Le-**van**-a) (Hebrew) moon. *Lavanah*
Levina (Le-**vee**-na) (Old English) shining.

Levona (Le-**vone**-a) (Hebrew) spice. *Levonah*
Lexi/Lexine (**Lex**-ee/**Lex**-een) (Greek) pet forms of Alexandra, the feminine version of Alexander, meaning defender of mankind. *Lexy*
Lia (**Lee**-a) (Greek) a diminutive of Evangelia, which means bringer of good news.
Liadain (Lee-**dahn**) (Irish) from the Irish word *liath*, meaning grey.
Lian (**Lee**-an) (Chinese) willow.
Liama (Lee-**ahm**-a) (English) faithful guard.
Liana (Lee-**an**-a) (French) to bind loyally together. *Lianna*
Liberty (**Lib**-er-tee) (Latin) free.
Lida (**Lye**-da) (Greek) happy. (Slavic) loved.
Lidia (**Lid**-ee-a) (Greek) a version of Lydia, meaning woman from Lydia (see Lydia entry).
Lila (**Lye**-la) (Sanskrit) playful, full of life. *Lilia*
Lilian/Liliana/Lillian (**Lil**-ee-an/Lil-ee-**ahn**-a) (Latin) from the name of the lily flower. Saint Lillian was martyred for practising her faith openly. Saint's day: 27 July.
Lilith (**Lil**-ith) (Persian) the name of the Persian goddess of the night.
Lily (**Lil**-ee) (Latin) from the name of the flower.
Linda (**Lin**-da) (Spanish) pretty. (Italian) neat.
Linette (Lin-**et**) (Welsh) idol. (French) bird.
Liona (Lye-**own**-a) German form of Leona, meaning lioness.
Lisa (**Lee**-za/**Lee**-sa) (Hebrew) consecrated to God. Originally a shortened version of Elisabeth, but now a name in its own right. *Liza*
Lisandra (Li-**san**-dra) (Greek) the feminine form of Lysander, meaning liberator of men.
Lisette (Liz-**et**) French shortened form of Elizabeth. *Lysette*
Lissa (**Liss**-a) (Greek) honey bee. Also a short form of Melissa.
Livona (Li-**voe**-na) based on the Hebrew word for incense. *Livonah*
Llian (**Lee**-an) (Welsh) linen.
Loila (**Loy**-la) (Australian) sky.
Lola (**Low**-la) (Spanish) a short form of Dolores, meaning sorrowful.
Lolita (Lol-**ee**-ta) (Spanish) diminutive of Lola, meaning sorrowful.
Lora (**Lor**-a) (American) a form of Laura, meaning laurel.
Lorelei (**Lor**-a-lye) (German) alluring. In legend, a siren of the River Rhine who lured sailors to their death on the rocks with her singing.
Lorelle (Lor-**el**) (Latin) little one.
Lorena (Lo-**ren**-a) (English) a form of Lauren (from Laura, which means laurel tree).
Loretta (Lor-**et**-a) (English) a form of Laura (laurel tree).

Lorinda (Lor-**in**-da) (American) combination of Laura (laurel) and Linda (pretty).
Lorna (**Lor**-na) (English) invented by R. D. Blackmore for his book *Lorna Doone*. Possibly from the Scottish place name of Lorn.
Lorraine (Lor-**ain**) (Latin) from the region of eastern France of the same name.
Lottie (**Lot**-ee) a shortened version of Charlotte, meaning free person.
Louisa/Louise (Loo-**eez**-a/Loo-**eez**) French feminine version of Louis, which was based on the German word for famous warrior. Often used in the form Louise, both names having the same origin. Saint Louisa is celebrated on 10 March.
Lourdes (**Lord**) (French) from the cathedral city and pilgrimage centre in France.
Luana (Loo-**an**-a) a name invented for the 1932 film *The Bird of Paradise*.
Luann (**Loo**-ann) (German) female warrior.
Luca (**Loo**-ca) Italian form of Lucy, meaning light.
Lucerne (Loo-**sern**) (Latin) circle of light. Also a lake in Switzerland.
Lucia (**Loo**-see-a) (Latin) light. The feminine form of Lucius.
Luciana (Lo-see-**ah**-na/Loo-**chah**-na) a form of Lucy used in Italy and parts of Spain. Means light.
Lucienne (Loo-see-**en**) French form of Lucy, meaning light
Lucina (Loo-**sin**-a) (Latin) grove.
Lucinda (Loo-**sin**-da) the most common Spanish form of Lucy, meaning light.
Lucretia (Loo-**cree**-shee-a) (Latin) rewarded.
Lucy (**Loo**-see) (Latin) light. Saint's day: 13 December. *Luce, Lucette, Lucia, Lucie, Lucien, Lucienne, Lucille, Lucina, Lucinda, Luz.*
Luiseach (Lee-**shock**) (Irish) the feminine form of Lugh, which means oath.
Lulu (**Loo**-loo) a short form of Louise. *Lula*
Luna (**Loo**-na) (Latin) of the moon. The name of the Roman goddess of the moon. *Lunete*
Lurlene (Lur-**lee**-na) (Scandinavian) war horn.
Lydia (**Lid**-ee-a) (Greek) woman from Lydia, which is in modern-day southwest Turkey. She was Saint Paul's first convert at Philippi. Saint's day: 3 August. *Lidia*
Lynda (**Lin**-da) (Spanish) pretty. *Linda*
Lynelle (Lin-**el**) (French) pretty.
Lynette (Lin-**et**) (Celtic) waterfall or pool. Also a Celtic goddess who rescued imprisoned knights. *Linet*
Lynn/Lynne derivations of Linda, meaning pretty.

Maaia (My-a) (Maori) courage.
Maaruu (Ma-roo) (Maori) gentleness.
Mab (Mab) (Celtic) joyful baby. In folk tradition, the Queen of the Fairies.
Mabel (May-bull) (Old French) delightful one. Scottish form: Moibeal; Irish form: Maible; Welsh form: Mabli. *Mable, Mabeline, Maybelle, Maybelline, Mayble*
Macaria (Ma-**car**-ee-a) (Greek) happy.
Madeleine (Mad-a-lin) French version of Magdalene. There are numerous variants, the most popular being Madalena, Marlene, Malena and Maddy.
Madge (Madj) (English) variant of Margaret, meaning pearl.
Madia (Mah-dee-a) (Arabic) praiseworthy. *Madiah*
Madonna (Ma-**don**-a) (Latin) Our Lady (i.e. the Virgin Mary).
Madra (Mad-ra) (Spanish) mother. Madonna is the Italian version of this name. Both refer to the Virgin Mary.
Maegan (May-gan) (American) a combination of May (the month) and Megan (short for Margaret).
Maeve (May-vuh) (Irish) intoxicating. In Irish folklore, a warrior queen who controlled the Irish sea. *Mave, Meave, Meadhbh*
Magdalene/Magdalena (Mag-da-**lane**-a) (Hebrew) from the biblical Mary Magdalene. Her name was probably based on the town of Magdala on the western side of Lake Galilee. Saint Mary Magdalene was delivered of seven demons by Jesus and became a close friend of his. She was the first to witness his empty tomb – and became the patron saint of hairdressers, perfumiers and prostitutes! Saint's day: 22 July.
Maggie (Mag-ee) (English) a pet form of Margaret, meaning pearl.
Magnolia (Mag-**no**-lee-a) (French) named after the flowering tree.
Mahala (Ma-**hay**-la) (Hebrew) tenderness. *Mahalah*
Mahila (Ma-**hee**-la) (Sanskrit) womanly.
Mahina (Ma-**hee**-na) (Hawaiian) the halo of the moon.
Mahira (Ma-**hee**-ra) (Hebrew) full of energy. *Mahirah*
Maia (My-a) (Greek) mother or nurse. The oldest and most beautiful of the daughters of Atlas, she was turned into a dove by Zeus. The month of May is named after her.
Maida (May-da) (English) maiden. *Maidie*
Maire (My-ra) (Irish) an Irish form of Mary, meaning bitter.
Mairead (Ma-**raid**) Gaelic form of Margaret, which means pearl.
Mairsail (Mare-**sayle**) (Irish) a feminine form of Marcus, meaning of warlike disposition.

Maisie (**May**-zee) (Scottish) a short version of Mairead (Gaelic for Margaret).
Mali (**Mah**-lee) (Greek) a short form of Magdalene, from Mary Magdalene.
Malia (**Mal**-ee-a) Hawaiian form of Mary, meaning bitter.
Malika (Ma-**lie**-ka) (Hungarian) hard-working.
Malina (Ma-**lee**-na) (Hebrew) tower. *Malinah*
Malvina (Mal-**vee**-na) invented by the Scottish poet James Macpherson, perhaps from the Gaelic for smooth brow.
Manal (Ma-**nal**) (Arabic) attainment, achievement.
Mandara (Man-**dar**-a) (Hindi) calm.
Mandy (**Man**-dee) a short version of Amanda, meaning fit to be loved. Now a name in its own right.
Manilla (Man-**ill**-a) (Australian) from the winding river. Manila is the capital of the Philippines.
Mara (**Ma**-ra) (Hebrew) bitter. *Marah, Marala*
Maranda (Ma-**ran**-da) (American) a combination of Mara and Miranda.
Marcella (Mar-**sell**-a) French feminine form of the Latin root name Marcus, meaning warlike. Saint's day: 31 January. *Marcelina, Marcelle, Marcia, Marsha*
Marcelline (Mar-sell-**een**) (French) warlike. Marcelyn is the English form.
Marcia (**Mar**-see-a) (Italian) a feminine form of the Roman name Marcus, meaning warlike. *Marcy*
Mardella (**Mar**-dell-a) (English) from the hill near the lake.
Marelda (Ma-**rel**-da) (German) renowned warrior. *Marella*
Marisol (Ma-ree-**sol**) (Spanish) loved by the sun.
Margaret (**Mar**-ga-ret) (Greek) pearl. There are dozens of derivations, the most popular being Margery, Meg and Marjorie. Others include Madge, Maggie, Marge, Margo, Margot, Margarita and Marguerite. Saint Margaret of Antioch's father was a pagan priest. Her escape from those beliefs was depicted in a story of her being swallowed by a dragon representing paganism, and then escaping from its belly as if being born anew. This made her the co-patron saint of pregnancy, labour, and childbirth (the other patron saint being a man!). Her saint's day is 20 July.
Margo (**Mar**-go) English form of the French name Margot, a derivative of Margaret, meaning pearl.
Maria (Ma-**ree**-a) originally a form of Mary, meaning bitter, but now a name in its own right.
Mariabella (**Ma**-ree-a-**bel**-a) (Italian) a compound name of Maria and Bella, meaning beautiful.
Mariah (Ma-**rye**-a) (English) a variant of Maria, which means bitter.
Marian (**Ma**-ree-an) from the root name Mary, meaning bitter.

Marianne (Ma-ree-**an**) (American) a combination of Mary (bitter) and Anne (graceful and merciful). Popular religiously because it combines the name of the Virgin Mary with her mother, Saint Anne.
Maribeth (**Mare**-ee-**beth**) (English) a combination of Mary (bitter) and Beth (from the house of God).
Maricia (Ma-**ree**-see-a) (Italian) a name from Roman mythology.
Maricruz (Ma-re-**crooz**) (Spanish) Mary's cross.
Marigold (**Ma**-ree-gold) (English) from the vibrant yellow/orange flower. The original English word for this flower was golde, the name Mary being added to it in the early medieval period.
Marie/Mariette (Ma-**ree**/Ma-ree-**et**) (French) forms of Mary, meaning bitter.
Mariene (**Ma**-ree-**en**) a German form of Mary, which means bitter.
Marietta (Mar-ee-**et**-a) an Italian form of Mary (bitter).
Marika (Ma-**ree**-ka) Scandinavian and Slavic form of Mary (bitter).
Marilena (Ma-re-**lee**-na) (English) an elaborated form of Mary (bitter).
Marilyn (**Ma**-ril-in) (American) a combination of Mary (bitter) and Lynn (pretty). Also means from the line of Mary. *Marylynn*
Marina (Ma-**ree**-na) (Latin) has two meanings. One refers to the sea, the other to Mars, the Roman god of war.
Marion (**Ma**-ree-on) a French form of Mary, meaning bitter.
Maris (**Ma**-ris) (Latin) from the sea. *Marisa, Marissa*
Marjorie (**Mar**-jor-ee) (English) a form of Margaret, meaning pearl.
Marla (**Mar**-la) (English) a pet form of Marlene.
Marlene (Mar-**lay**-na) a combined form of the name Mary Magdalene, the biblical friend of Jesus.
Marmara (**Mar**-ma-ra) (Greek) shining.
Marni (**Mar**-nee) (Hebrew) directly translates into rejoice. *Marlinia*
Marquita (Mar-**kee**-ta) (English) the feminine form of the masculine name Marquis, from a French aristocratic title.
Marsha (**Marsh**-a) (English) variant of Marcia, from Marcus, meaning warlike.
Marta (**Mar**-ta) (English) variant of Marcia, the feminine form of Marcus, meaning warlike.
Martha (**Mar**-tha) (Aramaic) lady or mistress. The sister of Lazarus who served Jesus when he stayed at their house. She became the patron saint of cooks, dieticians, home-makers, hotel-keepers, laundry-workers, servants, single laywomen, and those who put other people up in their house. Saint's day: 29 July. *Marthia*
Martina/Martine (Mar-**teen**-a/Mar-**teen**) (Latin) the feminine form of Martin, derived from Mars, the Roman god of war.

Mary (**Mare**-ee) (Hebrew) bitter. Actually a derivation of the earlier biblical name Miriam. Over the centuries it has been the most popular girl's name in the world. *Mae, Mara, Maime, Maria, Marian, Marianne, Maribel, Marie, Marietta, Mariette, Marilyn, Maureen, Moira*

Matilda (Mat-**ill**-da) (French) battle maiden. Saint's day: 14 March. *Maud, Maude, Tilda, Tillie*

Maud (English) a short form of Madeline, Matilda and Madison.

Maura (**More**-a) (Celtic) dark.

Maureen (**More**-een) (English) the anglicized version of the Irish Maire, which derives from Mary, meaning bitter.

Maurelle (Mor-**el**) (French) dark elf.

Mauve (**Mowve**) (French) light purple.

Mavia (**Mayv**-ya) (Irish) happy.

Mavourneen (Ma-**voor**-neen) (Irish) a term of affection, meaning dear one.

Maxine (**Max**-een) (Latin) the greatest.

May (**May**) named for the month, which is named after a figure in Greek mythology called Maia, meaning mother or nurse. *Mai, Mae*

Meagan (**Mare**-gan) a Welsh short form of Margaret, itself often shortened to Meg. *Megan*

Meara (**Mere**-a) (Irish) full of mirth.

Medea (Mi-**dee**-a) (Greek) ruler. In Greek mythology, a princess and sorceress who helped Jason win the golden fleece.

Melana (Mee-**la**-na) Russian and Slavic forms of Melanie, meaning dark. *Meliana*

Melanie (**Mel**-an-ee) (Greek) dark. Saint's day: 31 December. *Melinia*

Melantha (Mel-**an**-tha) (Greek) dark flower.

Melba (**Mel**-ba) (Greek) soft and slender. Also means a girl from Melbourne.

Melina (Mel-**ee**-na) from the Greek word for honey.

Melinda (Mel-**in**-da) (American) a combination of Melina and Linda (pretty).

Meliora (Mee-lee-**or**-a) (Latin) better.

Melissa (Mel-**iss**-a) (Greek) bee. A figure from Greek mythology who was the first person to discover how to collect honey from bees. She fed this to the baby Zeus who grew up to become king of the gods.

Melita (Me-**lee**-ta) (Greek) honey flower.

Melody (**Mel**-o-dee) (Greek) from the Greek word for song.

Melora (**Mel**-or-a) (Celtic) King Arthur's daughter, who rescued her lover from captivity.

Menora (Men-**or**-a) (Hebrew) the seven-branched candle-holder used in Jewish religious observances. *Menorah*

Mercedes (Mer-**say**-deez) (Spanish) mercy. *Merced, Mercy*

Mercia (**Mer**-see-a) (English/Latin) merciful. Also the name of a Dark Ages kingdom in the English Midlands.

Mercy (**Mer**-see) (Latin) mercy – although the original meaning of the word was reward.

Meri (**Mer**-ee) (Finnish) from the sea.

Meriel (**Mer**-ee-el) (Celtic) bright sea. *Meryl*

Merinda (Mer-**in**-da) (Australian) beautiful.

Merle (**Merl**) (Old French) blackbird.

Meryl (**Mer**-ull) (Celtic) a form of Meriel, meaning bright sea.

Mia (**Mee**-a) Scandinavian form of Maria (bitter) and the Italian word for mine (belonging to me).

Miana (Mee-**ah**-na) (Scandinavian) a combination of Maria (bitter) and Ann (graceful and merciful).

Michaela (Mi-**kye**-la) the feminine form of the Hebrew name Michael, which means he who is like God. *Micaela*

Michelle (Mee-**shell**) French feminine form of Michael (he who is like God).

Mila/Milah (**Mee**-la) (Slavonic) loved by all people. Also a short form of Camilla, meaning temple servant.

Milantia (Mi-**lan**-tee-a) (Italian) girl from Milan.

Mildred (**Mil**-dred) (Old English) gentle giant. Saint Mildred was an abbess with a reputation for great holiness and generosity, as well as compassion for the poor and rejected. She chose this life over marrying into nobility and wealth. *Millie, Milly*

Mileta (My-**lee**-ta) (German) merciful.

Milena (Mi-**lay**-na) (Old German) mild and peaceful.

Miliani (Mi-lee-**ahn**-ee) (Hawaiian) gentle caress.

Milissa (Mil-**iss**-a) Greek form of Melissa, meaning bee.

Millicent (**Mil**-li-sent) (German) strong worker. Often shortened to Milly or Millie.

Minerva (Mi-**nerve**-a) (Latin) the Roman goddess of wisdom, arts and crafts. Athene in Greek.

Minette (Min-**et**) (French) faithful defender.

Minnie (**Min**-ee) short for Wilhelmina. The feminine of Wilhelm, which is the German form of William, meaning strong protector.

Mirabella (Mi-ra-**bel**-a) (Latin) miracle. *Mirabel*

Miracle (**Mi**-ri-cull) (Latin) from the Latin word *miraculum*, meaning something to wonder at.

Miranda (Mi-**ran**-da) invented by Shakespeare for his play *The Tempest*. Miranda was wise beyond her years.

Mireille (Mi-**ray**) (French) but based on the Spanish word *mirar* meaning to look at, implying to admire.

Mirella (Mi-**rell**-a) Irish and German form of Meryl, meaning bright sea.

Miren (**Mi**-ren) (Hebrew) bitter. From the same root as Mary. *Mirien*

Miri (**Mi**-ree) (Romany) of me. Also a short form of Miriam.

Miriam (**Mi**-ree-um) (Hebrew) fertile. The sister of Moses and Aaron, she watched over the baby Moses hidden in the reeds.
Mirinda (Mi-**rin**-da) Esperanto word for wonderful.
Misaki (Mi-**sa**-kee) (Japanese) beautiful blossom.
Missie (**Miss**-ee) (English) a short form of Melissa, meaning bee.
Misty (**Miss**-tee) (English) misty.
Mocara (Ma-**ca**-ra) (Scottish) my friend.
Modesty (**Mod**-est-ee) (Latin) modest.
Moira (**Moy**-ra) (English) an anglicized version of the Irish Maire (bitter).
Moll/Molly (**Moll/Moll**-ee) Irish form of Mary (bitter).
Mona (**Moan**-a) (Irish) noble. Also a short form of Monica.
Monica (**Mon**-ik-a) (Latin) to advise or counsel. A popular French variation is Monique. Saint Monica was the mother of Saint Augustine, and for many years prayed and cried and did penances for her son. As a result, she became a Doctor of the Church and the patron saint of alcoholics. Her saint's day is 27 August.
Mora (**Mor**-a) (Spanish) blueberry.
Moriah (Mo-**rye**-ah) (Hebrew) pupil of God. *Moria*
Morena (More-**ray**-na) (Spanish) brown.
Morna (**Morn**-a) (Scottish) beloved and gentle.
Morrighan (**More**-a-han) (Irish) named after the Irish goddess of death and war.
Morwenna (Mor-**wane**-a) (Welsh) maiden of the sea, mermaid.
Muireann (**Mwi**-ren) (Irish) a character from Irish folklore. *Muir* means sea.
Muirgean (**Mwi**-gan) (Irish) a maiden in Irish folklore who was changed into a salmon.
Muirne (**Mur**-nee) (Irish) directly translates as beloved.
Mura (**Moo**-ra) (Japanese) girl from the village.
Muriel (**Myoor**-ee-el) (Irish) bright sea. Also the Arabic word for myrrh.
Musetta (Moo-**set**-a) from the French word for bagpipe (*musette*).
Musidora (Moo-see-**dore**-a) (Greek) beautiful muse.
Myfanwy (Mah-**van**-wee) (Welsh) literally, my fine one.
Mykala (My-**ka**-la) American form of Michaela, the feminine of Michael.
Myla (**My**-la) (Old English) gentle.
Mylene (**My**-leen) (Greek) dark.
Myra (**My**-ra) (Latin) wonderful. *Mira*
Myrtle (**Mert**-ull) (Greek) the myrtle bush or tree.
Mystique (Miss-**teek**) (French) mysterious.
Myune (Mee-**oon**) (Australian) from the clear water.

N

Nabila (Na-**bee**-la) (Arabic) noble. *Nabilah*
Nachine (Na-**sheen**) (Spanish) fiery.
Nadette (Na-**det**) (French) short form of Bernadette, the feminine form of Bernard.
Nadia (**Nah**-dee-a) (Russian) full of hope. *Nadida, Nadiyah, Nadja*
Nadine (Na-**deen/Nay**-deen) the French form of Nadia, meaning full of hope.
Nadira (Na-**dear**-a) (Arabic) precious. *Nadirah*
Nahida (Na-**hee**-da) (Persian) the name of the Persian goddess of beauty and love. *Nahidah*
Naida (Na-**ee**-da) (Greek) water nymph.
Nakia (Na-**kee**-a) (Arabic) pure. *Nakiah*
Nakita (Na-**kee**-ta) American form of the Russian Nikita, meaning of the victorious people.
Nami (**Na**-mee) (Japanese) wave.
Nancy (**Nan**-see) (English) gracious.
Nandalia (Nan-**day**-lee-a) (Australian) born of fire.
Nanette (Nan-**et**) (English) graceful. Originally a form of Hannah, introduced in the Middle Ages. *Nettie*
Nani (**Nan**-ee) (Greek) full of charm.
Naoimh (**Neev**) (Irish) holy or radiant beauty. In Irish legend, Niamh, a daughter of the sea god, took a shipwrecked sailor as her lover and carried him off to a timeless land. *Niamh*
Naomi (**Nay**-o-mee/Nay-**oh**-mee) (Hebrew) my delight. A widow from the Old Testament who travelled to Judea and married Boaz.
Nara (**Na**-ra) (Celtic) happy.
Narcissa (Nar-**sis**-a) (Greek) in Greek mythology, Narcissus was a beautiful youth who fell in love with his own reflection. This is the feminine version of that name.
Narda (**Nar**-da) (Greek) aromatic oil.
Narelle (Na-**rel**) (Australian) girl from the sea.
Natalie (**Nat**-a-lee) (Latin) birthday of the Lord (i.e. born at Christmas). Natalie's saint's day is 27 July. *Natalia, Nataline*
Natania (Na-**tahn**-ya) (Hebrew) a gift from God. *Nataniah*
Natara (Na-**tah**-ra) (Arabic) sacrifice. *Natarah*
Natasha (Na-**tash**-a) Russian diminutive form of Natalie, meaning birthday of the Lord.
Natividad (Na-ti-vi-**dad**) (Spanish) born at Christmas.
Nayana (Nay-**ah**-na) (Sanskrit) beautiful eyes.
Nazira (Na-**zee**-ra) (Arabic) an equal. *Nazirah*

Neala (**Neel**-a) (Irish) feminine form of Neal or Neil, meaning champion. *Neila, Nelia*
Neassa (**Ness**-a) (Irish) a female character from Irish folklore.
Neely (**Nee**-lee) (Irish) a form of Neala and Nelia, derived from the boy's name Neil.
Neema (**Nee**-ma) (Swahili) born in good times.
Neena (**Nee**-na) based on the Spanish name Nina, which means little girl. *Nena*
Nell/Nellie (**Nel/Nel**-ee) (English) a form of Eleanor, meaning foreign. (Greek) stone.
Nenet (**Neh**-net) (Egyptian) the name of the Egyptian goddess of the sea.
Neola (Nee-**oh**-la) (Greek) young and new.
Nerissa (Ne-**riss**-a) from the Greek *Nereid*. The Nereids were fifty beautiful sea nymphs in Greek mythology. Variations include Nereida, Nerine and Nerida.
Nerys (**Ne**-riss) (Welsh) lady.
Nessie (**Ness**-ee) (English) a pet form of Vanessa and Agnes.
Nettie (**Net**-ee) (French) a pet form of Annette, Antoinette and Nanette.
Nevada (Ne-**vah**-da) (Spanish) snowy. Also from the American state.
Neve (**Nev**) (Latin) snowy.
Nia (**Nee**-a) (Celtic) a short form of Neala/Neila, and the name of a woman in Celtic mythology.
Nicola (**Nik**-o-la) (Italian) a feminine version of Nicholas, meaning victory over the people. *Nicholie, Nicole, Nicolette, Nikolette*
Nike (**Nye**-kee) (Greek) the Greek goddess of victory, usually depicted with wings.
Nikki (**Nik**-ee) (English) a short form of Nicola. *Nicki, Niki*
Nikita (Nik-**ee**-ta) (Russian) of the victorious people.
Nima (**Nee**-mah) (Arabic) blessing. *Nimah*
Nina (**Nee**-na) (Russian) a pet form of Antonia, Agnes and Christine.
Ninette (Nin-**et**) (French) small.
Nirvana (Nir-**van**-a) (Sanskrit) the highest state of bliss.
Nisha (**Nee**-sha) (Sanskrit) night.
Nissa (**Niss**-a) (Scandinavian) elf.
Nitha (**Nith**-a) (Scandinavian) elf.
Noelani (No-el-**ah**-ni) (Hawaiian) beautiful one from heaven.
Noirin (**No**-reen) an Irish form of Nora, which means foreign.
Nola (**No**-la) (Irish) white-shouldered. Also a short form of Fionnuala. *Noleen, Nolana*
Nora/Norah (**Nor**-a) an Irish form of Eleanor, meaning foreign.
Nordica (**Nor**-di-ka) (Scandinavian) from the north.
Noreen (**Nor**-een) a diminutive of Nora, which is a diminutive of Eleanor, meaning foreign.

Norell (No-**rel**) (Scandinavian) from the north. *Norelle*
Norma (**Nor**-ma) based on the Latin word for pattern or model. Also the feminine version of Norman, meaning a man from the north.
Novella (No-**vel**-la) (Latin) newly-arrived.
Nuala (**New**-a-la) (Irish) short form of Fionnuala, meaning white-shouldered.
Nuna (**Noon**-a) (Native American) land. *Nunia*
Nuria (Noo-**ree**-a) (Aramaic) light. *Nura, Nuriah*
Nydai (Ni-**day**) (Latin) from the nest.
Nydia (Ni-**dee**-a) invented by Edward Bulwer-Lytton for his novel, *The Last Days of Pompeii.*
Nyree (Ni-**ree**) (Maori) from the sea.
Nyssa (**Niss**-a) (Greek) goal.

Obelia (O-**bee**-lee-a) (Greek) needle.
Octavia (Ok-**tay**-vee-a) (Latin) eighth child. The name of Mark Antony's wife.
Odeda (**Oh**-ded-a) (Hebrew) courageous. *Odedah*
Odele (O-**dell**-uh) (Greek) song. *Odelette, Odelita*
Odelia (O-**dee**-lee-a) (Greek) song.
Odella (O-**dell**-a) (English) from the wooded hill.
Odera (O-**dee**-ra) (Hebrew) from the ploughed land. *Oderah*
Odessa (O-**dess**-a) originally from the Greek word for journey or quest, but now associated with the Ukrainian Black Sea town. (The town itself was originally a Greek colony.)
Odette (O-**det**) (French) from a wealthy home. *Odelette, Odetta*
Ohanna (O-**han**-a) (Hebrew) God's gracious gift. *Ohannah*
Okalani (**Ok**-a-**lan**-ee) (Hawaiian) from heaven.
Ola (**Oo**-la) (Scandinavian) from the ancestors.
Olalla (**O**-la-la) (Greek) beautiful voice.
Oldina (**Ol**-din-a) (Australian) snow.
Oleander (O-lee-**an**-der) (Latin) an evergreen shrub with sweet-smelling flowers.

Oleda (O-**lee**-da/O-**lay**-da) Spanish form of Alida, which means winged one.
Olen (**O**-len) (Russian) deer.
Olena (O-**len**-a) (Russian) a form of Helen, meaning bright.
Olesia (O-**lee**-see-a) Greek feminine form of Alexander, meaning defender of mankind.
Oletha (**Oh**-leth-a) (Scandinavian) nimble-footed.
Olethia (**Ol**-thea) (Latin) honest and truthful.
Olga (**Ol**-ga) (Old Norse) holy. Saint Olga was married to a prince who was assassinated. She took her revenge by scalding her husband's murderers to death and killing hundreds of their followers. However, she later forgave them and so became a saint. Her feast day is 11 July.
Olina (O-**lee**-na) (Hawaiian) full of happiness.
Olive (**O**-liv) (Greek) named after the tree which is associated with peace and, in Greek tradition, was given by the goddess Athene to the citizens of Athens. Saint Oliva of Brescia was martyred in the persecutions of Hadrian in AD 138. Her relics are still in Saint Afra's church in Brescia, Italy. Her feast day is 5 March.
Olivia (O-**liv**-ee-a) first used by Shakespeare in *Twelfth Night*. Presumably, it was based on the name of the olive tree.
Olwen (**Ol**-wen) (Welsh) white footprints. In Welsh legend, a girl who leaves white flowers wherever her feet touch the ground.
Olympia (O-**lim**-pee-a) (Greek) heavenly.
Ona (**Oo**-na) (English) from the river. (Irish) a form of Oona, which means lamb.
Ondine (**On**-deen) (Latin) from the water sprite Undine, a figure in Roman mythology.
Oneida (Oh-**nye**-da) (Native American) sought-after one.
Onella/Onelle (O-**nell**-a/O-**nel**) (Greek) light.
Onora (Un-**oo**-ra) (Irish) honour.
Oonagh (**Oo**-na) Irish form of Una, which means lamb. *Oona*
Opal (**O**-pull) (Hindi) from the name of the gemstone.
Ophelia (O-**feel**-ya) (Greek) to help. A key character in Shakespeare's *Hamlet*, who tried to do just that.
Oprah (**O**-pra) (Hebrew) fawn. Also has a connotation of liveliness. *Ofra, Ophra, Ophrah*
Ora (**Or**-ra) (Spanish) gold. (Latin) prayer.
Oran (**Or**-an) (Irish) queen. *Orann*
Orana (**Or**-a-na) (Australian) welcome.
Orena (Or-**ee**-na) (Hebrew) pine tree. *Orenah, Orenne*
Oriana/Orianna (Or-ee-**ah**-na) (Latin) golden dawn.

Oriella (Oh-**ree**-la) (Latin) golden.
Orina (Or-**ee**-na) Russian form of Irene, meaning peace.
Oriole (Oh-**ree**-o-lay) (Latin) golden-feathered bird.
Orithna (Or-**ith**-na) invented by George Bernard Shaw for his play, *The Apple Cart*.
Orlaith (**Or**-la) (Irish) *Or* means gold and *laith* means princess. *Orla*
Orlanda (Or-**lan**-da) (Old German) famous in the land. A feminine form of Orlando.
Orlena (Or-**lee**-na) (Irish) golden girl. *Orlaine, Orlana, Orlina*
Orlenda (Or-**len**-da) (Russian) eagle.
Orly (**Or**-lee) (Hebrew) my light.
Ormonda (Or-**mon**-da) (Irish) the feminine form of Ormond, which means from the mountain of the bear. In early Irish history there was an area in Ireland called Ormond.
Orna (**Or**-na) (Irish) the colour of olives.
Ornice (**Or**-neece) (Irish) olive-coloured. (Hebrew) from the cedar tree.
Orsa (**Or**-sa) (Latin) little bear. Also short for Orsaline.
Osla (**Oss**-la) (Old Norse) consecrated to God.
Otilie (Oh-**till**-ee) (Czech) lucky and heroic. *Otily*
Owena (Oh-**wen**-a) (Welsh) born to a noble warrior.
Ozara (Oh-**za**-ra) (Hebrew) treasure. *Ozarah*

P

Pacifica (Pa-**sif**-ik-a) (Latin) peaceful.
Paidrigin (Paw-drig-**een**) (Irish) the feminine form of Padraigh (Patrick), meaning patrician or nobleman.
Palila (Pa-**lee**-la) (Tahitian) with a spirit as free as a bird.
Palma (**Pal**-ma) (Latin) palm tree.
Paloma (Pal-**oh**-ma) (Spanish) dove.
Pamela (**Pam**-el-a) invented by the Elizabethan poet Sir Philip Sidney. Probably based on the Greek words for all and honey. *Pam, Pamella, Pamina*
Pandora (Pan-**dor**-a) (Greek) all gifts. In Greek mythology, Pandora was given a box but told not to open it. Unable to resist, she did. It contained all the troubles of mankind, which promptly flew out, but she shut it just in time to keep hope inside. The story means that although humankind is plagued by all sorts of adversity, there's always hope.
Pansy (**Pan**-zee) based on the name of the flower and the French word for thoughts (*pensées*).
Panthea (**Pan**-thee-a) (Greek) of all the gods.
Parthenia (Par-**then**-ee-a) (Greek) virginal.
Parvati (Par-**vah**-ti) (Sanskrit) climber of mountains.

Pasha (**Pash**-a) (Greek) of the sea.
Passion (**Pash**-un) (Latin) passion.
Patience (**Pay**-shunss) originally from the Latin for to suffer, it now has the modern meaning of virtuous waiting.
Patricia female form of Patrick, meaning patrician or nobleman. *Pat, Patrina, Patsy,*
Patia (**Pat**-ee-a) (Spanish) leaf. (English) a short form of Patricia.
Paula (**Paw**-la) the female form of Paul, meaning little. *Paulette, Paulina, Pauline*
Peace (**Peace**) (English) peaceful.
Pearl (**Perl**) (Latin) the jewel.
Peggy (**Peg**-ee) a short form of Margaret, meaning pearl. *Pegeen*
Pela (Pe-**la**) (Polish) a short form of Penelope, meaning weaver of thread.
Pelagia (Pel-**aj**-ee-a) (Greek) of the sea.
Penda (**Pen**-da) (Swahili) loved.
Penelope (Pen-**el**-oh-pee) (Greek) weaver of thread. In Greek mythology, the wife of Odysseus. She was besieged by suitors during the ten years he took to return from the Trojan War. She held them off by saying she could not re-marry until she had finished weaving a garment. Each night she unwove the work she'd done that day. (Odysseus did eventually return.) *Penelopie, Penny*
Peony (**Pee**-oh-nee) (Greek) the flower. *Peonie, Piony*
Pera (**Pe**-ra) (Persian) elf. *Perah, Peri*
Perdita (**Per**-dit-a) invented by Shakespeare for *The Winter's Tale.* Probably derived from the Latin for lost.
Perfecta (Per-**fek**-ta) (Latin) perfect.
Perla (**Per**-la) (Latin) a form of Pearl. *Perlie, Perlina*
Persephone (Per-**sef**-on-e) (Greek) bearer of light. In Greek mythology, Persephone was the daughter of the harvest goddess Demeter. She was abducted by the god of the underworld, causing permanent winter across the Earth. Demeter and the god of the underworld struck a deal allowing Persephone to return for six months each year (spring and summer), and so the seasons came about.
Persis (**Per**-sis) (Latin) from Persia.
Peta (**Pee**-ta) a modern feminine version of Peter, meaning rock. Only in use since the 1930s.
Petra (**Pet**-ra) a feminine form of Peter, based on the Greek word for rock.
Petronella (Pet-ron-**el**-a) (Greek) small rock. *Petronilla*
Petula (Pet-**yoo**-la) (Latin) seeker. *Petunia*
Phaedra (**Fee**-dra) (Greek) shining bright. She was a figure from Greek mythology who fell in love with her stepson and killed herself when he rejected her.
Philana (Fil-**ah**-na) (Greek) lover of mankind. *Phila*
Philanthra (Fil-**an**-thra) (Greek) lover of flowers. *Philly*
Philippa (**Fil**-ip-a) (Greek) lover of horses. *Fillipa, Philise, Pip, Pippa*

Philomena (Fil-o-**mee**-na) (Greek) beloved. *Philly*
Phoebe (**Fee**-bee) (Greek) radiant. The daughter of heaven and Earth in Greek mythology. Also a figure in the Bible who helped Saint Paul.
Phyllida (**Fil**-id-a) (Greek) the direct translation is leafy.
Phyllis (**Fil**-iss) (Greek) based on the Greek word for leaf. In Greek mythology, her husband sailed away, promising to return. When he did not, she hanged herself and was transformed into the first almond tree. *Phylicia, Phylis*
Pia (**Pee**-a) (Italian) dutiful.
Pier (**Pee**-er) a form of Petra, meaning rock. *Pierette, Pierina*
Pippa (**Pip**-a) a short version of Philippa, meaning lover of horses. *Pip*
Pixie (**Pix**-ee) (English) a mischievous fairy. *Pixy*
Placida (Pla-**see**-dah) (Latin) serene.
Pleasance (Ple-**zohnce**) (French) pleasant.
Pocahontas (Po-ca-**hon**-tas) (Native American) playful.
Polly (**Pol**-ee) based on Molly, which is based on Mary, meaning bitter.
Pollyanna (Pol-ee-**an**-a) a combination of Polly and Anna (meaning graceful and merciful).
Pollydora (Pol-ee-**dor**-a) (Greek) one with many gifts.
Polyxena (Pol-ee-**zee**-na/ Pol-ee-**kseen**-a) (Greek) welcoming.
Pomona (Po-**moan**-a) (Latin) the Roman goddess of fruit. The god of changing seasons fell in love with Pomona and pursued her, disguised as a harvester, a herdsman and an old woman. He finally won her heart when he appeared as himself.
Poni (**Pon**-ee) (African) second daughter.
Poppy (**Pop**-ee) (Latin) the flower name.
Portia (**Por**-sha) (Latin) doorway, gateway. The wife of Brutus, who conspired against Julius Caesar. The name appears in two Shakespeare plays, *Julius Caesar* and *The Merchant of Venice*.
Prima (**Pree**-ma) (Latin) first. *Primalia*
Primavera (Pree-ma-**vair**-a) (Spanish) spring.
Primrose (**Prim**-rose) (English) from the name of the flower. *Primmie*
Princess (**Prin**-sess) (English) princess.
Priscilla (Pri-**sill**-a) (Latin) ancient. The biblical Priscilla travelled to Syria with Saint Paul. Her saint's day is 8 July. *Prissy*
Promise (**Prom**-iss) (Latin) promise.
Prudence (**Pru**-dense) (Latin) circumspect and cautious. *Prudy*
Prunella (Proo-**nell**-a) (Latin) plum.
Psyche (**Sye**-kee) (Greek) soul. In Greek mythology, she was a mortal so beautiful that she won the heart of Eros, the god of love.
Purity (**Pyoor**-it-ee) (English) purity.
Pyralis (Pi-**ral**-is) (Greek) fire. *Piralis, Pyrena*
Pythia (**Pith**-ee-a) (Greek) prophet.

Q

Quaralia (Kwa-**ray**-lee-a) (Australian) star.
Queenie (**Kween**-ee) (English) little queen. *Quenna*
Querida (Ker-**ee**-da) (Spanish) loved.
Questa (**Kwest**-a) (French) searcher.
Quiana (Kwee-**an**-a) Anna, meaning graceful and merciful, with the prefix Qu-.
Quillane (**Quill**-en) (Irish) fair maiden. *Quillaine, Quillayne*
Quinby (**Kwin**-bee) (Scandinavian) from the queen's estate.
Quintana (Kwin-**tan**-a) (Latin) fifth.
Quintessa (Kwin-**tess**-a) (Latin) essence.
Quinta (**Kwin**-ta) a feminine form of Quentin, meaning fifth.
Quitterie (**Kwit**-er-ree/Kee-ter-**ee**) (French) tranquil.

R

Raanana (Ra-**an**-an-na) (Hebrew) fresh. *Raananah, Ranana*
Rachel (**Ray**-chel) (Hebrew) ewe. The beautiful daughter of the biblical Laban. Jacob fell in love with her and promised to work for seven years to win her hand. He did so, but then he married her sister by mistake. To rectify matters, he agreed to work for another seven years and then marry Rachel. *Rachael, Rachelle*
Radha (**Rad**-ha) (Hindi) successful and prosperous.
Radhiya (Ra-**hee**-ya) (Swahili) pleasant and friendly.
Rafaela (Ra-**fel**-la) Spanish feminine form of Raphael, which means God heals. *Rafela*
Rainbow (**Rain**-bo) means... rainbow, and was most popular in the 1960s.
Raiona (Rye-**own**-a) (Maori) lion.
Raisa (**Rye**-sa) (Hebrew) rose. Saint Raisa was martyred in AD 308. *Raisah*
Ramla (**Ram**-la) (Swahili) one who can see the future.
Ramona (Ra-**moan**-a) (Old German) wise protector. Based on the masculine name Raymond. *Mona, Raimunda, Raymena*
Rana (Ra-**nah**) (Arabic) beautiful to gaze upon. *Ranah*

Ranielle (Ra-nee-**el**) (African-American) God is my judge.

Ranjana (Ran-**jah**-na) (Hindi) beloved.

Ranya (**Ran**-ya) (Hindi) to gaze.

Raquel (Ra-**kell**) Spanish form of Rachel, meaning ewe.

Rasheda (Ra-**shee**-da) (Turkish) a feminine form of Rashid, which means well-guided one.

Rasia (Ra-**see**-a) (Arabic) young gazelle. *Rasha, Rasiah*

Rathnait (**Raith**-na) (Irish) little graceful one.

Raya (**Ra**-ya) (Hebrew) friend. (Javanese) greater.

Rayna/Rayne (**Ray**-na/**Rayne**) (Scandinavian) mighty.

Raziah (Ra-**zee**-ah) (Arabic) contented. *Razia*

Reanne (**Ree**-an) based on the Welsh name Rhiannon, which means moon goddess or nymph.

Rebecca (Re-**bek**-a) (Hebrew) to join together. The beautiful wife of Isaac. She helped their younger son, Jacob, receive God's word and thus caused acrimony between her children. Jacob became father of the Israelites. *Becca, Becky*

Regina (Re-**jye**-na) from the Latin for queen.

Rehema (Re-**hee**-ma) (Swahili) compassionate.

Rei (**Rye**) (Maori) jewel.

Reika (**Ray**-ka) (Japanese) beautiful flower.

Rena (**Ren**-a) (Hebrew) joyful song. *Renah*

Renata (Ren-**ah**-ta) (Latin) re-born. *Renate, Renée, Renetta*

Renita (Re-**nee**-ta) (Latin) a combination of Renata (re-born) and Anita (graceful and merciful).

Reva (**Ree**-va) (Hindi) from the sacred river.

Rexanne (Rex-**an**) a combination of Rex, meaning king, and Roxanne, meaning dawn.

Reyna (**Ray**-na) (Greek) peaceful.

Rhea (**Ree**-a) (Greek) Earth Mother. From the goddess of that name. *Rhia*

Rheta (**Ret**-a) (Greek) eloquent.

Rhiannon (Ree-**an**-on) (Welsh) moon goddess or nymph. In Welsh legend, the beautiful daughter of the king of the underworld. Her story is close to that of the Greek goddess Persephone. *Rhianna*

Rhianwen (Ree-**an**-wen) (Welsh) pure maiden. *Rhianwyn*

Rhoda (**Road**-a) (Greek) either rose or woman from Rhodes. Also a maidservant in the Bible.

Rona (**Roh**-na) (Irish) little seal. The feminine form of Ronan.

Riane (Rye-**ah**-nay) (Irish) the feminine version of Ryan, meaning follower of Riaghan, an Irish king.

Rihana (Ree-**hah**-na) (Arabic) sweet basil. *Rihanah*

Rina (**Ree**-na) a short version of Katrina (see Catherine).

Rima (Re-**mah**) (Arabic) antelope. *Rimah*
Rioghnach (**Ree**-an-ock) (Irish) a female character from Irish folklore. *Rioghan* means queen in Irish.
Rissa (**Riss**-a) (English) a familiar form for Nerissa, which is the name of a water nymph in Greek mythology.
Rita (**Ree**-ta) (English) a familiar form of Margaret, which means pearl.
Rivka (**Riv**-ka) (Hebrew) noose. *Rivkah*
Roberta (Ro-**ber**-ta) the feminine version of Robert, which means famous.
Rochelle (Rosh-**el**) (French) little rock.
Roderica (Rod-er-**ee**-ka) French feminine form of Roderick, meaning famous and powerful.
Roha (**Ro**-wa) (Maori) a rose.
Rohana (Ro-**hah**-na) (Hindi) sandalwood.
Roisin (Roh-**sheen**) (Irish) little rose. *Rois* is the Irish for rose.
Rolanda (Roe-**lan**-da) (German) famous in the land. Feminine version of Roland.
Roma (**Ro**-ma) (Italian/Latin) a girl from Rome, the Eternal City. *Romaine, Romana, Romilla*
Romola (Ro-**mow**-la) (Welsh) a girl from Rome.
Rona (**Roe**-na) (Scandinavian) from the rough island. *Rhona, Ronelle, Ronna*
Roniya (Ro-**nee**-a) (Hebrew) the joy of God. *Roniyah*
Rosa (**Rose**-a) (Italian) a form of Rose, from the flower. *Rosabella, Rosabelle*
Rosalba (Ros-**alb**-a) (Latin) white rose.
Rosalind (**Roz**-a-lind) (German/Latin) the Latin root means lovely rose. The German root means, er, tender horse. She is the heroine in Shakespeare's *As You Like It*. *Rosalinda, Rosaline, Rosalyn.*
Rosamund (**Roz**-a-mund) (German/Latin) the Latin translates as rose of the world; the German as horse protector. *Rosemonde*
Rosanna (Rose-**an**-a) (American) a combination of Rose (the flower) and Anna (graceful and merciful). *Roseanna, Roseanne*
Rosaria (Ro-**sah**-ree-a) (Latin) means rosary (i.e beads used in prayer).
Rose (**Rose**) (English) from the name of the flower, and popular since Victorian times. Saint Rose of Lima received a special type of stigmata (bleeding from the palms) that was invisible to everyone but her. The condition was even invisible to doctors and so she was made a saint. Saint's day: 23 August. *Rosa, Rosalie, Rosalinda, Rosalyn, Rosemarie, Rosetta*
Roselani (Roe-se-**lah**-ni) (Hawaiian) heavenly rose.
Rosemary (**Rose**-ma-ree) (Latin) based on the name of the herb, which means sea dew.
Rosetta (Rose-**et**-a) Italian form of Rosa, meaning rose.
Rossalyn (**Ross**-a-lin) (Scottish) a feminine form of Ross. Ross means headland in Scottish Gaelic. *Rossalin*

Roula (**Roo**-la) (Greek) defiant. *Rula*
Rowena (Roe-**wee**-na/Roe-**wen**-a) The probable first use was in the 1819 novel *Ivanhoe* by Sir Walter Scott. The name is derived either from the Welsh for white lance or the German for fame and joy.
Roxanne (Rocks-**an**) (Persian) dawn. The name of the wife of Alexander the Great. *Roxane, Roxanna, Roxy*
Ruby (**Roo**-bee) (Latin) from the name of the gemstone, and the Latin word for red. *Rubi*
Rudelle (Roo-**del**) (German) famous. *Rudella*
Rufina (Ruf-**ee**-na) (Latin) feminine version of Rufus, which means red-haired.
Rukiya (Ruk-**ee**-ya) (Swahili) to arise.
Rusalka (Rus-**al**-ka) (Czech) wood nymph.
Ruth (**Rooth**) (Hebrew) friend. The name also means soft compassion, (i.e. the opposite of ruthless). In the Bible, she remained devoted to her mother-in-law, Naomi, after the death of her husband. The two of them travelled to Bethlehem, where Ruth married Boaz. She was great-grandmother to King David.
Ryanna (**Ree**-an-a) Irish feminine form of Ryan, meaning follower of Riaghan, an Irish king.

S

Saba (Sa-**bah**) (Arabic) dawn. *Sabah*
Sabina (Sab-**ee**-na) (Latin) Sabine woman. The Sabines were a tribe in northern Italy who were conquered by the Romans.
Sabra (**Sab**-ra) (Hebrew) rest. *Sabrah*
Sabrina (Sab-**ree**-na) (Latin) from the Latin name for the River Severn. Also a figure from Welsh legend who was the daughter of King Locrine by one of his lovers. She was drowned in the River Severn by Queen Gwendolen.
Sacha (**Sash**-a) (Russian) the feminine diminutive of Alexander, which means defender of men. *Sasha*
Sadhbh (**Siyve** – rhymes with 'five') (Irish) sweet. *Saidnb*
Sachi (**Sa**-shee) (Japanese) bliss.
Sadira (Sa-**dear**-a) (Persian) lotus tree. *Sadirah*
Saffa (**Saf**-a) (Arabic) pure. *Safa, Safiyya*
Saffron (**Saf**-ron) from the colour and name of the spice. The colour is yellow-brown and it's the most expensive spice in the world.
Safi (**Saff**-ee) (Hindi) friend. Also a diminutive of Saffron.
Safiyya (Sa-**fee**-ya) (Swahili) best friend.

Sagara (Sa-**gar**-a) (Hindi) ocean.
Sahar (Sa-**har**) from the Arabic word for sunrise. *Sahara*
Saida (Sye-**da**) (Arabic) happy. *Saidah*
Sakari (Sa-**kar**-ee) (Hindi) sweet one.
Sakuna (Sa-**koo**-na) (Hindi) bird.
Sakura (Sa-**koo**-ra) (Japanese) cherry.
Salama (Sa-la-**mah**) (Swahili) security.
Salena (Sa-**lay**-na) (Hindi) moon.
Salima (Sa-**lee**-mah) (Arabic) safe. *Salama, Salimah*
Sally (**Sal**-ee) originally a version of Sarah, meaning princess, but now a name in its own right.
Salome (Sa-**low**-me) (Hebrew) peace. Most famous as the stepdaughter of King Herod. He offered her anything she wanted and she demanded the head of John the Baptist.
Samantha (Sam-**an**-tha) a female form of Samuel, which means heard by God. *Sam*
Samara (Sa-**mar**-a) (Hebrew) protected by god. *Samarah, Samaria*
Samhradh (**Saw**-ra) (Irish) summer.
Samina (Sa-**mee**-na) (Hindi) happy.
Samira (Sa-**mere**-a) (Hebrew) evening talk. *Samirah*
Samuela (Sam-**wel**-a) (Hebrew) heard by God. A feminine form of Samuel.
Sancia (**San**-see-a) (Latin) holy.
Sandra (**San**-dra/**Sahn**-dra) (English) feminine diminutive of Alexander, meaning protector of men. *Sandi, Sandrea, Sandy*
Santana (San-**tah**-na) (Spanish) Saint Anne (Ana in Spanish).
Sanura (Sa-**nur**-a) (Swahili) kitten.
Saoirse (**Sair**-sher) (Irish) translates directly as saved.
Sapphire (**Saf**-ire) (Greek) from the blue gemstone.
Sarah (**Sair**-a) (Hebrew) princess. The wife of Abraham and mother of Isaac. *Sara*
Sarala (Sa-**rah**-la) (Hindi) straight.
Saril (Sa-**ril**) (Turkish) running water. *Sarilla*
Sarita (Sa-**ree**-ta) (Hindi) of the river.
Satin (**Sat**-in) (French) satin.
Savanna (Sa-**van**-a) (Spanish) treeless plain. *Savannah*
Scarlett (**Scar**-let) (English) bright red. Scarlett O'Hara is the heroine of *Gone with the Wind*.
Seda (**Se**-da) (Armenian) echo in the forest.
Sedna (**Sed**-na) (Inuit) goddess of the sea and animals, and the name of the tenth planet in our solar system.
Seini (**Sye**-nee) (Polynesian) God is gracious.
Sela (**See**-la) (Polynesian) princess.
Selene (Sel-**ee**-nee) (Greek) based on the original name for the Greek goddess of the moon, the name translates as either moon or bright light. Her role as moon goddess was eventually superseded by Artemis. *Selena, Selina*
Selima (Sel-**ee**-ma) (Hebrew) peace.

Semele (Sem-il-ee) (Greek) in Greek mythology, a beautiful girl who gave birth to Dionysus, the god of wine, celebration and excess.
Seona (See-**oh**-na) (Scottish) God is gracious.
Serach (Se-**rash**) (Hebrew) plenty.
Serena (Se-**ree**-na) (Latin) calm. *Serenity*
Serilda (Se-ril-da) (German) female soldier.
Shada (Shah-da) (Native American) pelican.
Shaela (Shay-uh-la) (Hindi) from the mountain.
Shaina (Shay-na) (Hebrew) beautiful.
Shamina (Sha-**mee**-na) (Hindi) beautiful.
Shamira (Sha-**mere**-a) (Hebrew) protector.
Shana (Shan-a) (English) diminutive of Shannon, Ireland's longest river.
Shanasa (Sha-**nass**-a) (Hindi) wished for.
Shani (Shan-ee) (Swahili) a marvel.
Shannon (Shan-un) (Irish) named after the longest river in Ireland. The direct translation is old one.
Shapira (Sha-**peer**-a) (Hebrew) good. *Shapirah*
Sharlene (Shar-leen) (American) a feminine version of Charles, meaning free man. *Charleen, Charlene, Sharleen*
Sharik (Sha-**reek**) (African) child of God.
Sharon (Sha-run) (Hebrew) from the flatland, from the plain. A place name for an area of flat land in Israel, which is referred to in the *Song of Solomon*. *Sharona*
Shauna (Shaw-na) a feminine form of Shaun, which is an Irish version of John, meaning favoured by God. *Shawna*
Shea (Shay-a) (Hebrew) asked for. *Sheah*
Sheba (Shee-ba) (Hebrew) pledged. Also short for Bathsheba, meaning beautiful daughter of Sheba (an ancient kingdom, probably situated in modern-day Ethiopia).
Sheena (Shee-na) (Hebrew) shining. *Sheenah*
Sheila (Shee-la) (Hebrew/Gaelic) the Hebrew derivation means longed-for; the Gaelic is a form of Cecilia, meaning unseeing. *Shelagh*
Sheina (Shy-na) (Hebrew) beautiful. *Sheinah*
Shekeda (Shek-**ee**-da) (Hebrew) from the almond tree.
Shelia (Shell-ee-a) (Gaelic) blind.
Shenandoah (Shen-an-daw) (Native American) beautiful girl from the stars. Also a place name in Virginia, in the eastern USA.
Shera (Shee-ra) (Hebrew) light.
Shiki (Shee-kee) (Japanese) gentle deer.
Shira (Sheer-ra) (Hebrew) song. *Shirah*
Shirin (Shi-rin) (Hindi) sweet.

Shirley (**Sher**-lee) (Old English) from the bright clearing. Originally it was a boy's name, but it switched genders in the mid-nineteenth century. *Shirlee, Shirlie*
Shobhana (**Show**-han-a) (Hindi) beautiful.
Shona (**Show**-na) (Irish) God is good. Also a feminine version of John, meaning favoured by God.
Shoshana (Shosh-**an**-a) (Hebrew) lily. *Shoshanah*
Shumana (Shoo-**man**-a) (Native American) rattlesnake girl.
Shyama (Shy-**ah**-ma) (Hindi) dark beauty.
Sian (**Shahn**) Welsh form of Jane, the feminine form of John, meaning favoured by God.
Siany (**Shah**-nee) (Irish) healthy.
Sibyl (**Sib**-ill) (Greek) legendary Greek prophetess. *Cybill*
Sidona (**Sid**-o-na) (Latin) woman from Sidon, a city in modern-day Lebanon. *Sidonie*
Sidra (**Sid**-ra) (Latin) of the stars.
Sienna (See-**en**-a) (Italian) from the Italian city of Sienna.
Sierra (See-**air**-a) (Irish) black. (Spanish) from the mountains.
Sigele (Si-**gee**-lee) (Malawian) left.
Signe (**Sig**-nuh) (Scandinavian) beautiful.
Sigrid (**Sig**-rid) (Scandinavian) beautiful victory.
Simone (Si-**moan**) French feminine version of Simon, which means God listens.
Sina (**Sheen**-a) (Irish) God is good.
Sinead (Shin-**aid**) (Irish) Irish for Janet, a form of Jane (favoured by God).
Siobhan (Shi-**vawn**) (Irish) Irish form of Joan, a variant of Jane (favoured by God).
Siofra (She-**off**-ra) (Irish) directly translates into elf.
Siomha (Shi-**va**) (Irish) from the root of the Irish word *maith*, meaning good.
Siren/Sirena (**Sye**-run/**Sye**-ren-a) (Greek) entangler of men. The Sirens were three sisters in Greek mythology, who lived on an island. The beauty of their singing lured men to their death.
Sivana (Siv-**ah**-na) (Hebrew) the ninth month of the Jewish calendar. *Sivanah*
Sita (**See**-ta) (Sanskrit) furrow. An Indian goddess born in a furrow and therefore the goddess of agriculture.
Sitara (Si-**tar**-a) (Sanskrit) morning star.
Slaina (**Sloin**-a) (Irish) from the Irish word *slain*, meaning health.
Socorro (So-**cor**-o) (Spanish) helpful.
Solana (So-**lahn**-a) (Spanish) sunshine.
Soline (So-**leen**) (French) solemn.
Soma (**So**-ma) (Hindi) of the moon.
Sona (**So**-na) (Hindi) of gold.
Sonia (**Son**-ya) anglicized version of Sophia, which is the Greek word for wisdom.
Sonya (Russian) Russian form of Sophia, meaning wisdom.

Sophia (So-**fee**-a/So-**fye**-a) (Greek) wisdom. Saint Sophia had three daughters called Faith, Hope and Charity. They, in turn, all became saints. *Sofia, Sophie*
Sora (Sore-a) (Native American) songbird.
Sorcha (Sor-cha) (Celtic) bright light.
Stella (Stel-a) (Latin) star.
Stepana (Step-**ah**-na) (Czech) crown.
Stephanie (Stef-an-ee) French feminine form of Stephen, meaning crown or garland. *Stephene*
Subira (Sub-**eer**-a) (Swahili) patience.
Suki (Soo-kee) a derivative of Susan, which means lily.
Sulwen (Sil-wen) (Welsh) bright sun.
Summer (Sum-er) (English) named after the season.
Surata (Soo-**rah**-ta) (Hindi) joy.
Susan (Soo-zan) (English) an anglicized version of Susannah, meaning lily.
Susannah (Soo-**zan**-a) (Hebrew) lily. A biblical figure who followed Jesus. *Susana, Suzanna, Suzanne*
Svannt (Svant) (Scandinavian) slender.
Svea (Svay-ya) (Scandinavian) of the kingdom.
Svetlana (Svet-**lah**-na) (Czech) star.
Sylvia (Sil-vee-a) (Latin) of the wood. *Silvia*
Symone (Si-**moan**) (Hebrew) one who listens well. A feminine form of Simon.

T

Tabia (Ta-**bee**-a) (Swahili) talented.
Tabina (Ta-**bee**-nah) (Arabic) follower of Muhammed. *Tabinah*
Tabitha (Tab-ith-a) (Aramaic) doe or roe deer. In the Bible, a Christian who worked with the poor. She died but was brought back to life by Saint Paul. *Tabatha, Tabithah*
Tacita (Tass-it-a) (Latin) quiet.
Tadita (Ta-**dee**-ta) (Native American) runner.
Taffline (Taf-leen) (Welsh) loved.
Tahira (Ta-**hee**-rah) (Arabic) pure. *Tahirah*
Tahiti (Ta-**hee**-tee) (Polynesian) rising sun. The native name for the South Pacific island.
Taima (Time-a) (Native American) thunder.
Taite (Tait) (English) cheerful.
Takara (Ta-**kar**-ra) (Japanese) treasure.
Takenya (Ta-**ken**-ya) (Hebrew) animal horn.
Takira (Ta-**kear**-a) (American) Kira, meaning light, with the prefix Ta-.
Tala (Tal-a) (Native American) stalking wolf. *Talah*
Taleebin (Ta-**lee**-bin) (Australian) youthful.
Talia (Tah-lee-a) (Greek) blooming.

Talitha (Ta-**lee**-tha) (Aramaic) little girl. *Talithah*
Tallis (**Tal**-iss) (French/English) from the forest.
Tallulah (Ta-**loo**-la) (Native American) leaping water.
Tama (**Tam**-a) (Japanese) jewel.
Tamaka (Ta-**mah**-ka) (Japanese) bracelet.
Tamanna (Ta-**man**-a) (Hindi) desired.
Tamara (Tam-**are**-a) (Hebrew) date tree. Also from the name of the river dividing Devon and Cornwall (the Tamar). There are three Tamaras in the Bible, respectively the daughters of Judah, Absolom and King David. *Tam, Tamarah, Tammi, Tammy*
Tameka (Ta-**mee**-ka) (Aramaic) twin. *Tamekah*
Tamsin (**Tam**-zin) a short form of Thomasina, which is based on the Greek word for twins.
Tamra (**Tam**-ra) (Hebrew) a short form of Tamara, meaning date tree. *Tamrah*
Tania (**Tan**-ya/**Tahn**-ya) (Slavic) fairy queen. *Tanina, Tanya*
Tanisha (Ta-**nee**-sha) (American) Nisha (meaning night) with the prefix Ta-.
Tanith (**Tan**-ith) (Phoenician) goddess of love in Phoenician mythology.
Tara (**Tah**-ra) (Irish) from the name of a hill fort in central Ireland from where the High King ruled.
Tarati (Ta-**rah**-ti) (Maori) gift from God.
Tarika (Ta-**ree**-ka) (Hindi) star.
Tasaria (Ta-**saar**-ee-a) (Romany) dawn.
Tasha (**Tash**-a) (Russian) short form of Natasha, meaning birthday of the Lord. (Greek) born on Christmas Day.
Tatiana (Ta-tee-**ah**-na/Tat-**ya**-na) (Greek/Russian) the Greek derivation means putting in order. The Russian is a version of the Roman name Tatius, and also the name of the fairy queen in Russian folklore. One of the daughters of the Tzar murdered in 1918.
Tavia (**Ta**-vee-a) (Latin) the short form of Octavia, meaning eighth.
Tavie (**Tav**-ee) (Scottish) twin.
Tawny (**Taw**-nee) (Old French) tanned. Now based on the modern word for light brown. *Tawnie*
Teagan (**Tee**-gun) (Welsh) attractive.
Tecla (**Tek**-la) (Greek) the fame of God. *Tekla*
Tegwen (**Teg**-win) (Welsh) beautiful and blessed.
Temira (Te-**mere**-ra) (Hebrew) tall. *Temirah*
Tempany (**Tem**-pan-ee) Australian form of Temperance, meaning sobriety.
Teresa/Theresa (Ter-**ee**-za) (Greek) reaper. *Terese*
Terrene (**Ter**-een) (Latin) smooth.
Tertia (**Ter**-shee-a) (Latin) third born.
Tessa (**Tess**-a) a short form of Teresa, meaning reaper. *Tessie*
Tetsu (**Tet**-soo) (Japanese) lioness.
Thaddea (**Thad**-ee-a) (Greek) courageous.

Thalassa (Tha-lass-a) (Greek) daughter of the sea.
Thalia (Thay-lee-a) (Greek) to bloom. A muse from Greek mythology, associated with poetry and comedy. *Talia, Talya*
Thana (Thah-nah) (Arabic) happy time. *Thanah*
Thadie (Tha-**dee**) (Zulu) loved one.
Thea (Thee-a) (Greek) a short form of Althea, meaning to heal.
Thelma (Thel-ma) (Greek) wish.
Thema (Thee-ma) (African) queen.
Theodora (Thee-oh-**dore**-a) (Greek) the feminine form of Theodore, which means gift of god.
Theodosia (Thee-oh-**doe**-see-a) (Greek) God-given.
Theone (Thee-**oh**-nee) (Greek) gift of God.
Theta (Thee-ta) (Greek) letter of the Greek alphabet.
Thetis (Thee-tiss) (Greek) Greek goddess of thought, and mother of the warrior Achilles.
Thora (Thor-a) (Scandinavian) thunder.
Tia (Tee-a) (Spanish) aunt. *Tiah*
Tiana (Tee-**ahn**-a) (Slavic) fairy queen. *Tyana*
Tiffany (Tiff-an-ee) (Greek) appearance or manifestation of God. The same root as the word Epiphany, and so is associated with 6 January. *Tiphanie*
Tilly (Till-ee) originally a short form of Matilda, meaning battle maiden. Tilly is now used as a name in its own right.
Tina (Tee-na) a short form of Christina, Martina and Valentina. Also a name in its own right.
Timi (Tim-ee) (English) short for Timothea, the feminine of Timothy, which means he who honours God.
Tira (Tear-a) (Hindi) arrow.
Tisa (Tiss-a) (Swahili) ninth child.
Tisha (Tish-a) (Latin) a short form of Leticia, which means joy.
Tonia (Ton-ya) a short form of Antonia, which means praiseworthy. *Tonya*
Topaz (Toe-paz) (Greek) a yellow gemstone.
Tori (Tore-ee) a short form of Victoria, meaning victory. Also Japanese for bird.
Tracy (Tray-see) (Latin) girl from Thrace. A name first introduced to Britain by the Normans. *Tracey, Tracie*
Treasa (Tra-sa) (Irish) directly translates into harvest.
Trevina (Tre-**vee**-na) (Irish) prudent. (Welsh) from the hearth.
Tricia (Trish-a) (Latin) noble woman. Pet form of Patricia. *Trisha*
Trina (Tree-na) (Greek) pure and virginal.
Trinity (Trin-it-ee) (Latin) of the three.
Trixie (Trix-ee) (American) short form of Beatrice, meaning she who is blessed.
Trudy (Troo-dee) (German) short form of Gertrude, meaning spear maiden.
Tullia (Tul-**ee**-a) (Irish) peaceful.
Twyla (Twy-la) (English) woven from two threads.

U

Ualani (Oo-a-**lah**-ni) (Hawaiian) heavenly rain.
Udele (**You**-dell) (English) wealthy. *Udelle*
Ujana (**Oo**-ja-na) (Breton) of noble birth. (African) youth.
Ula (**Oo**-la) (Irish) jewel of the sea, or apple of the sea.
Ulima (Oo-**lee**-mah) (Arabic) wise. *Ulimah*
Ulrica (**Ul**-ree-ka) (German) wolf ruler.
Ulrika (**Ul**-ree-ka) (Scandinavian) wolf ruler.
Uma (**Oo**-ma) (Hindi) motherly.
Una (**Yoo**-na/**Oo**-na) (Irish) from the Irish word for lamb, *uan*.
Unity (**Yoo**-nit-ee) (Latin) based on the Latin for one.
Urania (You-**ray**-nee-a) (Greek) of the heavens. In Greek mythology, the muse of astronomy. *Uranja, Urainia*
Urith (**You**-reeth) (German) worthy.
Ursula (**Ers**-yoo-la) (Latin) literally, she-bear. The name of a fourth-century saint martyred in Cologne. *Ursa*
Usha (**Oo**-sha) (Hindi) dawn.
Uta (**Oo**-ta) (German) rich. (Japanese) poem.
Utano (You-**tah**-no) (Japanese) from the field of songs.

V

Vailea (**Vye**-lee-a) (Polynesian) talking water.
Val (**Val**) (Latin) short for Valentina and Valerie, both meaning strong.
Vala (**Val**-a) (German) the single one.
Valda (**Val**-da) (German) famous ruler.
Valencia (Va-**len**-see-a) (Spanish) means both strong, and a girl from the Spanish region of that name.
Valentina (Val-en-**tee**-na) (Latin) strong. Name of the first woman in space.
Valerie (**Val**-er-ee) (Latin) to be strong. *Valera, Valeria, Valery, Valora, Valoria*
Valeska (Va-**less**-ka) (Slavic) glorious ruler.
Valetta (Va-**let**-a) named after the capital of Malta.
Valonia (Va-**low**-nee-a) (Latin) valley in the shadows.
Vanda (**Von**-da) (German) a form of Wanda, meaning wanderer.
Vanessa (Van-**ess**-a) invented by the novelist Jonathan Swift. Thought to mean butterfly. *Venesa, Venessa, Nessie*
Vania (**Vah**-nee-a) (Russian) pet form of Anna, meaning graceful and merciful. *Vanna, Vanya*
Vanora (Va-**nor**-a) (Welsh) from the white wave.
Vara (**Va**-ra) (Scandinavian) cautious.

Varda (**Var**-da) (Hebrew) rose. *Vardah*
Veda (**Vey**-da) (Sanskrit) sacred knowledge. The Vedas are the sacred writings of Hinduism.
Vedette (Vuh-**dette**) (Italian) horse scout.
Vega (**Vey**-ga) (Arabic) falling star. *Vegah*
Velinda (Ve-**lin**-da) (American) prefix Ve- and Linda, meaning pretty.
Velma (**Vel**-ma) (German) a short form of Velhelmina or Wilhelmina.
Velvet (**Vel**-vit) from the English word for the soft, lustrous material, velvet.
Venice (**Ven**-iss) (Italian) named after the Italian city. *Venetia, Venitia*
Venus (**Vee**-nuss) (Latin) the name of the Roman goddess of beauty and love.
Vera (**Vee**-ra) (Russian) faith. (Latin) true.
Verena (Ve-**ree**-na) Swiss form of Vera.
Verity (**Ve**-rit-ee) (Latin) truth.
Verlene (**Ver**-leen) (Latin) a blend of Veronica and Lena.
Verna (**Vern**-a) (Latin) spring. (French) short for Laverne (verdant as the spring).
Vernice (**Ver**-neece) (Latin) a form of Bernice or Berenice (bringer of victory).
Veronica (Ver-**on**-ik-a) (Latin) from the Latin *vera icon* meaning true image. Saint Veronica wiped the face of Jesus with a cloth as he carried his cross to Calvary. Later, she found the cloth bore an image of his face. *Veronique*
Vesta (**Vess**-ta) (Latin) Roman goddess of hearth and home. *Vestia*
Vevina (Ve-**vee**-na) (Irish) pleasant and sweet.
Vianne (Vee-**an**-a) (American) prefix Vi- and Anne, which means graceful and merciful.
Victoria (Vik-**tore**-ee-a) (Latin) victory. Named after the Roman goddess of victory. *Tori, Vicky*
Vidella (Vid-**el**-a) (Latin) full of life.
Vienna (Vee-**en**-a) from the name of the Austrian capital.
Vincentia (Vin-**sent**-ee-a) (Latin) female form of Vincent, which means to be victorious.
Viola (Vye-**oh**-la) Latin for the colour violet, and the flower. The heroine of Shakespeare's *Twelfth Night*.
Violet (**Vye**-o-let) the anglicized version of Viola.
Virginia (Ver-**jin**-ee-a) (Latin) virgin. The original meaning of this word was child. The first child born in America to English parents (in 1587) was called Virginia. *Ginny, Jinny*
Virtue (**Ver**-tyoo) (Latin) virtuous.
Vita (**Vee**-ta) (Latin) spirited and full of life. *Vivianna*
Vivecca (**Viv**-ek-a) (Scandinavian) a form of Vivien. *Viveca*
Viviane, Vivien, Vivienne (Viv-ee-**an**/**Viv**-ee-en/Viv-ee-**en**) see gender-neutral names list.
Voletta (Vo-**let**-a) (Greek) veiled. *Voleta, Volette*

Wakana (Wa-**kah**-na) (Japanese) plant.
Walda (**Val**-da) (German) powerful and famous.
Wanda (**Wand**-a) (German) wanderer.
Wenda (**Wen**-da) Welsh form of Wendy, a name invented by J. M. Barrie in *Peter Pan*.
Wendelle (**Wen**-del) (English) wanderer.
Wendy (**Wen**-dee) invented by J. M. Barrie for his 1904 story *Peter Pan.*
Whoopi (**Woop**-ee) (American) happy and excitable.
Wilda (**Vil**-da) (German) untamed. (English) willow.
Wilhelmina (Vil-hel-**mee**-na/ Wil-hel-**mee**-na) (German) feminine form of Wilhelm, the German form of William, which means strong protector.
Willa (**Will**-a) (German) a short form of Wilhelmina.
Willow (**Will**-o) (English) from the name of the tree, which has connotations both of femininity and passive sorrow.
Wilma (**Will**-ma) (German) a short form of Wilhelmina.
Wilona (Wi-**low**-na) (English) desired.
Winda (**Win**-da) (Swahili) hunter.
Winifred (**Win**-ee-fred) (German) peaceful friend.
Winola (Win-**o**-la) (German) charming friend. *Wynola*
Winona (Win-**own**-a) (Native American) oldest daughter.
Wyanet (**Wye**-an-et) (Native American) legendary beauty.
Wynne (**Win**) (Welsh) fair. *Wyne, Wynn*

Xanthe (**Zan**-tay) (Greek) bright yellow.
Xena (**Zay**-na) (Greek) hospitable. *Xenia, Zena, Zina*
Xylene (**Zy**-lean) (Greek) forest dweller. *Zylenna, Zylina.*
Xylia (**Zy**-lee-a) a Greek form of Sylvia, meaning of the woods.

Yachne (**Yak**-nee) (Hebrew) hospitable. *Yachnee*

Yakira (Ya-**keer**-ra) (Hebrew) dear and precious. *Yahaira*

Yana (**Yah**-na) (Slavic) a form of Jana, which is from Jan, the Slavic form of John, meaning favoured by God.

Yara (**Ya**-ra) (Persian) courageous.

Yasmin (**Yaz**-min) a form of Jasmine, the name of the fragrant climbing flower.

Yedida (Ye-**dee**-da) (Hebrew) dear friend. *Yedidah*

Yenifer (**Yen**-if-er) Welsh form of Jennifer, meaning fair and beautiful.

Yoko (**Yo**-ko) (Japanese) good girl.

Yolanda (Yo-**land**-a) (Greek) violet flower. *Iolanthe, Jolanda*

Yordana (Yor-**dah**-na) (Basque) descendent.

Yvette (Ee-**vet**) (French) a familiar form of Yvonne.

Yvonne (Ee-**von**) the French feminine form of Yves, which is Ivor in English, meaning army of archers.

Z

Zana (**Zah**-na) (Persian) womanly. *Zenia*

Zara (**Zah**-ra) both a version of Sara, meaning princess, and a name based on the Arabic word for bright dawn.

Zefiryn (**Zif**-rin) Polish form of Zephyr, the Greek god of the west wind.

Zephyr (**Zef**-ear) (Greek) the Greek god of the west wind. *Zephir*

Zerlina (Zer-**lee**-na) (Spanish) beautiful dawn.

Zeta (**Zee**-ta) (Greek) the sixth letter of the Greek alphabet.

Zia (**Zee**-a) (Latin) grain. (Arabic) light. *Sia, Zea*

Zina (**Zee**-na) (Russian) form of Zinaida, from the name of the Greek god Zeus.

Zirina (Ze-**ree**-na) (Greek) a form of Serena, meaning calm.

Zita (**Zee**-ta) means rose in Spanish, and mistress in Arabic.

Zoe (**Zoe**-ee) based on the Greek word for life. The implication of eternal life made it popular with early Christians.

Zola (**Zoe**-la) (Italian) piece of earth. *Zolema*

Zora (**Zore**-a) (Slavic) dawn. *Sora*

Zoriana (Zo-**ree**-an-a) (Slavic) golden. *Sorina, Zoralle, Zoreen, Zorina*

Zsa Zsa (**Zah**-zah) Hungarian form of Susan, meaning lily.

A–Z
of
Boys' names

Aaron (**Air**-on) (Hebrew) mountain of strength. In the Bible, Aaron was the first High Priest of the Israelites, and famous for his peacemaking abilities. *Aaran, Ahren, Ahron, Arin*

Abasi (**Ah**-bas-ee) (Swahili) stern.

Abban (**Ah**-ban) (Persian) god of water and the arts. Also from the Latin for white.

Abbott (**Ab**-ot) (Hebrew) father. From which our word for the religious rank and title of abbott comes. *Abbitt, Abott, Abotte*

Abdi (**Ab**-dee) (African) servant.

Abdul (**Ab**-dull) (Arabic) servant. *Ab, Abdel, Abul*

Abdullah (Ab-**dull**-a) (Arabic) servant of Allah. *Abdallah, Abdulah, Abdulla*

Abel (**Abe**-el) (Hebrew) son. The second son of Adam and Eve. He was murdered by his jealous brother, Cain. *Abe, Abele, Abell, Able*

Abelard (**Ab**-ell-ard) (German) noble and indomitable. *Abbey, Abby, Abe, Abel, Abelerd*

Abiah (Ab-**eye**-ah) (Hebrew) God is my father.

Abidan (Ab-**bee**-dan) (Hebrew) father of judgement.

Abisha (Ab-**ish**-a) (Hebrew) gift of God.

Abner (**Ab**-ner) (Hebrew) father of light. Abner was a general in Saul's army (Saul being the father of King David). *Abnir, Abnor*

Abraham (**Abe**-ra-ham) (Hebrew) exalted father or father of the nation. He features prominently in the Christian, Muslim and Jewish faiths. *Abe, Abrahim, Abrahm, Abram*

Absalom (**Ab**-sal-om) (Hebrew) peaceful father. Third son of King David. *Abe, Absolon, Abs*

Ace (**Ace**) (Latin) actually the Latin for unity, rather than top or number one.

Achilles (A-**kill**-eez) (Greek) in Greek mythology, the premier fighter in the Greek army at Troy. *Achille, Ackill, Akilles*

Ackerley (**Ak**-er-lee) (Old English) from the clearing of oak trees. *Ackley*

Acton (**Ak**-ton) (Old English) town in the oak trees.

Adair (A-**dare**) (Scottish) from the ford surrounded by oak trees. (Irish) Derived from the Irish *doire* meaning oak wood. *Adaire, Adare, Ade*

Adal (**Ah**-del) the Spanish and Portuguese form of Al, short for Alexander, meaning defender of mankind.

Adam (**Ad**-am) (Hebrew) meanings differ, with red, fire, earth and likeness being the most common. The first man created by God. *Ad, Adahm, Adamo, Adamson, Addam, Addy*

Adar (Aid-**are**) (Syrian) prince. (Hebrew) noble.
Addison (**Ad**-iss-un) (English) son of Adam.
Ade (**Ad**-day) (Yoroba) royal.
Adel (**Aid**-el) (German) a short form of Adelard, which means brave and noble. *Adal, Addey, Addie, Addy*
Aden (**Aid**-en) (Irish) a form of Aidan, meaning fire. (Arabic) from the country of Aden.
Adham (**Ah**-dam) (Arabic) black.
Adir (**Ad**-ir) (Hebrew) majestic.
Adlai (**Add**-lie) (Hebrew) ornament.
Adler (**Add**-ler) (German) eagle-spirited. *Adlar*
Adli (**Add**-lee) (Turkish) wise and just.
Adney (**Ad**-nee) (Old English) from the island of the nobleman.
Adonis (A-**don**-iss) (Greek) in mythology, Adonis was a beautiful young man who won the heart of Aphrodite, the goddess of love. *Addonis, Adones, Adonys*
Adrian (**Aid**-ree-an) (Latin) black. Although in use since Roman times, it did not become popular until the 1930s. *Addie, Ade, Adriann, Adrien, Adrion, Adryan*
Adriel (**Aid**-ree-el) (Hebrew) a praised member of the Lord's flock. *Ade, Adriene, Adrienn*
Aemilius (Em-**ee**-lee-us) (Latin) rival.
Aeneas (Ee-**nee**-us) (Greek) a Trojan hero who went on to found Rome. *Aineas, Eneas*

Agamemnon (Ag-a-**mem**-non) (Greek) the king of Mycenae who led the Greek armies in the Trojan War. *Agamem*
Agrippa (Ag-**rip**-a) (Latin) born feet-first. The commander of the Roman fleet that defeated Antony and Cleopatra.
Ahearn (A-**hern**) (English) heron. (Scottish) horse lord. *Ahern*
Ahmed (**Ah**-med) (Swahili) worthy of praise. *Achmed, Amad, Amed*
Aiken (**Ake**-en) (English) heart of oak, made of oak. *Aikin, Ayken, Aykin*
Ailmer (**Ail**-mer) a version of Aylmer, meaning famous noble.
Aimery (**Aim**-er-ee) the French form of Emery, meaning hard-working leader.
Aindrea (An-**drey**-a) the Irish form of Andrew, which means strong man.
Ajay (**A**-jay) (Punjabi) indomitable. *AJ*
Ajit (**A**-jit) (Sanskrit) unconquerable.
Akbar (**Ak**-bar) (Arabic) the greatest.
Akemi (**A-kem-i**) (Japanese) dawn.
Akio (**A-kee-o**) (Japanese) bright.
Akira (**A-kee-ra**) (Japanese) intelligent.
Akiva (A-**kee**-va) (Hebrew) a form of Jacob, which means supplanter.
Aksell (**Ak**-sell) (Scandinavian) father of peace.
Al (**Al**) short form of Alistair or Alexander.
Aladdin (A-**lad**-in) (Arabic) the height of faith. The key character in *The Arabian Nights*.
Alain (Ah-**layne**/A-**lan**) French version of Alan, meaning cheerful.

Alaire (A-**lair**) (French) full of joy.
Alan (**Al**-an) (English/Celtic) its English form translates as cheerful. In Celtic it means good-looking.
Alante (A-**lan**-te) Spanish form of Alan, meaning cheerful.
Alaric (Al-**a**-rik) (Old German) ruler of all. The Visigoth King Alaric sacked Rome in AD 410.
Alban (**All**-ban) (Latin) white. Saint Alban was the first recorded British martyr. He was beheaded for sheltering a fleeing Christian, and Saint Alban's Abbey now stands on the site of the execution.
Albert (**Al**-bert) (Old German) noble knight. Also the patron saint of scientists. Saint's day is 15 November. *Al, Alberto, Albie, Alby, Ally, Bert, Bertie*
Albion (**Al**-bee-on) (Latin) white cliffs. It was the Roman's name for England. *Albyon*
Alburn (**All**-burn) (Geman) noble and courageous.
Alcandor (**Al**-can-dore) (Greek) strong and manly. *Alkandor*
Alcott (**All**-cott) (Old English) from the oak cottage.
Alden (**All**-den) (Old English) wise protector.
Alder (**All**-der) (Old English) from the alder tree. *Aldair*
Aldis (**All**-diss) (Old English) from the old house.
Aldo (**Al**-doe) (German) old. *Aldoh*
Aldred (**All**-dred) (Old English) wise counsellor. *Al, Aldrich, Aldrid, Aldy, Alldred*
Aldwin (**All**-dwin) (Old English) wise counsellor.
Alec (**Al**-ek) a diminutive of Alexander, meaning defender of mankind. *Al, Aleck, Alic*
Aleron (**Al**-er-on) (Latin) winged.
Alexander (Al-ex-**and**-er) (Greek) defender of mankind. Most languages have a version of this name. *Al, Alec, Alex, Alexandar*
Alexei (Al-**ex**-ee) Russian form of Alexander, which means defender of mankind.
Alford (**All**-ford) (Old English) from the old ford.
Alfred (**Al**-fred) (Old English) elf counsel. King Alfred the Great (reigned 871–99) saved England from being overrun by the Vikings. *Al, Alf, Alfie, Alfrede, Alfryd*
Alger (**Al**-gur) (German) noble spearman. Also a short form of the name Algernon, which means with whiskers. *Algar*
Algernon (**Al**-jer-non) (French) with whiskers. *Al, Alger, Algie, Algy*
Algis (**Al**-giss) (German) of the spear.
Ali (**Al**-ee) (Swahili) exalted. (Arabic) greatest. *Alee, Aly*
Alistair (**Al**-iss-ter) (Gaelic) a version of Alexander, meaning defender of mankind. *Al, Alee, Aly*

Allambee (Al-**am**-bee) (Australian) from a quiet place.
Allarde (Al-**ard**) (French) brave and noble. *Allard*
Almer (**Al**-mer) (Old English) noble. *Al, Almarr*
Almon (**Al**-mon) (Hebrew) widower. *Almo*
Alon (**Al**-on) (Hebrew) like an oak tree. *Lon*
Alonso (Al-**onz**-o) the Spanish form of the German Alphonso. The name of the King of Naples in Shakespeare's *The Tempest*.
Aloysius (Al-oo-**ish**-us) Latinized form of Lewis, meaning famous warrior.
Alphonso (Al-**fon**-so) (German) ready and willing. *Alfonsie, Alphonse, Alphonso, Fonsi*
Alpin (**Al**-pin) (Irish) good-looking.
Alroy (**Al**-roy) (Spanish) kingly. *Al, Alroi*
Alston (**All**-ston) (Old English) from the noble's town. *Allston, Alsten, Alstin*
Alton (**All**-ton) (Old English) from the old town. *Allton, Alten, Altyn*
Alva (**Al**-va) (Hebrew) sublime. *Alvah*
Alvern (**All**-vern) (Latin) spring. *Al, Alverne, Alvurn*
Alvin (**Al**-vin) (German) great friend. *Alwin*
Amadeus (Am-a-**day**-us) (Latin) lover of God. Wolfgang Amadeus Mozart (1756–1791) was a famous composer. *Amad, Amaddayus*
Amal (Ah-**mal**) (Arabic) helpful. (Hebrew) worker. *Amahl, Amahll*
Amato (Am-**ah**-toe) (French) loved. *Amahto, Amatoh*
Ambrose (**Am**-broze) (Greek) of or pertaining to the immortals. A name based on the word ambrosia, which was the heavenly food of the Greek gods. His saint's day is 7 December. *Amba, Ambie, Amby*
Amiel (A-**meal**) (Hebrew) God is of the people. *Ameal, Amheel, Ammiel*
Amir (A-**meer**) (Hebrew) proclaimed. (Arabic) prince. *Ameer, Amire*
Amish (**Am**-ish) (Sanskrit) honesty.
Amol (**Am**-ol) (Hindi) priceless.
Amos (**Aim**-oss) (Hebrew) bearer of a burden. A prophet from the Bible. *Amus*
Amrit (**Am**-rit) (Sanskrit) nectar.
Anand (**Ah**-nand) (Hindi) bliss.
Ander/Anders (**An**-der/**An**-derz) Swedish forms of Andrew, meaning strong man.
André (**On**-dray) French form of Andrew, meaning strong man. *Andree*
Andreas (An-**dree**-us) Greek form of Andrew, meaning strong man. *Andrieas, Andy*
Andrew (**An**-droo) (Greek) strong man. The first Apostle of Jesus, and an enthusiastic converter of others, starting with his brother, Saint Peter. He is patron saint of Scotland and is celebrated on 30 November. *Aindrew, Anders, Andreas, Andres, Andy*

Aneurin (An-**eye**-rin) (Welsh) gold.
Angelo (**An**-jell-o) (Italian) angel.
Angus (**An**-gus) (Gaelic) one choice. One of three legendary Irish brothers who invaded Scotland and brought the Stone of Scone with them. The Stone is still placed beneath the throne when British monarchs are crowned. *Ange, Angos*
Anil (**An**-ill) (Hindi) the Hindu god of the wind.
Annan (**An**-an) (Swahili) fourth son. (Scottish) brook.
Annas (**An**-ass) (Greek) gift of God.
Ansel (**An**-sell) (French) follower of a noble. *Ancell, Anse, Ansell*
Anselm (**An**-selm) (German) divine protector. *Anse, Ansehlm, Ansellm*
Antares (An-**tar**-eez) (Greek) large red star. Also the brightest star in the constellation of Scorpio.
Anthony (**An**-ton-ee) (Latin) praiseworthy and priceless. The 'h' is a recent addition to the name and is now the more common spelling. Mark Antony was immortalized as the lover of Cleopatra by Shakespeare. Saint Anthony is the patron saint for finding lost things. Saint's day: 13 December. *Antony, Tony*
Apollo (A-**poll**-o) (Greek) the god of the sun in Greek mythology, and also the patron of music and healing. *Apolloh, Apolo*
Aquila (**Ak**-will-a) (Latin) eagle.
Aramis (**A**-ram-iss) (French) one of the three musketeers. *Arames, Aramyse*
Archer (**Arch**-er) (English) longbowman. *Arch, Archie*
Archibald (**Arch**-ee-bald) (Old German) very bold. First introduced by the Normans. *Arch, Archie*
Ardal (**Are**-dul) Irish form of Arnold, which means powerful eagle.
Ardell (**Are**-dell) (Latin) keen and eager. *Ardel*
Aren (**A**-ren) (Danish) of the eagle.
Argus (**Are**-gus) (Danish) vigilant watcher. *Arjus*
Aric (**A**-ric) (Scandinavian) a form of Eric, meaning king of all. *Arec*
Aries (**Air**-eez) (Latin) ram. Zodiac sign for those born between 21 March and 21 April.
Arion/Arien (A-**ree**-on) (A-**ree**-en) (Greek) enchanted. *Ari, Arie, Ariohn, Arrian*
Aristides (A-**riss**-tee-dees) (Greek) son of the finest. *Ari, Aris*
Aristotle (A-riss-**tot**-ul) (Greek) the wisest. A Greek philosopher who taught the young Alexander the Great. *Ari, Aris, Aristie*
Arjun (**Ar**-jun) (Hindi) as white as morning milk (i.e. before the cream has risen).
Arkin (**Are**-kin) (Scandinavian) son of the eternal king. *Ark, Arken*
Arlen (**Are**-lun) derived from the Irish verb to pledge. *Arle*

Arley (**Are**-lee) (English) a form of Harley, which means from the clearing of the army. *Arle, Arlee*
Arlo (**Are**-low) (English) fortified hill. (German) a form of Charles, meaning free man. *Arloh*
Arman (**Are-**man) (Persian) desire.
Armand (Are-**mand**) (German/Latin) a form of Herman, which means soldier. *Armando, Arme, Ormand*
Armani (Are-**mah**-nee) the Italian form of Herman, which means soldier. *Amani, Arman, Armarnie, Armoni*
Armon (**Are**-mon) (Hebrew) high castle.
Armstrong (**Arm**-strong) (English) strong-armed. *Arme, Army*
Arnold (**Are**-nold) (Old German) powerful eagle. *Arnald, Arney, Arny*
Arthur (**Are**-thur) (Celtic) bear. The name is forever associated with the legendary British war leader of the fifth and sixth centuries, described as 'the once and future king'. *Art, Arther, Artie, Artur*
Arun (**A**-run) (Hindi) sun.
Arundel (**A**-run-dell) (English) from the valley of the eagle. *Ari*
Arvel (**Are**-vel) (Welsh) brings forth tears.
Arvin (**Are**-vin) (German) friend of the people. *Arv, Arven, Arvy*
Asgard (**Ass**-gard) (Scandinavian) from the name of the court of the gods in Norse mythology.
Ashby (**Ash**-bee) (Scandinavian) from the farm of the ash trees. *Ashbee, Ashbey, Ashbie*
Ashwin (**Ash**-win) (Hindi) star.
Aston (**Ass**-ton) (English) from the name of the English town.
Athan (**A**-than) (Greek) immortal.
Athol (**Ath**-ol) (Scottish) from Ireland.
Atwell (**At**-well) (English) from the well.
Atwood (**At**-wood) (English) from the wood.
Auberon (**Awe**-ber-on) German form of Oberon, which means noble bear. *Aube*
Auburn (**Awe**-burn) (Latin) reddish-brown. *Aubern, Aubie, Auburne*
Audley (**Awd**-lee) (English) strong and noble.
Augustine (**Aw**-gust-in) (Latin) venerable. Saint Augustine was the first Archbishop of Canterbury. *Auge, Gus*
Augustus (Aw-**gust**-us) (Latin) venerable. The adopted son of Julius Caesar and the first hereditary Roman Emperor. The month of August is named after him. *Auge, Gus*
Aurelius (Awe-**ree**-lee-us) (Latin) golden. The name of a second-century Roman Emperor. *Aurel, Aurie, Aury*
Ayers (**Airs**) from the Old English word meaning heir, but now most commonly associated with Ayers Rock in Australia.
Aylmer (**Ail**-mer) (German) famous noble. *Ailmer*
Azizi (A-**zee**-zee) (Swahili) precious.

B

Baden (**Bay**-den) (German) bather.
Baeddan (**Bye**-than) (Welsh) boar.
Baez (**By**-ez) (Welsh) boar.
Bainbridge (**Bain**-bridge) (Irish) fair bridge. *Bain, Banebridge*
Baird (**Baird**) (Irish) bard or poet. *Bard, Bayrde*
Baldwin (**Bald**-win) (Old English) bold friend.
Balfour (**Bal**-four) (Scottish) from the pastures.
Balin (**Ba**-lin) (Hindi) famous soldier.
Balthazar (**Bal**-tha-zar) (Greek) God saves the king. Name of one of the three Wise Men who visited the baby Jesus.
Banan (**Ban**-on) (Irish) based on the Irish word for white.
Bancroft (**Ban**-croft) (English) from the beanfield. *Banc, Bankie, Beanie*
Bandit (**Ban**-dit) (German) outlaw.
Banner (**Ban**-er) (Scottish/English) flag-bearer.
Baradine (**Ba**-ra-din) (Australian) small kangaroo.
Barak (**Ba**-rak) (Hebrew) lightning bolt.
Barclay (**Bar**-clay/**Bar**-clee) (British) clearing surrounded by birch trees. *Bar, Barclaye, Barky*
Barden (**Bar**-den) (Old English) from the valley of barley. *Bardon*
Barlow (**Bar**-low) (English) from the bare hillside. *Barloe, Barlowe*
Barnaby (**Bar**-na-bee) (English) son of consolation. This is an anglicized version of the Aramaic name Barnabas. Barnabas was a companion of Saint Paul's who converted to Christianity. *Barn, Barnabee, Barnabie*
Barnes (**Barns**) (English) son of Barnett, which means from the land cleared by burning.
Barney (**Bar**-nee) (English) the familiar form of Barnaby and Bartholomew. *Barnie, Barny*
Barric (**Ba**-rik) (English) from the grain farm.
Barry (**Ba**-ree) (Celtic) spear-born. (French) from the gate or barrier. *Barre, Barrie, Bary*
Bartholomew (Bar-**thol**-o-myoo) (Aramaic) son of Tolmai. One of the twelve Apostles. Sometimes shortened to Bart. Saint's day: 24 August. *Bart, Bartie*
Bartram (**Bart**-rum) English form of Bertram, an Old German name meaning bright raven. *Bart*
Basil (**Baz**-ill) (Greek) royal. The patron saint of hospital administrators. Saint's day: 2 January. *Basel, Basey, Basile*
Bassett (**Bass**-it) (English) little boy. *Baset, Basett, Basse*
Baxter (**Bax**-ter) (English) baker. *Bax, Baxey, Baxie, Baxther*
Bayard (Bay-**ard**) (English) with reddish-brown hair. *Bay, Baye, Bayerd*

Beacher (**Beach**-er) (English) from the beech trees. *Beach, Beachie, Beachy, Beecher*

Beagàn (Beeg-**ahn**) (Irish) little. *Beagan*

Beamer (**Bee**-mer) (English) player of a trumpet.

Beattie (**Bee**-tee) (Latin) bringer of happiness.

Beau (**Bo**) (French) beautiful.

Beaumont (**Bo**-mon) (French) from the beautiful mountain.

Becker (**Beck**-er) (Scandinavian) from the brook. *Beck, Beckett*

Belden (**Bel**-den) (Anglo-French) from the beautiful valley. *Beldon*

Belen (Beh-**len**) (Greek) arrow.

Bellamy (**Bell**-am-ee) (French) beautiful friend. *Belamie, Bell, Bellamie*

Belvedere (**Bell**-ved-eer) (Italian) of beauty.

Benedict (**Ben**-a-dict) (Latin) blessed. A popular name among both saints and popes; and the name of the most famous order of monks, the Benedictines. *Ben, Benedikt, Bennie, Benny*

Benjamin (**Ben**-jam-in) (Hebrew) son of sorrow. Also interpreted as son of the south and son of the right hand. One of Jacob's twelve sons, and therefore a patrician of one of the Twelve Tribes of Israel. *Ben, Benjy, Benny, Benyamin*

Benton (**Ben**-ton) (English) from the town on the moor. *Bentan, Bentone*

Berenger (**Ber**-in-jer) (French) from the town of the bear.

Bergen (**Berg**-en) (Scandinavian/German) from the mountain.

Berkeley (English) birch wood. Also a place name, originally from Gloucestershire. *Berk, Berkley, Berkly*

Bernard (**Bern**-ard) (Old German) bold as a bear. A name introduced by the Normans. *Bern, Bernarde, Bernee, Bernie, Berny*

Bert (**Bert**) (German/English) short form of Albert, Bertram, Bertrand, Burton and Egbert.

Bertram (**Bert**-ram) (German) bright raven. The raven bird was associated with death and wisdom in Germanic and Scandinavian folklore. *Bert, Bertie, Bertrem*

Bertrand (**Bert**-rand) the French form of Bertram, meaning bright raven.

Berwyn (**Bear**-win) (Welsh) white-headed. *Berrie, Berwin*

Bevan (**Bev**-an) (Welsh) son of Evan, the Welsh form of John, meaning favoured by God. *Bev, Bevahn, Beven, Bevin*

Bill/Billie/Billy (**Bill/Bill**-ee) short forms of William , which means strong protector.

Bijan (**Bee**-shan) (Persian) ancient hero.

Birger (**Ber**-ger) (Scandinavian) rescued.

Birin (**Bi**-rin) (Australian) cliff.

Birley (**Bur**-lee) (English) from the cow barn in the clearing. *Berl, Birl, Birlee, Birly*

Bjørn (Be-**yawn**) (Scandinavian) a form of Bernard, meaning bold as a bear.
Blade (Blayd) (English) knife. *Bladie, Blayd*
Blue (Bloo) (English) named after the colour.
Boaz (Bo-az) (Hebrew) strength within him. Husband of Ruth in the Old Testament.
Bobby (Bob-ee) diminutive of Robert, meaning famous.
Bodie (Bo-dee) (Scandinavian) a short form of the name Boden, which means sheltered.
Bogart (Bo-gart) (German) strong as a bow – although the Welsh and Irish derivations mean from the bog. *Bo, Boge, Bogert, Bogey, Bogie*
Bond (Bond) (English) tied to the earth.
Boone (Boon) (French) good and fortunate. *Boon*
Boris (Bor-iss) (Slavonic) to fight. Saint Boris helped Christianize Russia. His saint's day is 24 July. *Boras, Bore, Bores*
Bors (Borss) (Celtic) Knight of the Round Table and cousin of Sir Lancelot. A form of Boris.
Bowen (Bo-wen) (Welsh) son of Owen, meaning well-born. *Bowie, Bowin*
Bowie (Bo-wee) (Celtic) yellow-haired, or son of Owen (well-born).
Boyce (Boyss) (French) from the woods. *Boice, Boy*
Boyd (Boyd) (Celtic) blond or yellow. *Boide, Boy, Boydie*
Braden (Braid-en) (English) from the broad valley. *Bradon*
Bradley (Brad-lee) (English) broad meadow. Recently popularized almost entirely thanks to the American film actor Brad Pitt. *Brad, Bradie, Bradlee, Bradlie, Bradly*
Bradshaw (Brad-shaw) (English) from the broad forest. *Brad*
Brady (Braid-ee) (English) from the broad island. (Irish) spirited. *Brade, Bradee, Bradey*
Bram (Bram) (Scottish) from the bramble. *Brahm, Bramm*
Brand (Brand) (English) from the word for lit firewood. *Brandd, Brande, Brandy, Brann*
Brandon/Branden/Brayden (Bran-don/**Bran**-den) (Old English) beacon hill.
Brannon (Bran-on) Irish form of Brandon, meaning beacon hill. *Bran, Brans, Bransen*
Brant (Brant) (English) proud. From the root word brag. *Brandt*
Breck (Breck) (Irish) freckled.
Brendan (Bren-dan) (Celtic) royal prince. The name of several Irish saints. *Brennan, Brenner, Brennon*
Brent (Brent) (English) hill. *Bren, Brint*
Brett (Bret) (French) son of Brittany. (Celtic) son of the ardent one. *Bret, Brit, Britt, Britton*
Brewster (Broo-ster) (English) brewer. *Brew, Brewer*

Brian (**Bry**-an) (Celtic) high or royal. King Brian was a High King of Ireland who defeated invading Vikings, but died in the winning battle. *Briann, Brien, Brienn, Bryan*
Bridgely (**Bridge**-lee) (English) from the clearing by the bridge. *Bridger*
Brinley (**Brin**-lee) (English) tawny-coloured.
Brodie (**Broe**-dee) (Scottish) from the muddy place or ditch.
Brody (**Broe**-dee) (Irish) one who digs a ditch. *Broden*
Brogan (Bro-**gahn**) (Irish) shoe.
Bronson (**Bron**-sun) (English) son of someone named Brown.
Brooklyn (**Brook**-lin) (Dutch) named after the part of New York that was originally named after a Dutch village.
Bruce (**Brooce**) (Scottish) originally a place name from Normandy. Now it is most closely associated with the famous Scots King Robert the Bruce who defeated the invading English at Bannockburn in 1314. *Bru, Brucie, Brucy, Brue*
Bruno (**Broo**-no) (German) brown. *Brune, Brunne, Brunoh*
Bryce (**Brice**) Welsh form of Brice, which means alert and ambitious. *Brycen, Bryceton, Bryson*
Brynmor (**Brin**-more) (Welsh) from the large mountain.
Buck (**Buck**) (English) male deer. *Buckey, Buckie, Bucko, Bucky*
Bud (**Bud**) (Old English) herald. The Anglo-Saxons gave the word this meaning because the bud heralds the coming of the flower. *Budd, Buddie*
Buddy (**Bud**-ee) (American) a form of Bud, meaning herald.
Burleigh (**Bur**-lee) (English) from the clearing of knotted tree trunks.
Burt (**Bert**) see Bert.
Burton (**Bert**-on) (English) fortified town. *Burt, Burty, Brutie*
Buster (**Bus**-ter) (American) puncher.
Butch (**Butch**) (American) short form of the name Butcher, meaning, er, butcher.
Byrne/Burne (**Burn**) (English) brook or stream.
Byron (**By**-ron) (Old English) actually means cattleshed, but the romantic poet Lord Byron moved the name considerably up-market. *Biron, Biryn, Byren, Byryn*

C

Caddock (**Cad**-ock) (Welsh) ready and eager for war.
Cadell (**Cad**-ell) (Welsh) from the small battle.
Cadhla (**Cow**-la) (Irish) handsome
Cadmar (**Cad**-mar) (Irish) brave warrior.
Cadmus (**Cad**-mus) (Greek) from the east. The legendary founder of Thebes in central Greece.
Cadwallon (Cad-**wall**-on) (Welsh) arranger of battle.
Caelan (**Kell**-an) (Irish) strong in battle.
Caerwyn (**Care**-win) (Welsh) from the white fortress.
Cahir (**Care**) (Irish) warrior.
Cai (**Kye**) (Welsh) joy.
Cailean (**Cale**-ee-an) (Scottish) victorious warrior.
Cain (**Cane**) (Hebrew) possessed. Son of Adam and Eve who murdered his brother, Abel, and so reduced the popularity of the name.
Cairbre (**Kahr**-bra) (Irish) chariot warrior. Also the name of the lion mascot of Metro Goldwyn Mayer films.
Calder (**Called**-er) (Gaelic) one who lives by the oak tree. (English) from the cold stream.
Caldwell (**Called**-well) (English) from the cold well.
Caleb (**Cay**-leb) (Hebrew) bold. A biblical figure who played a key role in finding the promised land of Israel.
Calhoun (Cal-**oon**) (Irish) from the small forest. (Scottish) warrior. *Cal, Calhoon, Calhoune, Callie*
Callum (**Cal**-um) (Gaelic) dove. *Cal, Calum, Calym*
Calvin (**Cal**-vin) (Norman) little bald one. *Cal, Calvie, Kal*
Camden (**Cam**-dun) (English) from the twisting valley. Also an area of London. *Cam, Camdan, Camdon*
Camlo (**Cam**-lo) (Romany) beautiful. *Cam*
Canice (**Can**-iss) (Irish) handsome.
Caradoc (Ca-**rad**-ock) (Welsh) full of warmth.
Carden (**Car**-den) (Irish) from the black castle. (Norman) wool-comber.
Carl (**Carl**) German form of Charles, meaning free man. Also one of the Knights of the Round Table.
Carling (**Car**-ling) (Old English) from the hill where old women gather.
Carlos (**Car**-loss) Spanish form of Charles, meaning free man. *Carlo*
Carlton (**Carl**-tun) (English) from the farmer's place. *Carlten, Carltown*
Carnell (**Car**-nell) (English) defender of the castle. *Car, Carny, Kar, Karnell, Karney*
Carney (**Car**-nee) (Irish) champion. *Carn, Carnee, Carnie*
Carrick (**Ca**-rik) (Irish) from the rocky place.

Carter (**Car**-ter) (English) driver of a cart. *Cart, Cartie*
Carthach (Car-**thack**) (Irish) loving.
Carvel (Car-**vell**) (French) from the marsh. *Carvell, Karvel*
Carver (**Carve**-er) (English) carver. *Carve, Carvey, Karver, Karvey*
Cashlin (**Cash**-lin) (Irish) from the little castle.
Caspar/Casper (**Cass**-par/**Cass**-per) Dutch version of Jasper. Also based on the Persian words for treasurer and secretive. One of the three Wise Men who brought gifts to the baby Jesus. *Cass*
Castor (**Cass**-tor) (Greek) beaver. One of the twins that make up the constellation of Gemini. Also the patron saint of sailors. *Cass, Caster, Castie*
Cathal (**Ca**-hal) (Irish) ready for war.
Cathmor (**Cath**-more) (Irish) great fighter.
Cavan (**Cav**-an) (Gaelic) handsome. *Cavahn, Caven, Cavin*
Cavell (**Kay**-vel) (German) bold.
Cearbhall (**Car**-val) (Irish) of the war.
Cecil (**Sess**-ill) (Welsh) sixth. *Cecel*
Cedric (**Sed**-rik) (Welsh) war leader.
Cerdic (**Sir**-dik) (Old German) a sixth-century English king who is the earliest traceable ancestor of the current British royal family.
Chad (**Chad**) (Old English) warlike. *Chadd, Chadwick*
Chai (**Chai** – rhymes with 'eye') (Hebrew) life.
Chal (**Chal**) (Romany) life. *Chall*
Chand (**Chand**) (Hindi) shining like the moon.
Chandler (**Chand**-ler) (English) supplier of ships' goods. (French) candle-maker. *Chand, Chandey*
Chane (**Sha**-nay) (Swahili) reliable man.
Charles (**Charlz**) (German) free man. Curiously, the name is derived from the word 'churlish'. A churl was a free man in the medieval social system – but also one who gained an unfortunate reputation for being curmudgeonly. Charles has strong royal connotations, too. *Charley, Charlie, Chas*
Charlton (**Charl**-ton) (Old English) from the farm of free peasants. Charlton Heston (or, technically, his parents) are almost single-handedly responsible for making this into a first name. *Charles, Charley, Charlie*
Chase (**Chase**) (French) hunter. *Chace*
Che (**Chay**) Spanish short form of Joseph, which means God will add.
Chenzira (Shen-**zee**-ra) (South African) born while travelling.
Chester (**Chess**-ter) (Latin) Roman legionary camp. *Ches*
Chevalier (She-**val**-ee-yay) (French) knight. *Chevi, Chevy*
Chilton (**Chill**-ton) (English) from the farm near the stream.
Chip (**Chip**) (English) short for Charles.
Chiram (**Khi**-ram) (Hebrew) exalted brother.

Christopher (**Criss**-tof-er) (Greek) bearer of Christ. Saint Christopher carried the baby Jesus across a stream and so became the patron saint of travellers. His saint's day is celebrated on 25 July. *Chris, Crista, Christofer, Cristos, Kristopher*
Chuck (**Chuck**) American short form of Charles, meaning free man.
Chui (**Shu**) (Swahili) leopard.
Cian (**Kee**-an) (Irish) ancient.
Ciaràn (**Keer**-an) (Irish) black-haired.
Clarence (**Cla**-rence) (Latin) from Clare. Clare is both the name of an Irish county and of an aristocratic English family. *Clarance, Clarens, Clarense, Clarrence, Klarence, Klarens*
Clark (**Clark**) (English) one who can read and write. *Clarke*
Claude (**Clawd**) (Latin) crippled. *Claude, Claudie, Claudy, Klaud, Klaude*
Clay (**Clay**) (English) one who works with clay. *Klay*
Clayborne (**Clay**-born) (English) from the stream in the clay.
Clayton (**Clay**-ton) (English) from a settlement on clay land.
Cleary (**Clear**-ee) (Irish) scholar.
Clement (**Clem**-ent) (Latin) merciful.
Cleon (**Klee**-on) (Greek) famous.
Clifford (**Cliff**-ord) (Old English) meaning the steep edge of a ford. *Cliff*
Clinton (**Clin**-ton) (English) settlement near a hill. *Clint, Clinten, Clyton, Klinten, Klyton*
Clive (**Clive**) (English) cliff. Popularized by Clive of India (Clive was his surname), who was a key figure in the British conquest of India. *Cleve, Clyve*
Cluny (**Cloon**-ee) (Irish) from the meadow. *Cloone, Cloonie, Cloony, Clune, Cluney, Clunie*
Clyde (**Clyde**) (Scottish) named after the Scottish river.
Coel (**Cole**) (Celtic) an ancient British king who was the supposed ancestor of King Arthur and the source of the rhyme 'Old King Cole'.
Coilean (Quill-**ahn**) (Irish) puppy.
Colbert (**Coll**-bert) (English) renowned sailor. *Colbey, Colbi, Colbie, Colburt, Colby*
Colin (**Coll**-in) (Celtic) young chieftain. *Colan, Cole, Colen, Collin, Collyn*
Colm (**Coll**-um) (Irish) dove.
Colson (**Coll**-son) (English) son of Nicholas, which means victory over the people. *Cole, Colsan, Colsen*
Colt (**Colt**) (English) young horse. *Colter*
Colton (**Colt**-on) (English) from the coal town. *Cole, Collton, Colt, Coltan, Colty*
Colwyn (**Coll**-win) (Welsh) from the name of the Welsh river.
Conall (**Cun**-all) (Irish) mighty. *Conal*
Conan (**Co**-nan) (Irish) derived from the Irish word *cú*, meaning hound. *Conen, Connie, Conny, Conon*
Conlan (**Con**-lan) (Irish) hero. *Con, Conland, Conlen, Connie, Conny*
Connell (**Con**-ull) (Gaelic) courageous. *Con, Conal, Connall, Connel, Conny*

Conrad (**Con**-rad) (German) bold counsel. Also a Christian bishop who charged King Arthur's magician Merlin with heresy. *Con, Connie, Conny, Konrad*
Conroy (**Con**-roy) (Irish) wise adviser to the king. *Conrie, Conroye, Conry, Roy*
Constantine (**Con**-stan-tine) (Latin) constant. The first Christian Emperor of Rome and the founder of Constantinople. *Con, Conn, Constance, Constant*
Conway (**Con**-way) (Welsh) from the holy river. *Con, Connie, Kon, Konway*
Corcoran (Cor-**cuh**-ran) (Irish) from the city of Cork. *Corky*
Cordell (Cor-**dell**) (French) rope-maker. *Cordel, Cordelle, Cordie, Cordill, Cordy*
Cornelius (Cor-**nee**-lee-us) (Latin) the colour of horn. Also a courtier in Shakespeare's *Hamlet*. *Conny, Kornelius*
Cornell (**Cor**-nell) (French) short form of Cornelius. Now most commonly associated with the American Ivy League University. *Corne, Cornelle, Kornell*
Corrigan (**Cor**-ig-an) (Irish) spearman. *Coregan, Corie, Correghan, Koregan, Korrigan*
Corwin (**Core**-win) (English) friend of the heart. *Corwyn, Corwynne*
Cosgrove (**Coz**-grove) (Irish) he who triumphs. *Cosgrave, Kosgrove*
Cosmo (**Coz**-mo) (Greek) beautiful and ordered. The Greek word for universe. *Cosimon, Cosmos, Kosmo*
Covell (**Cuv**-el) (English) from the cave on the hill. *Covelle*
Craddock (**Crad**-ock) (Welsh) loving.
Craig (**Craig**) (Scottish) crag or rock. *Kraig*
Cranley (**Cran**-lee) (English) from the clearing of the cranes.
Creon (**Cree**-on) (Greek) prince.
Creighton (**Cray**-ton) (English) from the rocky place. *Criton*
Crevan (**Crev**-an) (Irish) fox.
Crispin (**Criss**-pin) (Latin) curly-haired. Saint's day: 25 October. *Crespen, Krispen*
Crosby (**Croz**-bee) (Scandinavian) from the shrine of the cross. *Crosbie, Krosbie, Krosby*
Crosland (**Cross**-land) (English) from the land of the cross (i.e. Christendom).
Crosley (**Cross**-lee) (English) from the field of the cross.
Cullen (**Cull**-en) (Irish) good-looking. *Culen, Cullan, Kullen*
Culver (**Cull**-ver) (English) dove. *Colver*
Curran (**Cuh**-run) (Irish) hero.
Curtis (**Cur**-tiss) (Anglo-Norman) has two origins: Old English for short stockings; Norman French for courteous. *Curt*
Cuthbert (**Cuth**-bert) (Old English) bright and famous.
Cutler (**Cut**-ler) (Norman) maker of knives. *Cutlar*
Cynan (**Kun**-an) (Welsh) chief.
Cyrano (**See**-rah-no) (Greek) from the island of Cyrene. *Cyranoh, Cyrno*
Cyril (**Si**-rill) (Greek) lord. *Cyral, Cyrell*
Cyrus (**Sye**-rus) (Persian) of the throne. The name of several Persian kings. *Syrus*

D

Dacian (**Day**-see-an) (Latin) from Dacia, an ancient country which equates approximately to modern-day Romania and parts of surroounding countries. (Irish) from the southern part of Ireland.
Daegan (**Day**-gan) (Irish) dark-haired.
Dafydd (**Da**-vith) this is the Welsh form of David, which means beloved.
Dag (**Dag**) (Scandinavian) bright as day. *Dagg*
Daithe (**Da**-hee) (Irish) capable. The name is often anglicized to Dahy, which is how it is pronounced.
Dalbert (**Dal**-bert) (English) bright as day.
Dale (**Dale**) (English) from the valley. *Daley, Dallon, Dalon*
Dalfon (**Dal**-fon) (Hebrew) raindrop.
Dalibor (Dal-ee-**bore**) (Czech) warrior from afar.
Dallin (**Dall**-in) (English) of the proud people. *Dallen*
Dalman (**Dal**-man) (Australian) from the bountiful place.
Dalton (**Doll**-ton) (English) from the town in the valley. *Dalton, Delten*
Dalziel (Dee-**yel**) (Scottish) from the small field.
Damario (Da-**mah**-ree-oh) (Greek) gentle and kind. *Damarius*
Damian (**Day**-mee-an) (Greek) to tame. Damian and Cosmas were twin brothers and doctors who charged no fees to the poor. They were martyred for their Christian faith. Their saints' day is 27 September. *Damean, Dameon, Damion, Damyon*
Damon (**Day**-mon) (Greek) to tame. It is also the name of a Greek hero who stood in for a friend who had been sentenced to death. When his actions were discovered, the king was so impressed by his courage and loyalty that the two were let off. *Daemon, Damonn, Damyn*
Dane (**Dane**) (English) from the brook.
Daniel (**Dan**-yell) (Hebrew) God is my judge. Famous for surviving the lion's den, thanks to his faith in God. *Dan, Danny*
Dante (**Dan**-tay) (Latin) everlasting, eternal.
Dario (**Da**-ree-oh) (Spanish) wealthy.
Darius (**Da**-ree-us) (Persian) good man. The name of several Persian kings who were not called Cyrus. *Dareas, Dareus*
Darton (**Dar**-ton) (English) from the town of the deer.
Darwin (**Dar**-win) (English) dear friend. *Darwen*
Darryl (**Da**-rull) (Norman) introduced to Britain during the Norman Conquest by a family that came from Airelle (*d'Airelle* in French) in Normandy. *Darrell, Darren, Daryl*

David (**Day**-vid) (Hebrew) beloved. King of Israel and patron saint of Wales. *Davad, Daved, Davide, Davydd*

Dawson (**Daw**-sun) (English) son of David. *Dawsan, Dawsin*

Dean (**Deen**) (English) meaning both someone who lives in a valley and someone who serves as a dean. *Deane*

Declan (**Deck**-lan) (Gaelic) full of goodness. The name of a fifth-century saint. *Deklan*

Delroy (**Del**-roy) (French) of the king. *Dellroy, Delroi*

Delvin (**Dell**-vin) (English) friend from the valley. *Delven*

Demetrius (De-**mee**-tree-us) (Greek) lover of the Earth. In Greek mythology, Demetrius followed Demeter, goddess of the harvest, wherever she went. *Demetri, Dimitrios*

Dempsey (**Demp**-see) (Irish) proud. *Dempsie, Dempsy*

Denholm (**Den**-holm) (Scottish) from the Scottish town of Denholm.

Denley (**Den**-lee) (English) from the clearing in the valley.

Denman (**Den**-man) (English) man from the valley.

Dennis (**Den**-iss) (Greek) derived from Dionysus, the Greek god of revelry and excess. The patron saint of France, who was martyred in AD 258. Saint's day: 9 October. *Denis, Dennison*

Denton (**Den**-ton) (English) from a happy home. *Dentan, Denten*

Denver (**Den**-ver) (English) from the green valley. Also the name of the capital of the US state of Colorado.

Denzel (**Den**-zel) (Cornish) either based on the Celtic goddess Don or the Cornish word for stronghold. May also be based on the name of the Greek god Dionysus, god of wine and celebration. *Denzell, Denzil*

Derek (**Deh**-rik) (English) an anglicized version of the German name Theodoric, which means people's ruler. *Darrick, Dernas*

Derfel (**Der**-vell) (Welsh) Derfel Cadarn fought with King Arthur and later became a monk.

Dermot (**Der**-mot) (Celtic) without envy. A figure in Irish mythology who eloped with Grainne, who was the wife of the superbly-named Finn MacCool. *Dermod*

Desmond (**Dez**-mond) (Irish) someone who originates from Deas-Mhumhan, a region on the south coast of Ireland. *Desmund, Dezmond*

Destin (**Des**-tin) (French) destiny. *Desten*

Devlin (**Dev**-lin) (Irish) brave and fiery. *Devlan, Devland*

Dewey (**Doo**-ee) (Welsh) prized. *Dewie, Dewy*

Dick (**Dick**) short for Richard, meaning brave ruler.

Didier (Did-ee-**yay**) (French) greatly desired.

Diego (Dee-**yay**-go) Spanish form of Jacob, meaning supplanter. *Diago*
Dieter (**Dee**-ter) (German) from the people's army.
Digby (**Dig**-bee) (English) a place name which means settlement by the ditch.
Dionysus (Die-on-**eye**-suss) (Greek) in Greek mythology, Dionysus is the god of celebration, wine and excess. *Dionysius*
Dirk (**Derk**) Dutch form of Derek, meaning people's ruler. (The actor Dirk Bogarde was of Dutch descent.) It's also the name of a small, straight-bladed knife carried by soldiers of Scottish infantry regiments. *Derke, Dirke*
Dixon (**Dix**-on) (English) son of Dick. *Dickson*
Dob (**Dob**) this is an English shortened form, or nickname, for Robert, which means famous.
Doherty (**Do**-her-tee) (Irish) harmful.
Dolan (**Doe**-lan) (Irish) with dark hair.
Dominic (**Dom**-in-ik) (Latin) lord. The Spanish Saint Dominic de Guzman founded the Dominican Order of monks, which went on to found Oxford University. Dominic's saint's day is 8 August. *Dom*
Donald (**Don**-ald) (Scottish) proud ruler. *Doneld, Donild*
Donnell (**Don**-ell) (Irish) brave and dark. *Donell, Donnelly*
Donovan (**Don**-o-vun) (Irish) anglicized version of Donnell, which means brave and dark.
Dooley (**Doo**-lee) (Irish) dark hero.
Doran (**Do**-ran) (Greek) gift. (Irish) stranger. *Dorian*
Dorral (**Dor**-al) (Scottish) the king's gatekeeper.
Dotan (**Doe**-tan) (Hebrew) law. *Dotann*
Dougal (**Doo**-gal) (Irish) dark stranger.
Douglas (**Dug**-lass) (Scottish) dark waters. Also the name of the most powerful family in medieval Scotland. *Douglace, Douglis*
Dowan (**Doe**-wan) (Irish) dark-haired.
Doyle (**Doil**) (Irish) a form of Dougal, meaning dark stranger.
Drake (**Drake**) (English) dragon. Thanks to the swashbuckling activities of Sir Francis Drake, and especially his success against the Spanish Armada, some Spanish children are still told today that if they misbehave '*El Drago*' will come. (*El Drago* means the Dragon in Spanish.)
Driscoll (**Driss**-coll) (Irish) interpreter of dreams. *Driskell*
Dryden (**Dry**-den) (English) meaning from the dry valley. *Driden, Drydan, Drydin*
Duane (**Dwayne**) (Celtic) little and dark.
Dudley (**Dud**-lee) (English) named after Dudley in the English Midlands. The probable meaning is Dudda's clearing. *Dudlee*
Duff (**Duff**) (Irish) dark-skinned.
Dugan (**Dugg**-an) (Irish) dark.

Duke (**Dyook**) (French) aristocratic leader. Duke is the highest of the five grades of peerage in the British Commonwealth.
Duman (**Doo**-man) (Turkish) misty.
Duncan (**Dun**-can) (Scottish) dark warrior prince. Three Scottish kings have borne this name – all were murdered shortly after ascending the throne. After that, future aspirants tried other names. *Dunkan*
Dunley (**Dun**-lee) (English) from the clearing on the hill. *Dunlea, Dunlee, Dunleigh, Dunly*
Dunstan (**Dun**-stan) (Old English) dark stone. Saint Dunstan became Archbishop of Canterbury in AD 959 and wrote the coronation rites that are still used when British monarchs are crowned. *Dunsten, Dunstin, Dunston*
Dunton (**Dun**-ton) (English) from the town on the hill.
Dustin (**Dust**-in) (Old Norse) warrior. Often shortened to Dusty. *Dustan, Dusten, Dustyn*
Dwight (**Dwite**) English form of De Witt (a Flemish name, meaning white-haired, or blond). *Dwite*
Dyson (**Die**-son) (English) short form of Dennison, which means son of Dennis. *Dysan, Dysen*

E

Eachann (**Ak**-an) (Irish) horse.
Eagan (**Ee**-gan) (Irish) mighty.
Eamonn (**Aim**-on) (Irish) successful protector. *Amon, Eamon*
Eardley (**Erd**-ley) (Old English) from the clearing by the home.
Earl (**Erl**) (Old English) nobleman. The second-highest of the five ranks of peerage. (The other four are baron, marquis, viscount and duke, all of which were introduced by the Normans.) *Earle, Earley, Earlie, Early, Eril, Eri*
Easton (**East**-on) (English) from the town in the east. *Easten*
Eaton (**Eat**-on) (English) from the estate on the river. *Eton*
Eben (**Ebb**-en/**Ee**-ben) (Hebrew) rock.
Ebenezer (Ebb-en-**eez**-er) (Hebrew) stone of help. Named after the place at which the Israelites secured victory over the Philistines. *Eb, Ebbie, Ebby, Eben, Ebeneezer, Ebeneser*
Edan (**Ee**-dan) (Scottish) fire. *Edon*
Edbert (**Ed**-bert) (English) intelligent.
Edel (**Ee**-dell) (German) noble.
Eder (**Ee**-der) (Hebrew) of the flock.
Edgar (**Ed**-gar) (Old English) literally, prosperous spear. King Edgar (944–75) was the first King of all England. *Ed, Eddie, Edghur, Edgur*

Edison (**Eddy**-son) (English) son of Edward. *Ed, Eddie, Edisen, Edyson*
Edmund (**Ed**-mund) (Old English) successful defender. A king and martyr (841–69), murdered by the Danes. His body is enshrined at Bury St Edmunds. *Ed, Eddie, Edmond*
Edric (**Ed**-rik) (English) prosperous ruler. *Ed, Edri, Edrik, Edry*
Edryd (**Ed**-rid) (Welsh) teller of history.
Edward (**Ed**-ward) (Old English) guardian of prosperity. The name of eight English kings. Edward the Confessor was the original patron saint of England before Saint George, and had the advantage of actually being English; Saint George was Armenian. Edward's saint's day is 13 October. *Ed, Eddey, Eddi, Eddie, Eddy, Edwar, Edwerd*
Edwin (**Ed**-win) (Old English) prosperous friend. *Ed, Edwinn, Edwynn*
Efrain (Ef-ra-**een**) (Hebrew) fertile. *Efren*
Egan (**Ee**-gan) (Irish) ardent, spirited. *Eggie, Egin, Egon*
Egbert (**Egg**-bert) (Old English) prosperous sword. *Egber, Egburt, Eggie, Eggy*
Egerton (**Edge**-er-ton) (English) from Edgar's town.
Egon (**Egg**-on) (German) formidable.
Eilwyn (**Ail**-win) (Welsh) white-browed.
Einar (**Eye**-nar) (Scandinavian) solitary.
Elder (**El**-der) (English) from the elder trees. *El, Eldor*
Eldred (**El**-dred) (Old English) old counsel. One of many Anglo-Saxon names revived by the Victorians. *El, Eldrid*
Elgin (**El**-gin) (English) nobleman. *Elgen*
Eli (**Ee**-lie) (Hebrew) of great height. A high priest in the Old Testament. *El, Elie, Eloy, Ely*
Elias (**El**-ee-as) (Greek) Jehovah is God.
Elior (**El**-lee-or) (Hebrew) God is my light.
Elijah (El-**eye**-ja) (Hebrew) the Lord is my God. A prophet in the Bible. *El, Elie, Elija*
Elisha (El-**eye**-sha) (Hebrew) God is my salvation. Yet another prophet from the Old Testament.
Elliott (**El**-ee-ot) (Old English) noble battle. *Elie, Elio, Ell, Elliot*
Ellison (**El**-iss-on) (English) son of Ellis, meaning the Lord is God. *Ell, Ellason, Ellissen, Ells, Ellyson*
Elmer (**El**-mer) (Old English) famous noble. *Ell, Elm, Elmar, Elmir, Elmo, Elmoh*
Elmo (**El**-mo) (Greek) amiable. *Ellmo, Elmoh*
Elmore (**El**-more) (English) from the moor where elm trees grow. *Elm, Elmie, Elmoor, Elmor*
Eloy (**El**-oy) (Latin) chosen one. *Eloi, Eloie*
Elrad (**El**-rad) (Hebrew) God rules.
Elvin (**El**-vin) (English) of the elves. *El, Elv, Elven*
Elvis (**El**-viss) (Scandinavian) wise.

Elwen (**El**-wen) (Celtic) fair and kind. *Elwy, Elwyn, Elwynn, Elwynt*
Emerson (**Em**-er-son) (English) son of Elmer. *Emersen*
Emery (**Em**-er-ee) (German) hard-working leader. *Em, Emeri, Emerie, Emmerie, Emory, Emrie*
Emil (**Em**-eel) (German) hard-working. (Latin) smooth-tongued. *Emile*
Emlyn (**Em**-lin) (Welsh) from the waterfall.
Emry (**Em**-ree) (Welsh) honourable.
Enan (**Ee**-nun) (Welsh) hammer.
Enoch (**Ee**-nock) (Hebrew) teacher. The son of Cain and the father of Methuselah in the Bible. *Enoc, Enok*
Enos (**Ee**-nos) (Hebrew) man.
Enrico (En-**ree**-co) Italian form of Henry (ruler of the home). *Enrike, Enriko*
Erasmus (Ee-**raz**-mus) (Greek) beloved. *Eras, Erasmis*
Ercole (**Air**-cole) (Italian) wonderful gift.
Eric (**Air**-ik) (Norse) king or ruler of all. Eric Bloodaxe was a famous Viking king. *Ehrick, Erek, Erick, Eryke*
Erin (**Air**-in) (Irish) peaceful. Also the name of Ireland before the Romans renamed it Hibernia. *Eryn*
Erland (**Er**-land) (Old English) from the earl's land. *Earlan, Earland, Erlind*
Erling (**Er**-ling) (Old English) the first-born son of the earl.
Ernest (**Earn**-est) (German) determined. *Earnest, Ernie*
Errol (**Air**-oll) (Scottish) a place name. (English) a form of Earl. *Eral, Eril, Erol*
Ervin (**Er**-vin) (English) friend of the sea. *Ervine, Erwin*
Esau (**Ee**-saw) Hebrew) rough. Brother of Jacob in the Bible. *Esa, Esaw*
Esteban (Ess-**tay**-ban) Spanish form of Stephen, meaning crown or garland. *Estabon, Estebann, Estevan*
Ethan (**Ee**-than) (Hebrew) strong. Four men of this name are mentioned in the Old Testament. *Ethen, Ethin, Ethon*
Etienne (Ate-**yen**) French form of Stephen, meaning crown or garland.
Ettore (Et-**or**-ray) Italian form of Hector, which means one who holds fast.
Eugene (**You**-jean) (Greek) noble. The name of four popes and several saints. *Eugean, Eugenie, Ugene*
Eustace (**You**-stas) (Greek) good harvest. *Eustice, Eustis, Ustace*
Evan (**Ev**-an) the Welsh form of John, meaning favoured by God.
Evander (**Ee**-van-der) (Greek) preacher. *Evand, Evandir*
Everett (**Ev**-er-et) English form of Eberhard, meaning brave as a boar. *Everet, Everitt, Evret*
Everley (**Ev**-er-lee) (English) from the clearing of the boar. *Everly, Everlee, Everlie*
Ewan (**You**-an) (Celtic) yew tree. The Celts considered the yew to have many special qualities. *Euan, Ewon*
Ezra (**Ez**-ra) (Hebrew) help. An Old Testament prophet who led exiles back to Jerusalem. *Esra, Ezrah*

F

Fabian (**Fay**-bee-an) (Latin) bean. Saint Fabian was a farmer who went shopping in Rome on the day a new pope was being chosen. He joined the crowd to watch the proceedings and a dove landed on his head. This was taken to be a sign from God and he was promptly made pope. He ruled from AD 236 until his death 14 years later. Fabian's saint's day is 20 January. *Faber, Fabean, Fabiano*

Fabrice (**Fab**-reece) (Italian) a form of Fabrizio, meaning craftsman.

Fabrizio (Fab-**ritz**-ee-oh) (Italian) craftsman. One who makes or fabricates things. *Fabryce*

Fabron (Fab-**ron**) (French) little blacksmith.

Fadil (Fad-**ill**) (Arabic) one who gives freely.

Fagan (**Fay**-gin) (Irish) little and fiery. *Fagen, Fagin, Fegan*

Fairfax (**Fair**-fax) (English) blond-haired. *Fax*

Falco (**Fal**-co) (Latin) one who keeps falcons.

Falkner (**Fol**-kner) (English) one who looks after falcons.

Fane (**Fane**) (English) full of happiness.

Faolàn (Fay-**lahn**) (Gaelic) little wolf.

Farlane (**Far**-lun) (English) from the distant lane.

Farley (**Far**-lee) (Old English) from the clearing of the bull. *Farlee, Farleigh, Farlie, Farly, Farlye*

Farnell (**Far**-nell) (English) from the fern-covered hill. *Farnel*

Farnley (**Farn**-lee) (English) from the fern-covered clearing. *Farnlee*

Farold (**Fa**-rold) (English) bold traveller.

Farquar (**Far**-kwar) (Scottish) dear to the heart. *Farquhar*

Farr (**Far**) (English) traveller. *Far*

Farrar (**Fa**-rar) (English) blacksmith. *Farr, Farrah*

Farrell (**Fa**-rell) (Irish) brave hero. *Farrel*

Faust (**Fowst**) (Latin) fortunate. The best-known bearer of this name made a pact with the devil, which proved rather *un*fortunate. *Faustino, Fausto, Faustus*

Favian (**Fay**-vee-an) (Italian) one who understands.

Feagh (**Fee**-a) (Irish) raven.

Fearghal (**Fer**-gal) (Irish) brave and courageous. Fergal MacMaolduin was an eighth-century High King of Ireland with a reputation for these qualities in battle. *Fergal, Ferghal*

Felipe (Fe-**lee**-pay) Spanish form of Philip (lover of horses). *Felepe, Filipe*

Felix (**Fee**-liks) (Latin) happy and lucky. The name of sixty-seven martyrs. Also a character from Arthurian legend, and a popular name for cats. *Felixce, Filix, Phelix, Philix*

Fenton (**Fen**-ton) (English) from the town in the marsh. *Fen, Fenn, Fennie, Fenny*
Feoras (**Fee**-o-rass) (Greek) polished rock.
Ferdinand (**Fur**-din-and) (German) ready in peace. Also has the connotation of daring. Shakespeare used this name in two of his plays, *Love's Labour's Lost* and *The Tempest*.
Fergus (**Fur**-gus) (Irish) brave man. One of the Knights of the Round Table and, separately, in Irish legend, a hero from Ulster. *Feargus, Fergie, Fergis, Fergus, Fergy*
Feroz (**Fe**-rose) (Persian) fortunate.
Ferrand (Fe-**ron**) (French) with iron-coloured hair.
Fidel (**Fee**-del) Latin) faithful and trusting. *Fidele, Fidell, Fydel*
Fielding (**Field**-ing) English) a name for someone who works in a field.
Fife (**Fife**) (Scottish) from the county of Fife. *Fyfe*
Finian (**Fin**-ee-an) (Gaelic) pale-coloured man. *Finan, Fineen*
Finlay (**Fin**-lee) (Gaelic) fair warrior. *Finley*
Finnegan (**Fin**-i-gan) (Irish) fair. Finn MacCool was a legendary Irish hero who, with his band of warriors, gave help to one and all. *Finegan, Finigan, Finn, Finny*
Fintan (**Fin**-tan) (Irish) from Finn's town. *Finn, Finten, Finton*
Firman (**Fur**-man) (Norman) resolute and steady.
Fitzroy (**Fitz**-roy) (Norman/Gaelic) son of Roy. *Fitz*
Flannery (**Flan**-er-ee) (Irish) red-haired. *Flann, Flannon, Flanyn*
Flavian (**Flay**-vee-an) (Latin) blond-haired.
Fletcher (**Fletch**-er) (English) maker of arrows. *Fletch*
Flint (**Flint**) (Old English) name of the stone.
Flynn (**Flin**) (Irish) son of a red-haired man. *Flin, Flinn, Flyne*
Forbes (**Forbs**) (Irish) prosperous. *Forb*
Ford (**Ford**) (English) one who lives by a ford. *Forde*
Fordel (For-**dell**) (Romany) forgiving.
Forest (**For**-est) (English) one who lives in a forest. Woodsman. *Forrest*
Forester (**For**-est-er) (English) one who guards or keeps a forest.
Foster (**Foss**-ter) (English) a form of Forester.
Francis (**France**-iss) (Latin) a Frenchman. Closely associated with Saint Francis of Assisi whose actual name was Giovanni. Saint Francis is most famous for his descriptions of serenity, but he's also reported to have preached to birds and evangelized to wolves. *Francisco, Franco, François, Frans*
Frank (**Frank**) (German) of the Frankish tribe, after whom France is named. *Franc, Franco, Frankee, Frankey, Frankie, Franky*

Franklin (**Frank**-lin) (English) freeman. A rank which means a landholder, but not of noble birth. *Francklin, Franclin, Frank, Frankie, Franklinn, Franklyn*
Fraser (**Fraze**-er) (Scottish) originally named after a town in Normandy, but now associated with Scotland. The aristocratic Scottish Fraser family was of Norman descent. *Frasier, Frazer*
Frayne (**Frain**) (English) foreigner or stranger. (French) from the ash wood.
Frederick (**Fred**-er-ik) (German) peaceful ruler. *Fred, Frederic, Freddy*
Freeborn (**Free**-born) (English) not born a slave or a peasant.
Frewin (**Frew**-in) (English) freeman and friend.
Friend (**Frend**) (English) friend.
Frode (**Froo**-duh) (Scandinavian) wise one.
Fuller (**Full**-er) (English) one who thickens cloth. *Fuler*
Fulton (**Full**-ton) (English) from the field near the town.

Gabor (Ga-**boor**) (Hungarian) my strength is God.
Gadiel (**Gay**-dee-el) (Arabic) my fortune is God.
Gaines (**Gains**) (English) one whose possessions will increase. *Gaynes*
Gair (**Gair**) (Irish) small. (Old English) spear.
Gaius (**Guy**-us) (Latin) rejoicer.
Galahad (**Gal**-a-had) (French) tall. One of the Knights of the Round Table. Brother to Sir Lancelot.
Galbraith (Gal-**braith**) Irish word for a Scotsman.
Galen (**Gay**-len) (Greek) healer. Named after the famous Greek physician (AD 129–200). (Irish) lively. *Gailen, Gaylen*
Gallagher (**Gal**-a-her) (Irish) helped by the eagles. *Gallager*
Galloway (**Gal**-o-way) Another Irish word for a Scotsman. Also a county in southwest Scotland. *Gallie, Gally, Galoway, Galway*
Galton (**Gall**-ton) (English) from the high town. *Galt*
Galvin (**Gal**-vin) (Irish) like a sparrow.
Gamlyn (**Gam**-lin) (Scandinavian) small and wise.
Gar (**Gar**) (English) a short form of Gareth, meaning gentle.

Garbhan (**Gar**-van) (Irish) rough.
Garek (**Ga**-rek) (Polish) a form of Edgar, which means prosperous spear.
Gareth (**Ga**-reth) (Welsh) gentle. Gareth was a nephew of legendary King Arthur who was killed unwittingly by Sir Lancelot. *Gare*
Garfield (**Gar**-field) (English) from the field of spears. *Garfeld*
Garner (**Gar**-ner) (French) ribboned or wreathed. *Gar, Garn, Garnir*
Garnock (**Gar**-nok) (Welsh) from the alder by the river.
Garrett (**Ga**-ret) (Old English) brave spearman. *Gare, Garet, Garitt, Garritt, Gerret*
Garrick (**Ga**-rik) (Old English) oaken spear. *Garey, Garic, Garick, Garik, Garreck, Gerrick*
Garrison (**Ga**-riss-un) (French) soldier of the fort.
Garson (**Gar**-sun) (Old English) son of the spear.
Garth (**Garth**) (Norse) a person living in an enclosure. *Garthe*
Garton (**Gar**-ton) (Old English) from the town of spears.
Garvey (**Gar**-vee) (French) a form of Gervaise, who is the patron saint of haymaking and those trying to discover thieves. *Garvy*
Gary (**Ga**-ree) (German) spear carrier. *Gare, Garry*
Gaston (Gas-**ton**) (French) from Gascony. *Gastowyn*
Gautier (**Go**-tee-yay) (French) a form of Walter, meaning leader of an army.
Gavin (**Gav**-in) (Welsh) small, white falcon. A form of the medieval name Gawain. *Gaven, Gavino, Gavyn, Gavynn*
Gavriel (**Gav**-ree-el) (Hebrew) man of God.
Gawain (Ga-**wayne**) (Welsh) form of Gavin. Also a knight from the Arthurian legends. *Gawaine, Gawayne, Gwayne*
Gearoid (**Gar**-ode) (Irish) form of Gerald, meaning spear ruler.
Geno (**Jeen**-oh) (Italian) a form of John, meaning favoured by God. Also a short form of Genovese, meaning from Genoa in Italy.
Gent (**Jent**) (English) gentleman. *Gynt, Jent*
Geoffrey (**Jef**-ree) (English) translates as either God-fearing, or peaceful ruler. *Geoff, Jeff, Jeffrey*
George (**Jorj**) (Greek) farmer. Patron saint of England and, er, Georgia. *Georg, Georgi, Jorg, Jorge*
Geraint (Gair-**aint** – rhymes with 'pint') (Greek) wise old man. Despite its Greek origins, it is now most popular as a Celtic name.
Gerald (**Jer**-ald) (Old German) spear ruler.
Gerard (**Jer**-rard) (German) spear ruler. *Geralde, Gerrald, Gerry*
Gerlach (**Gur**-lock) (Scandinavian) spear sport.

Gerwyn (**Gur**-win) (Celtic) fair love.
Gianni (Jee-**ahn**-ee) Italian form of John, meaning favoured by God. *Giannii, Gianny*
Gibson (**Gib**-sun) (English) son of Gilbert. *Gibbson, Gibsan, Gibsen, Gibsyn*
Gideon (**Gid**-ee-un) Hebrew) he who cuts down. In the Bible, Gideon saved the Israelites from the Midianites in a daring attack. *Gideone, Gidion, Gidyn*
Gifford (**Gif**-ford) (English) generous giver.
Gilbert (**Gil**-bert) (German) bright promise. *Gilburt*
Gilchrist (**Gil**-krist) (Greek) bearer of the shield of Christ.
Gilen (**Guy**-len) (German) pledged.
Giles (**Jiles**) (Greek) literally, young goat.
Gill (**Gill**) (Irish) servant.
Gillespie (Gil-**ess**-pee) (Irish) son of the bishop's servant. *Gilespie*
Gilmore (**Gil**-more) (Irish) devoted to the Virgin Mary. *Gillmore, Gilmohr*
Giona (Jee-**ohn**-a) Italian form of Jonah, which means dove.
Giórbheann (**Gur**-vin) (Irish) tough. *Girvin*
Giovanni (Jee-o-**vah**-nee) Italian form of John, which means favoured by God. *Geovanni, Giovani, Vanny*
Gipsy (**Jip**-see) (English) traveller.
Giuseppe (Jyoo-**sepp**-ee) Italian form of the name Joseph, which means God will add.
Gladstone (**Glad**-ston) (Old English) kite-shaped stone. Gladstone was a famous nineteenth-century Liberal Prime Minister.
Glasson (**Glass**-un) (Scottish) from Glasgow.
Glenrowan (Glen-**roe**-un) (Irish) from the valley of the rowan trees.
Glenville (**Glen**-vil) (Irish/French) from the town on the glen.
Godfrey (**God**-free) (German) God's peace, or peaceful ruler. The German form of Geoffrey. *Godfre, Godfry*
Godwin (**God**-win) (Old English) God's friend. *Godwinn, Godwyn, Godwynn*
Goldwin (**Gold**-win) (English) golden friend.
Gomer (**Go**-mer) (Hebrew) complete. In the bible, she was the wife of the Old Testament prophet Hosea. *Gomar, Gomher, Gomor*
Gonzalo (Gon-**zah**-lo) (Spanish) wolf.
Goran (**Go**-ran) (Greek) a form of George, meaning farmer.
Gordon (**Gor**-don) (Scottish) large fort. Originally derived from English, it is now strongly associated with Scotland. *Gordan, Gorden*
Gore (**Gore**) (English) from the wedge-shaped piece of land.
Gower (**Gow**-er – rhymes with 'power') (Welsh) pure. Also the name of the famous Welsh peninsula.
Grady (**Grade**-ee) (Irish) high-born and illustrious.

Graham (**Gray**-am) (English) from the grand home. *Graeham, Graeme*
Grant (**Grant**) (French) big and tall. *Grandt, Grannt*
Granville (**Gran**-vil) (French) from the large village. *Granvel, Granvelle*
Greenwood (**Green**-wood) (English) from the green wood. *Grenwood*
Gregory (**Greg**-or-ee) (Latin) watchman. *Gregor*
Gresham (**Gresh**-am) (English) from the village in the fields.
Griffin (**Griff**-in) (Latin) griffin: a mythical beast with the body of a lion and the head and wings of an eagle. *Greffen, Griff, Griffen, Griffon*
Griffith (**Griff**-ith) (Welsh) fierce leader.
Grover (**Grove**-er) (English) from the grove.
Gunner (**Gun**-er) (English) artilleryman. (Scandinavian) a form of Gunther.
Gunther (**Gun**-ter) (Scandinavian) soldier. *Guntar, Gunthar*
Gus (**Guss**) (English) short form of Angus, Augustine and Gustav.
Gustav (**Gus**-tahv) (Scandinavian) staff of the Goths. *Gustaf, Gustave*
Guthrie (**Guth**-ree) (Irish) from a windy place. (German) hero in war. *Guthree, Guthry*
Guy (**Guy**) (French) guide.
Gwidon (**Gwi**-don) (Polish) full of life.

Hackett (**Hack**-it) (French) cutter of wood.
Hadar (**Hay**-dar) (Hebrew) glory.
Hadwin (**Had**-win) (English) a friend in wartime.
Hagar (**Hay**-gar) (Hebrew) stranger.
Hagen (**Hay**-gen) (Irish) youthful. *Hagan, Hagin*
Haig (**Hayg**) (English) from the field surrounded by hedges.
Haines (**Hanes**) (English) from the vine-covered house.
Hal (**Hal**) (English) short form of Halden, Harold and Henry.
Halbert (**Hal**-bert) (English) shining hero.
Halden (**Hal**-den) (Scandinavian) half Danish. *Haldane*
Halen (**Hay**-len) (Scandinavian) from the hall. *Hailen, Hale, Haley, Hallen, Haylen, Haylin*
Halford (**Hall**-ford) (English) from the ford near the hall.
Halley (**Hal**-ee) (English) holy. From the clearing near the hall. (Irish) clever. *Hailey, Haley, Hayley*
Halliwell (**Hal**-ee-well) (English) from the holy well.
Halsten (**Hall**-sten) (English) from the grounds of the manor.

Halton (**Hall**-ton) (English) from the town on the hill.
Hamlet (**Ham**-let) (German) little village. Hero of Shakespeare's most famous play, which was written shortly after the death of his only son, Hamnett.
Hamill (**Ham**-ill) (English) scarred. *Hamel, Hamell*
Hamilton (**Ham**-ill-ton) (Old English) from the flat-topped hill. Also the family name of a famous Scottish aristocratic family. Possibly an early form of the name Hamlet. *Hamel, Hamelton, Hamil, Hamill*
Hamish (**Hay**-mish) Scottish form of James, a disciple to Jesus.
Hammond (**Ham**-ond) (English) home protector.
Hanan (**Han**-an) (Hebrew) grace.
Handel (**Hand**-ul) German form of John, meaning favoured by God.
Hank (**Hank**) American form of John.
Hanley (**Han**-lee) (English) from the high clearing.
Hannes (**Hahn**-us) Finnish form of John, meaning favoured by God.
Hannibal (**Han**-ee-bul) (Punic) grace. Associated with the Carthaginian general who came within an ace of conquering the Roman Empire in the third century BC. *Hanibel, Hannibel*
Hans (**Hanss**) German and Scandinavian form of John, meaning favoured by God.
Hansen (**Han**-sen) (Scandinavian) son of Hans.
Hanson (**Han**-son) (English) son of Hans. *Hansan, Hansen, Hannsan, Hannsen*
Harbin (**Har**-bin) (Norman) small, bright soldier. *Harden*
Harding (**Hard**-ing) (English) hardy. *Harden*
Hardwin (**Hard**-win) (English) brave friend.
Harford (**Har**-ford) (English) from the army's ford. *Harferd*
Hargrove (**Har**-grove) (English) from the grove of the army.
Harkin (**Har**-kin) (Irish) little red one.
Harlan (**Har**-lan) (English) from the land of the army. *Harlen, Harlon*
Harley (**Har**-lee) (Old English) from the clearing of the hares, or from the clearing of the army. *Arlea, Arleigh, Arley, Harlea, Harlee, Harleigh, Harly*
Harold (**Ha**-rold) (Old English) ruler of an army. *Hal, Harald, Hareld, Harry*
Harris (**Ha**-riss) (English) a short form of Harrison, which means son of Harry.
Harrison (**Ha**-riss-un) (English) son of Harry.
Harrod (**Ha**-rod) (Hebrew) conquering hero. *Harod*
Harry (**Ha**-ree) (English) a pet form of Henry, which means ruler of the home.
Hartley (**Hart**-lee) (English) from the clearing of the deer. *Hartlee, Hartleigh, Hartly*
Hartman (**Hart**-man) (Old English) strong man. *Hart, Hartmann*

Harvey (Har-vee) (Breton) battle-worthy. *Harv, Harvie, Harvy*
Hasani (Ha-san-ee) (Swahili) handsome.
Haslett (Haz-let) (English) from the clearing of the hazel trees.
Hastings (Haste-ings) (English) home council. (Latin) spear-born. *Haste*
Haswell (Haz-well) (Dutch/German) from the hare forest. *Has, Haz*
Havelock (Hay-veh-lock) (Scandinavian) sea fighter.
Hawk (Hawk) (English) hawk. *Hawke*
Hawley (Haw-lee) (English) from the hedged clearing.
Hayden (Hay-den) (English) from the hedged valley. *Haydn, Haydon, Heyes*
Hayward (Hay-ward) (English) guard of the hedged place. *Hay*
Haywood (Hay-wood) (English) guard of the wood. *Hay*
Heathcliff (Heath-cliff) (English) from the heath near the cliff. The hero of Emily Brontë's *Wuthering Heights*.
Heaton (Heat-on) (English) from the high place. *Heat, Heaten*
Hector (Hek-ter) (Greek) one who holds fast. The greatest warrior of Troy, he was killed in battle by Achilles. *Hec, Hectar, Hecter*
Hedley (Hed-lee) (English) from the heather-covered clearing.
Hedwyn (Hed-win) (Welsh) peaceful and blessed.
Helmer (Hel-mer) (German) soldier's anger.
Henry (Hen-ree) (Old German) ruler of the home. The name of eight English kings, a record equalled only by the name Edward. *Hank, Harry, Henri*
Herbert (Her-bert) (Old English) famous within the army. *Herb, Herbart, Herby, Hurbert*
Hercules (Her-kyoo-leez) (Greek) glory of Hera (queen of the gods). A strong man in Greek mythology, who became a god after performing twelve labours. Heracles is the Greek version. *Herkules*
Hereward (Hair-eh-wood) (Old English) guardian of the army. An eleventh-century Englishman who led a rebellion against the Norman rulers.
Hermes (Her-meez) (Greek) messenger. In Greek mythology, the god of communication and business. *Hermez*
Herman (Her-man) (German) man of the army, soldier.
Hershel (Her-shel) (Hebrew) deer. *Herschel, Hershell, Hirsch, Hirshel*
Hew (Hew) Welsh form of Hugh, from Hughbert (German for bright of mind).
Hilliard (Hill-yard) (German) brave soldier.
Hippolyte (Hip-pol-**lie**-tee) (Greek) cavalryman. *Hipp*
Hiram (Hi-ram) (Hebrew) the most noble. *Hirom, Hirym*
Hogan (Ho-gan) (Irish) full of youth. *Hoge, Hoghan*
Holbrook (Hol-brook) (English) from the brook in the hollow.

Holcomb (**Hol**-com) (English) from the hollow in the valley.
Holden (**Hol**-den) (English) from the hollow in the valley.
Holmes (**Holmes**) (English) from the island in the river.
Holt (**Holt**) (Old English) from the wood. *Holte*
Horace (**Ho**-riss) (Latin) keeper of the hours.
Homer (**Home**-er) (Greek) pledge of safety. An Ancient Greek, famous for writing the *Iliad* and the *Odyssey. Home*
Houghton (**How**-ton) (English) from the town on the headland.
Howard (**How**-erd) (Norse) high guardian. Watchman. *How, Howerd, Howie*
Howell (**How**-ell) (Welsh) remarkable. *Howel, Howey, Howill, Hywel*
Hudson (**Hud**-son) (English) son of Hud. *Hud, Hudsen*
Hugh (**Hew**) (English) short form of Hughbert, which is German for bright of mind. *Hue, Huey, Hughie, Hughy*
Hunter (**Hun-**ter) (English) hunter. *Hunt*
Huntley (**Hunt**-lee) (English) the hunter from the clearing. *Hunt*
Humphrey (**Hum**-free) (German) strong and peaceful.
Hurley (**Her**-lee) (Irish) from the sea tide.
Huxley (**Hux**-lee) (English) from Hugh's clearing.
Hyde (**Hide**) (English) animal skin. Also a measure of land (a hyde is 120 acres).
Hyder (**Hide**-er) (English) tanner.

I

Ian/Iain (**Ee**-an) (Scottish) a Scottish form of John. Ian is the English spelling, Iain the Scottish. *Ean*
Ianos (**Yan**-oss) Slavic form of Ian.
Iarla (**Ear**-la) the Irish form of Henry, meaning ruler of the home.
Ibrahim (**Ee**-bra-heem) (Hebrew) a form of Abraham, meaning exalted father or father of the nation.
Ibsen (**Ib**-sen) (German) son of the archer.
Icarus (**Ik**-er-us) (Greek) follower. In Greek mythology, the son of the inventor Daedelus, who invented wings that allowed men to fly. Icarus flew too close to the sun, which melted the wax in his wings and caused him to crash to earth. *Ikarus*
Iden (**Ide**-en) (English) from the pasture in the woods.
Idwal (**Id**-wal) (Welsh) protected by the chief.
Iestyn (**Yes**-tin) Welsh form of Justin, which means just.
Ignatius (Ig-**nay**-shuss) (Latin) fiery and ardent. The name of the founder of the Jesuits. *Iggy*
Igor (**Ee**-gor) (Russian) originally derived from the name of the Scandinavian goddess of fertility.

Ike (Ike) (Hebrew) a short form of Isaac. Nickname of US General and President, Eisenhower.
Ilias (Ee-**lee**-us) Greek form of Elijah, meaning the Lord is my God.
Ilya (Eel-ya) (Russian) a form of Elijah, meaning the Lord is my God.
Imran (Im-rahn) (Arabic) host. Imran Khan is Pakistan's most famous cricketer.
Ingmar (Ing-mar) (Scandinavian) famous son. *Ing, Ingemar, Ingmer*
Ingram (Ing-ram) (English) angel. *Ing, Ingra, Ingre, Ingry*
Inir (In-**eer**) (Welsh) man of honour.
Innis (In-iss) (Irish) from the island. *Innes*
Ira (Eye-ra) (Hebrew) watchful. The name of one of King David's guards in the Bible. *Irae, Irah*
Iram (Eye-ram) (English) shining. *Irem, Irham, Irum*
Irvin (Er-vin) English, Welsh and Irish form of Irving, which means green water.
Irving (Er-ving) (Scottish) green water.
Irwin (Er-win) another English form of Irving, meaning green water. *Irwen*
Isaac (Eye-zak) (Hebrew) he who laughs. The son of Abraham and Sarah, he was saved from sacrifice at the last moment. *Isaak, Isack, Izak*
Isaiah (Eye-**zye**-a) (Hebrew) God is my salvation. A prophet from the Bible. *Isa, Isayah, Iziah*
Ishmael (Ish-mail) (Hebrew) God will hear. *Ismael, Ismail*
Israel (Iz-rail) (Hebrew) wrestled with God. This was the name given to Jacob after he wrestled with God's angel. *Israyel*
Ithel (Ith-ill) (Welsh) generous lord.
Ittamar (It-**ta**-mar) (Hebrew) from the island of palms.
Ivan (Eye-van) Russian form of John, meaning favoured by God. *Ivahn, Ive, Ivie*
Ivanhoe (Eye-van-hoe) (Hebrew) God's tiller.
Ives (Ives) (English) young archer.
Ivo (Eye-vo) (German) yew tree.
Ivor (Eye-ver) (Norse) army of archers. The name is an amalgam of the Scandinavian words for yew (from which bows are made) and army. *Iver*

J

Jabin (Ya-**bin**) (Hebrew) created by God.
Jack (**Jak**) (English) a pet name for John, which means favoured by God. The most popular name for male leads in Hollywood films.
Jackson (**Jak**-son) (English) son of Jack.
Jacob (**Jake**-ob) (Hebrew) supplanter. His name comes from his birth, when he emerged grabbing his twin brother's heels as they fought for first place. He tricked his father to gain an inheritance and was the father of Joseph of the coat of many colours. Most famous for 'Jacob's ladder', which was his vision of climbing to heaven. *Jaccob, Jakob*
Jacques (**Zjak** – Zj like the middle sound in leisure) (French) form of James (Jesus' disciple) and Jacob.
Jadon (**Jadd**-on) (Hebrew) heard by God. *Jaden, Jaedon*
Jagger (**Jag**-er) (German) hunter. *Jager*
Jake (**Jake**) (Hebrew) short form of Jacob, meaning supplanter.
Jalil (Ja-**lil**) (Arabic) exalted and sublime.
Jamal (Jam-**ahl**) (Arabic) handsome.
James (**James**) (Latin) the name of one of Jesus' disciples. A hugely popular name across the world. *Jaimes, Jaymes, Jim, Jimmy*
Jameson (**Jame**-a-son) (English) son of James.
Jamie (**Jay**-mee) (English) a short form of James.
Janson (**Yan**-son) (Scandinavian) son of Jan, the Scandinavian form of John, (favoured by God). *Jansen, Jannsen*
Janus (**Jay**-nuss) (Latin) the Roman god who gave his name to January. Usually shown looking back to the old year and forward to the new. God of gateways.
Jarah (**Ja**-rah) (Hebrew) honey-sweet.
Jared (**Ja**-red) Hebrew word for Jordan (the river). *Jarad, Jarod, Jarret, Jarrett, Jerod, Jerrad, Jerrod*
Jarek (**Ya**-rek) (Slavic) January's child. *Jarec*
Jarell (**Ya**-rell) (Scandinavian) Gerald. *Jarel*
Jarl (**Yarl**) (Scandinavian) earl. *Jarle*
Jaromil (**Ya**-ro-mill) (Latin) a form of Jerome, which means holy.
Jaron (**Jar**-on/Ja-**rahn**) (Hebrew) one who sings loudly.
Jarrell (**Ja**-rel) (English) a form of Gerald, meaning spear ruler.
Jarrod (**Ja**-rod) (English) a form of Gerald, which means spear ruler.
Jarvis (**Jar**-viss) (Norman) a derivation of Gervaise, patron saint of haymaking and those trying to discover thieves.
Jason (**Jay**-sun) (Greek) one who heals. In Greek mythology he was the leader of the Argonauts, who retrieved the golden fleece. *Jace, Jaison, Jayson*

Jasper (**Jass**-per) (Persian) treasurer, secretive. The name of one of the three Wise Men.

Javier (**Hav**-ee-air) (Spanish) a form of the more common Xavier. Both mean boy from the new house.

Jed (**Jed**) (Hebrew) short form of Jediah, meaning the hand of God.

Jediah (Jed-**eye**-a) (Hebrew) the hand of God.

Jedrek (**Yed**-rek) (Polish) manly. *Jedrec*

Jefferson (**Jef**-er-son) (English) son of Jeff (see Geoffrey). Also the name of the third US President.

Jens (**Yens**) (Scandinavian) a form of John, meaning favoured by God.

Jensen (**Jen**-sen) (Scandinavian) John's son. *Jenson*

Jeremy (**Je**-rem-ee) (Hebrew) raised up by God. Based on the name Jeremiah, who was a gloomy prophet in the Old Testament. *Jaramie, Jereme, Jeremee, Jerrey, Jerry*

Jerome (Je-**rome**) (Greek) holy. Saint Jerome was a secretary to the pope who translated the Bible from its original languages into Latin – the Vulgate. His saint's day is 30 September. *Jarome, Jerohm, Jerry*

Jerry (**Je**-ree) (English) short form of Gerald, Jeremy and Jerome.

Jesse (**Jess**-ee) (Hebrew) God sees. The father of King David in the Bible. *Jessey, Jessie, Jessy*

Jestin (**Yes**-tin) (Welsh) form of Justin.

Jesus (**Jee**-zuss) (Greek) God saves. The spelling of Jesus with which we are familiar is actually a Greek version of the original Aramaic.

Jethro (**Jeth**-roe) (Greek) excellence. Father-in-law to Moses. *Jett*

Jim/Jimmy (**Jim/Jim**-ee) (English) short form of James, a disciple of Jesus.

Joachim (**Jo**-a-kim) (Hebrew) founded by God.

Joe (**Joe**) (Hebrew) a short form of Joseph, which means God will add.

Joel (**Jo**-el) (Hebrew) God is willing. Another Old Testament prophet. *Joell*

John (**Jon**) (Hebrew) favoured by God. The most popular name, historically, in the world. Also the writer of the fourth gospel. *Jahn, Johne, Johnie, Johnnie, Jonnie, Jon*

Jonah (**Joe**-na) (Hebrew) dove. A reluctant prophet who faced aquatic challenges. *Joneh*

Jonas (**Joe**-nass) (Greek) Greek form of Jonah, meaning dove.

Jonathan (**Jon**-a-than) (Hebrew) God has given. Name of a son of King Saul. *Johnathan*

Jontae (**Jon**-tee) A form of John/Jon, meaning favoured by God.

Jorge (**Jorj**, or **Hor**-ghay in Spanish – 'gh' is like 'ch' in the Scottish word, 'loch') Spanish form of George, which means farmer.

Jørgen (**Yur**-gen) Scandinavian form of George, which means farmer.

Joseph (**Jo**-sef) (Hebrew) God will add. This name appears in both the Old and New Testaments. *Jodie, Joe, Joey, Josef, Josep, Jozef, Yusif*

Josh (**Josh**) (Hebrew) a short form of Joshua, meaning God saves.

Joshua (**Josh**-yoo-a) (Hebrew) God saves. Following the death of Moses, he led the Israelites to the Promised Land.

Josiah (Joss-**eye**-a) (Hebrew) supported by God. A seventh-century-BC King of Judah. *Josia, Josea*

Joss (**Joss**) (Chinese) fated to be lucky.

Juan (**Hwann**) Spanish form of John, meaning favoured by God.

Judah (**Joo**-da) (Hebrew) praised. The fourth of Jacob's twelve sons. *Juda*

Judas (**Joo**-duss) (Greek) praised. The Apostle who betrayed Jesus. The name has been rather unpopular since then.

Julian (**Joo**-lee-an) (Latin) fair-skinned. One of the few names to switch from a female to a male name. Saint Julian is the patron saint of circus workers, innkeepers and murderers. His saint's day is 12 February. *Juliane, Julien*

Julius (**Joo**-lee-us) (Latin) youthful. Most closely associated with Julius Caesar (100–44 BC).

Juri (**Yure**-ee) (Hebrew) a form of Uriah, which means God is my light.

Justin (**Just**-in) (Latin) just. *Justan, Justen*

Kadar (Kah-**dar**) (Arabic) powerful.

Kade (**Kade**) (Scottish) from the marshlands. *Kayde*

Kadir (Kah-**deer**) (Arabic) verdant springtime.

Kahana (Ka-**hahn**-a) (Hawaiian) priest.

Kahil (Kah-**hill**) (Turkish) youthful.

Kalea (Ka-**lee**-a) (Hawaiian) full of happiness.

Kana (**Ka-na**) (Japanese) powerful.

Kane (**Cane**) (Irish) offering. (Welsh) good-looking. Also a form of the biblical Cain. *Kain, Kaine, Kayne*

Kanaloa (Ka-na-**low**-ah) (Hawaiian) the name of a major Hawaiian god.

Kardal (Kar-**dal**) (Arabic) mustard seed.

Karel (**Ka**-rel) Czech form of Carl, which means free man.

Karl (**Karl**) German form of Carl, meaning free man.

Karney (**Kar**-nee) American form of the Irish name Carney, meaning champion.

Kaj (**Kye**) (Scandinavian) from the Earth.

Kalani (Ka-**lah**-nee) (Hawaiian) lord of the sky.

Kalmin (**Kal**-min) (Scandinavian) strong man.

Kaniel (Kan-**eel**) (Hebrew) reed.

Karsten (**Kar**-sten) (Greek) anointed by God.

Kaulana (Cow-**lah**-na) (Hawaiian) famous.
Kauri (Cow-ree) (Polynesian) tree.
Kavanagh (Kav-an-a) (Irish) a follower of Kavan. *Cavanagh*
Kay (Kye) (Greek) one who rejoices. There was also a Knight of the Round Table called Kay. *Cai*
Kayam (Kay-am) (Hebrew) stable and steady. *Cayam*
Kayle (Kale) (Hebrew) faithful. *Kail, Kaile, Kayl*
Keandre (Key-**and**-ra) (American) André with the Ke- prefix.
Keane (Keen) (Irish) handsome. (German) bold. *Kean, Keen, Keene, Kiene*
Keanu (Kee-**ahn**-oo) (Irish) a form of Keenan. (Hawaiian) cool breeze. *Keahnu*
Kearn (Kaarn) (Irish) a form of Kearney, which means champion. *Kern, Kerne, Kerney*
Kearney (Keer-ney) (Irish) a form of Carney, meaning champion.
Keefe (Keef) (Irish) handsome and admired. *Keaf, Keafe, Keef, Kief*
Keenan (Keen-an) (Irish) little Keene or Keane. *Kenan*
Kieffer (Keef-er) (German) barrel-maker.
Keir (Keer) (Gaelic) a form of Kieran, which means dark-haired.
Keith (Keeth) (Scottish) wood. Originally a surname. *Keath, Keeth, Keithe*
Kelby (Kell-bee) (Scandinavian) from the village of the ships. *Kel, Kelbey, Kell, Kelly*
Kellagh (Kel-ock) (Gaelic) from the wood. Saint Celsus, the Latinized version of Kellagh, was a ninth-century Bishop of Armagh in Ireland.
Kellen (Kell-en) (Irish) bold warrior. *Kel, Kelen, Kelin, Kell, Kellan, Kellin, Kelly*
Kelton (Kell-ton) (Scandinavian/ English) from the harbour town.
Kelvin (Kell-vin) (British) narrow river. Lord Kelvin was a famous nineteenth-century scientist. Also the name of a Scottish river. *Kelvan, Kelven, Kelvun, Kilvin*
Kemal (Kem-al) (Turkish) the most honoured.
Kemp (Kemp) (Scandinavian/English) champion.
Kempton (Kemp-ton) (English) from the town of the soldiers. Also a racecourse in Brighton.
Ken (Ken) (Scottish) the short form of Kendall, Kenrick and Kenneth.
Kendall (Ken-dall) (Norse) water spring. From the valley of the River Ken. Also a town in Cumbria, northwest England. *Ken, Kendahl, Kendal, Kendoll, Kendy, Kindal*
Kenley (Ken-lee) (English) from the king's clearing. *Kenlee, Kenlie, Kenly*
Kennan (Ken-an) (Scottish) little Ken, which is short for many names beginning Ken-.

Kennard (**Ken**-ard) (Irish) brave chief.
Kennedy (**Ken**-a-dee) (Irish) head wearing a helmet.
Kenneth (**Ken**-ith) (Gaelic) handsome. *Ken, Keneth, Kenith, Kennath, Kennie, Kenny*
Kenric/Kenrick (**Ken**-rik) (English) bold ruler.
Kent (**Kent**) (Celtic) from the county name, which originally meant borderland.
Kenton (**Kent**-on) (Celtic/English) from the English county of Kent. Also, from the king's town.
Kenward (**Ken**-ward) (English) of the king's guard.
Kenyon (**Ken**-yon) (Irish) blond-haired. *Kenyan, Kenyen*
Keola (**Kay**-o-la) (Hawaiian) full of life.
Keon (Ke-**oon**) Irish form of Ewan, meaning yew tree. *Keonne*
Kerel (**Ke**-rel) (Afrikaans) youthful.
Kerey (**Ke**-ree) (Romany) home-loving.
Kerr (**Care**) Scandinavian form of the English Carr, meaning one who dwells by the marsh. *Ker*
Kerrick (**Ke**-rik) (English) the rule of the king.
Kerwin (**Cur**-win) (English) friend from the marshes. *Kers, Kerwen, Kerwyn, Kir, Kirwin*
Kes (**Kez/Kess**) (English) short form of Kesley, Kester and Kestrel.
Kesley (**Kez**-lee) (English) from the kestrel's clearing.
Kester (**Kess**-ter) (English) a form of Christopher, which means bearer of Christ.
Kestrel (**Kess**-trel) (English) kestrel.
Kevin (**Kev**-in) (Irish) handsome. Saint Kevin renounced his royal birth to live as a hermit. He is said to have died at 120 and is celebrated on 3 June. *Kev, Kevan, Keven*
Kidd (**Kid**) (English) young goat, youthful.
Kiel (**Kyle**) (Irish) a form of Kyle, which means from the land of the cattle.
Kieran (**Keer**-an) (Irish) dark-haired. Anglicized form of the original Irish Ciaràn. *Keirnan, Kier, Kieren, Kierin, Kiers, Kyran*
Killian (**Kill**-ee-an) (Irish) little Kelly. His saint's day is celebrated on 8 July. *Killyum, Kylian*
Kimball (**Kim**-ball) (English) warrior chief.
Kin (**Kin**) (English) of the family. (Japanese) gold.
Kincaid (Kin-**kade**) (Scottish) leader in war. *Kincaide*
Kingsley (**Kings**-lee) (English) from the king's clearing. *Kingsleigh*
Kingston (**Kings**-ton) (English) from the king's town.
Kingswell (**Kings**-well) (English) from the king's well.
Kinnard (**Kin**-ard) (Irish) from the steep slope.
Kiral (Ki-**ral**) (Turkish) the high king.

Kirby (**Cur**-by) (Scandinavian) from the village with the church. *Kirbey, Kyrby*
Kirk (**Kirk**) (Scandinavian) from the church. *Kyrke, Kurk*
Kirkland (**Kirk**-land) (Scandinavian) from the church's land.
Kirkley (**Kirk**-lee) (Scandinavian/English) from the church clearing. *Kirkly*
Kirkwood (**Kirk**-wood) (Scandinavian/English) from the church wood.
Kirton (**Cur**-ton) (Scandinavian/English) from the church town.
Klemens (**Klem**-mentz) (Scandinavian/German) clement, merciful. *Clemens*
Knight (**Nite**) (English) knight.
Knowles (**Nowls**) (English) from the grassy slope.
Knox (**Nox**) (English) from the hill.
Kofi (**Ko**-fee) (West African) born on Thursday.
Kojo (**Ko-jo**) (West African) born on Monday.
Kondo (**Kon**-doe) (Swahili) warlike.
Koren (**Kor**-en) (Hebrew) shining or gleaming. *Coren*
Koresh (Ko-**resh**) (Hebrew) one who cultivates and digs.
Kyan (**Kye**-an) (African-American) little king.
Kyle (**Kyle**) (Irish) from the land of the cattle. *Kiel, Kye*
Kynan (**Kun**-nan) (Welsh) chieftain.
Kyros (**Ky**-ros) (Greek) master.

L

Laban (**La**-ban) (Hawaiian) white.
Lachlan (**Lock**-lan) (Scottish) from the land of the lochs. One of the most popular boy's names in Australia. *Lacklan, Lackland, Laughlin, Lock, Locklan*
Lader (**Lay**-der) (German) one who summons.
Laird (**Laird**) (Scottish) lord, landowner. *Layrd, Layrde*
Laith (**Layth**) (English/Scandinavian) a form of Latham meaning district (English), or barn (Scandinavian).
Laker (**Lake**-er) (English) from the lake.
Lambert (**Lam**-bert) (German) from the bright land. *Lamb, Lamber, Lamburt, Lammy*
Lamont (**La**-mont) (Scandinavian) lawyer. *Lamon*
Lance (**Lance**) (French or Celtic) a short form of Lancelot. *Lanse, Lantz, Lanz*
Lancelot (**Lance**-a-lot) (French or Celtic) the name could be based on the French for spear or the Celtic for church. A Knight of the Round Table who fell in love with Guinevere, which led to the fall of Camelot. Sir Lancelot's other achievements include inadvertently killing Sir Gareth, and accidentally fighting on the wrong side in a battle. *Lance, Lancelott, Launcelot, Launcey*

Lander (Land-er) (English) landowner. *Land, Landers*

Lando (Land-oh) Spanish form of Roland, meaning famous in the land. *Land*

Landon (Land-on) (Old English) from the long hill. *Land, Landen, Landun*

Landric (Land-rik) (German) ruler of the land. *Land*

Landry (Land-ree) (Norman) ruler. *Land*

Lane (Lane) (English) lane. *Layne*

Langdon (Lang-don) (English) from the long hill. *Langden, Langdun*

Langford (Lang-ford) (English) from the long ford. *Lanford*

Langley (Lang-lee) (English) from the long clearing. *Land, Langly*

Langston (Lang-ston) (English) from the long town. *Lang, Langstan, Langsten*

Langworth (Lang-worth) (English) from the long paddock.

Lansing (Lan-sing) (Dutch) from the low lands. *Lance, Lans*

Lanty (Lan-tee) (Irish) a short form of Leachlainn, which means devotee or follower of Saint Seachnall.

Laoghaire (Leer-ee) (Irish) one who herds calves. Name of a town to the south of Dublin.

Larkin (Lar-kin) (Irish) rough and warlike. *Lark, Larkan, Larken*

Larimore (La-ree-more) (French) armourer.

Larry (La-ree) short form of Laurence, meaning laurel. *Larrie*

Lars/Larson (Lars/Lar-son) Swedish form of Laurence, meaning laurel.

Latham (Lay-tham) (English) district. (Scandinavian) barn.

Latimer (Lat-im-er) (English) one who speaks Latin. *Latymer*

Laughlin (Lock-lin) (Irish) follower of Saint Secundinus who was a Spanish martyr put to death in AD 306. His feast day is 21 May.

Laurence/Lawrence (Law-rence) (Italian) meaning either laurel or from the city of Lauretum. Saint Lawrence was martyred for giving the Church's money to the poor. Saint's day: 10 August. *Larence, Laurance, Laurans, Lorence*

Laurent (Law-**ron/Lor**-ent) French form of Laurence, meaning laurel. *Laurynt*

Lavan (La-van) (Hebrew) white.

Lawler (Law-ler) (Irish) soft-voiced.

Lawley (Law-lee) (English) from the low clearing.

Lawson (Law-son) (English) son of Laurence. *Law, Laws, Lawsan, Lawsen*

Layton (Lay-ton) (English) a form of Leighton, meaning from the farm next to the river.

Lazarus (La-za-russ) (Hebrew) helped by God. A figure from the Bible brought back to life by Jesus. *Lasarus, Lazerus*

Leander (Lee-**an**-der) (Greek) lion man. A figure from Greek mythology who loved a priestess. He swam the sea each night to see her. *Anders, Leand, Leann, Leannder*

Leif (Leaf) (Scandinavian) greatly loved. *Laif, Leaf, Leife*
Leighton (Lay-ton) (Old English) from the farm next to the river. *Laytan, Layton, Leighten*
Leks (Lex) form of Alexander (defender of mankind) used in the Baltic States.
Leland (Lel-and) (English) from the fallow land. *Leeland, Leiland, Lelan*
Lennon (Len-on) (Irish) from the meadow. *Lenn, Lennan, Lennen*
Lennox (Len-ox) (Irish) from the elm grove. *Lenn, Lennix, Lenox, Linnox*
Lenny (Len-ee) (English) short form of Leonard, meaning strong lion. *Len, Lenney, Lenni, Lennie, Leny, Linn*
Leo (Lee-o) (Latin) lion. Popular for boys born between 21 July and 21 August, although the saint's day is 20 November.
Leonard/Leon (Len-ard/**Lee**-on) (German) strong lion. *Lee, Leo, Leonar, Leonard, Lynar, Lynard*
Leondre (Lee-**on**-dray) American form of Leon, meaning strong lion. *Leonid*
Leonidas (Lee-o-**nee**-dass) Greek form of Leonard, meaning strong lion. A famous Spartan king who, with 300 soldiers, defended the pass of Thermopylae against tens of thousands of Persians. *Leon, Leonidus, Leonydus*
Leopold (Lee-o-pold) (German) strong people or brave people. *Lee, Leo*
Leron (Le-ron) (French) circle. (American) Ron with the prefix Le-.
Leroy (Lee-roy) (French) literally, the king. *Elroy*
Lester (Less-ter) (English) man from Leicester. *Les, Lestor*
Levar (Le-var) (Hebrew) attached or joined. *Levarr*
Leverett (Lev-rett) (French) young hare.
Levi (Leave-eye) (Hebrew) associated. One of the sons of Jacob. The actual name of the Apostle Matthew.
Lewin (Loo-win) (English) well-loved friend.
Lewis (Loo-iss) (French) but based on the German for famous warrior. *Lewe, Lewie, Lewy*
Liam (Lee-um) (Irish) Irish for William, which means strong protector. *Leam, Liem*
Lincoln (Link-on) (English) man from Lincoln, which means town by the lake.
Lindell (Lin-del) (English) from the valley of linden (lime) trees.
Lindford (Lind-ford) (English) a man from a ford near linden (lime) trees.
Linford (Lin-ford) (English) the ford of the linden (lime) trees. *Lynford*
Linley (Lin-lee) (English) from the clearing in the linden trees. *Linlee, Linleigh, Lynlie*
Lionel (Lie-on-el) (French) little lion. *Lion, Lionell, Loyonel, Lyon, Lyonell*
Liron (Li-ron) (Hebrew) my song.
Litton (Lit-on) (English) from the town on the hill, from the lit town. *Lyten, Lyton, Lytton*

Llewellyn (Lew-**ell**-in) (Welsh) like a lion. A famous Welsh prince who fought against English invaders. *Lew, Lewellen*
Lloyd (**Loyd**) (Welsh) grey-haired, religious. *Loyd, Loydde*
Lochlain (**Loch**-lan) (Scottish) from the land of the lochs. *Lochlaine, Lochlane, Locklain*
Lock (**Lock**) (Scottish) lake.
Locke (**Lock**) (English) forest.
Lomán (Low-**man**) (Slavic) sensitive. (Irish) bare.
Lombard (**Lom**-bard) (Latin) long beard.
Lon (**Lon**) a short form of Alonso and Leonard. (Irish) fierce.
Lonny (**Lon**-ee) familiar form of Alonso, the Spanish form of Alphonso, meaning ready and willing.
Lono (**Lon**-o) (Hawaiian) the name of the Hawaiian god of learning and thought.
Lorcan (**Lor**-can) (Irish) small and feisty.
Lorenzo (Lo-**ren**-zo) Spanish and Italian forms of Laurence, meaning laurel. *Larenzo, Loranzo, Lore, Lorenso, Lorry*
Lorimer (**Lor**-rim-er) (Latin) one who makes harnesses.
Loring (**Lor**-ring) (German) son of a great soldier.
Loudon (**Loud**-on) (English) from the low hill.
Louis/Lou (**Loo**-ee/**Loo**) (French) but based on the German word for famous warrior. The name of 18 French kings. Often anglicized to Lewis. *Lew, Lou, Louie, Lue, Luie, Luis*
Lovell/Lowell (**Love**-el/**Low**-el) (English) loved one. *Lovall, Lovelle*
Lucas (**Loo**-cass) Latin form of Luke. *Luces, Lukas, Luke, Lukus*
Lucian/Lucius (**Loo**-see-an/**Loo**-see-us) (Latin) light. Saint Lucian is the patron saint of possessed people. Saint's day is 26 October. *Lew, Luciyan*
Lucky (**Luck**-ee) (American) fortunate.
Ludovic (**Loo**-do-vic) Scottish form of Louis. *Ludo, Ludovick, Ludvik*
Luka (**Loo**-ca) Italian form of Luke.
Luke (**Luke**) (Greek) man from Lucania. An Apostle of Jesus and writer of the third gospel. The patron saint of doctors. Saint's day: 18 October. *Luc, Luk*
Lukman (**Luck**-man) (Arabic) prophet.
Lunn (**Lun**) (Irish) warlike. *Lun, Lunne*
Luther (**Loo**-ther) (German) famous soldier. Martin Luther (1483–1546) was a key figure in the Protestant Reformation. *Luthar, Luthur*
Lynch (**Linch**) (Irish) sailor.
Lyndal (**Lin**-dal) (English) from the valley of the linden (lime) trees.
Lyndon (**Lin**-don) (English) man from the hill of linden (lime) trees. *Lindon, Lyndonn*
Lynwood (**Lin**-wood) (Old English) from the linden (lime) wood near the stream. *Linwood*
Lysander (Lie-**sand**-er) (Greek) liberator of men. A hero of Greek mythology. *Lysand*

Mac (**Mack**) (Scottish) son of. Mc is the Irish form.

Macalla (**Ma**-cal-a) (Australian) born at the full moon.

Maccabee (**Mac**-a-bee) (Hebrew) hammer.

Maccrea (Mac-**ree**) (Irish) son of grace.

Macdonald (Mac-**don**-ald) (Scottish) son of Donald.

Mace (**Mace**) (English) a short form of Mason (stone-cutter). (French) iron club.

Mack (**Mack**) a short form of names beginning Mac and Mc.

Mackinley (Mac-**kin**-lee) (Gaelic) son of the wise one. Also the name of the highest mountain in the USA. *MacKinlay, McKinlay*

Maclean (Mac-**lane**) (Gaelic) son of Leander, which means lion man. *Maclain, Mclaine*

Maddox (**Mad**-ux) (Welsh) son of the benefactor. *Maddy*

Magee (Ma-**gee**) (Irish) the son of Hugh. *McGee*

Magner (**Mag**-ner) (Scandinavian) strong man, great.

Magnus (**Mag**-nuss) (Latin) great one. *Magnes*

Maguire (Mag-**wire**) (Irish) son of a brown father. *McGuire*

Mahon (**Ma**-hon/**Mahn**) from the Irish word *hón* meaning bare. *Mahan*

Maitland (**Mate**-land) (English) from the meadowland.

Malachi (**Mal**-a-kye) (Hebrew) angel of God. Another prophet from the Bible. *Malachy, Maleki*

Malcolm (**Mal**-com) (Gaelic) follower of Columba. Saint Columba was a sixth-century missionary who converted parts of Scotland to Christianity, hence the name is most popular in Scotland and among those of Scottish descent. *Mal, Malkalm, Malkelm*

Mallin (**Mal**-in) (English) small soldier. *Malen, Malin, Mallan, Mallen, Mally*

Maloney (Mal-**own**-ee) (Irish) follower of Saint John. *Mal, Malonie, Malony*

Mandel (**Man**-del) (German) almond. *Mandela, Mandell, Mandy*

Mander (**Man**-der) (Romany) of my own self.

Manfred (**Man**-fred) (German) man of peace. *Mannfred*

Manley (**Man**-lee) (English) from the hero's clearing. *Man, Manlee, Manlie, Manly*

Mannig (**Man**-ig) (Scandinavian) brave and resourceful.

Mansel (**Man**-sell) (English/Scottish) from the house of the clergyman. Manse is the Scottish for rectory or vicarage.

Mansfield (**Mans**-field) (English) from the field of the heroes. *Manesfeld, Mansfeld*

Manton (**Man**-ton) (Old English) from the hero's village.
Marcel (Mar-**sell**) (French) but derived from the Latin word for virile. *Marcell, Mars, Marsel*
Marcher (**Mar**-cher) (English) guardian of the border. *March*
Marcus (**Mar**-cus) (Latin) of a warlike disposition. *Markus*
Marden (**Mar**-den) (English) from the valley of the lake.
Mario (**Ma**-ree-o) Italian version of the Latin Marcus, meaning warlike.
Mark (**Mark**) (Latin) anglicized version of Marcus. Means virile, or of Mars (i.e. warlike). Writer of the second gospel.
Marland (**Mar**-land) (English) from the land of lakes.
Marley (**Mar**-lee) (English) from the clearing by the lake.
Marmaduke (**Mar**-ma-duke) (Gaelic) follower of Saint Maedoc. The most famous saint of this name was the sixth-century Abbot of Clonmore in Ireland.
Marquis (**Mar**-kwiss/Mar-**kee**) (Norman) nobleman. The third of the five ranks of aristocracy.
Marsdon (**Mars**-don) (English) from the valley of the marsh. *Marr, Mars*
Marsh (**Marsh**) (English) from the marsh. (French) marshall.
Marshall (**Mar**-shall) (French) steward of cavalry horses. The highest military rank. (General is the second highest.) *Marsh, Marshal, Marshel, Marshell*
Marston (**Mars**-ton) (English) from the town by the marsh. *Marstan, Marsten*
Martell (Mar-**tell**) (French) hammer. *Martel*
Martin (**Mar**-tin) anglicized version of Martius, which is derived from Mars, the Roman god of war. Saint Martin de Porres studied medicine, entered the Dominican Order and focused his life on curing others. Saint's day: 3 November. *Martyn*
Marvin (**Mar**-vin) (English) at one with the sea. *Marv, Marven*
Mason (**Mace**-on) from the Old French word for stone-cutter. or stone-mason. *Mace, Mase*
Mattan (**Mat**-an) (Hebrew) gift.
Matthew (**Math**-yoo) (Hebrew) gift of God. Originally a tax collector, he became one of the Apostles and author of one of the four gospels. Saint's day: 21 September. *Matheu, Mathieu, Matt, Mattie, Matty*
Maurice (**Mor**-iss) (Latin) dark-skinned. His saint's day is celebrated on 22 September. *Maur, Maurie, Maurise, Morice, Morrie, Morry*
Maverick (**Mav**-er-ick) (American) independent, unconventional and free. Originally named from the Texan Samuel Maverick who did not brand his cattle. It's a name that rather appropriately lends itself to unconventional spellings. *Mav, Mavarick, Mavereck, Mavreck, Mavvy*

Maximilian (**Max**-ee-**mill**-ee-on) (Latin) greatest. Commonly shortened to Max. Saint Maximilian was imprisoned in Auschwitz where he ministered to the captives. He voluntarily took the place of a young married prisoner condemned to die. Saint's day: 14 August. *Max, Maxie, Maxy*

Maxwell (**Max**-well) (Scottish) from the stream of Maccus. Also shortened to Max. The name of a sixth-century king of the Isle of Man. *Maxe, Maxie, Maxwel, Maxy*

Mayhew (**May**-hew) (English) a form of Matthew, meaning gift of God.

Maynard (**May**-nard) (English) strong and brave. *Mayne, Maynerd*

Mayo (**May**-oh) (Irish) from the plain of the yew trees. Also the name of an Irish county. *Maio*

Meldon (**Mel**-don) (Old English) from the mill on the hill. *Melden, Meldin, Meldyn*

Mendel (**Men**-del) (English) one who mends.

Mered (**Meh**-red) (Hebrew) rebellious.

Merlin (**Mur**-lin) (Welsh) sea fort. Name of the famous wizard to the legendary King Arthur. *Merl, Merlan, Merlinn, Merlyn*

Merrick (**Mer**-rik) Welsh form of Maurice, meaning dark-skinned. *Mere, Meric, Merik, Merrack*

Mervin (**Mur**-vin) (Welsh) great lord. Often written as Marvin in the USA.

Michael (**Mike**-al) (Hebrew) he who is like God. *Mical, Mick, Mickey, Mikael, Mike, Mikey, Miko*

Miguel (Mig-**ell**) Spanish and Portuguese form of Michael, meaning he who is like God. *Migelle*

Milan (Mi-**lan**) (Slavonic) greatly loved. *Milano*

Miles (**Miles**) (German) generous. (Latin) soldier. *Myles*

Milhouse (**Mill**-house) (English) from the mill house. The middle name of famous US President, Richard Nixon. *Milhous*

Millard (**Mill**-ard) (Latin) mill-keeper. *Milard, Mill, Millerd*

Miller (**Mill**-er) (English) miller. *Myller*

Milo (**My**-low) German form of Miles, meaning generous or soldier. *Milos, Mylo*

Miloslav (**Mill**-oh-slav) (Czech) one who seeks glory.

Milson (**Mill**-son) (English) son of the miller.

Milton (**Mill**-ton) (Old English) from the mill by the farm. *Melton, Milt, Miltey, Mylton*

Mohammed (Mo-**ham**-ed) (Arabic) praiseworthy. The name of the seventh-century founder of Islam. *Mohamad, Mohamid, Mohamud, Muhammad*

Monahan (**Mon**-a-han) (Irish) monk. *Managhan, Mon, Monehan, Monnahan*

Montgomery/Monty (Mont-**gom**-er-ree/**Mon**-tee) (Norman) powerful man on a hill. The Montgomery family came to Britain with William the Conqueror, and the famous World War II field marshal – Monty – was a scion of that family.
Moran (Mo-**ran**) From the Irish word *mór* meaning big or great.
Moray (Mo-**ray**) (Gaelic) lord and master. Also a Scottish place name.
Mordecai (**More**-de-kye) (Hebrew) soldierly. In the Bible he was a counsellor to Queen Ester. *Morde, Mordekai*
Mordred (**More**-dred) (Welsh) takes his own path. A nephew of King Arthur. He severely wounded Arthur, causing him to be taken to the Isle of Avalon.
Moreland (**More**-land) (English) from the moor.
Morfans (**More**-vans) (Welsh) another of the Knights of the Round Table. Morfans was unfortunately famous for being ugly.
Mori (**Mo**-ri) (Ugandan) the literal translation of this name is born before the loan on the wife's dowry has been paid off.
Morley (**More**-lee) (Old English) from the clearing by the moor.
Morris/Morrison (**Mor**-iss-on) English forms of Maurice, meaning dark-skinned. *Maurice, Moris, Morse, Mouris*
Morse (**Morse**) (English) son of Maurice. *Morce, Morcey, Morsey*
Morten (**Mor**-ten) (Old English) from the farm by the moor.
Mortimer (**Mort**-im-er) (French) from the still water. *Mort, Mortemer, Mortie, Morty, Mortymer*
Morton (**Mor**-ton) (Old English) from the town by the moor. *Mort, Mortan, Mortun, Morty*
Morven (**More**-ven) (Scottish) sailor.
Moses (**Moe**-ziz) (Hebrew) saviour. Famously led the Israelites out of Egypt and brought the Ten Commandments down from Mount Sinai.
Mostyn (**Moss**-tin) (English/Welsh) from the moss settlement.
Mungo (**Mun**-go) (Scottish) likeable.
Murat (**Mur**-rat) (Turkish) wish. The name of the general who commanded Napoleon's cavalry.
Murdoch (**Mur**-dock) (Scottish) rich sailor. *Merdock, Murdock*
Murray (**Mu**-ree) (Scottish) settlement by the sea. *Muray, Murrey, Murry*
Myron (**My**-ron/**Mi**-ron) (Greek) the Greek word for myrrh. *Miron*

N

Nadim (Na-**deem**) (Arabic) friend.
Nagid (Na-**geed**) (Hebrew) ruler, prince.
Nailah (Na-**ee**-lah) (Arabic) successful. *Naila*
Nairn (**Nairn**) (Irish) from the alder tree.
Naldo (**Nal**-doe) Spanish short form of Fernando, itself derived from the German Ferdinand, meaning ready in peace.
Namid (Na-**mid**) (Native American) dancer of the stars.
Namir (Na-**meer**) (Hebrew) leopard.
Nando (**Nan**-doe) (German) a short form of Ferdinand (ready in peace).
Nansen (**Nan**-sen) (Scandinavian) son of Nancy. *Nance, Nansan, Nanson*
Napier (**Nay**-pee-er) (Old French) linen-maker.
Napoleon (Na-**pole**-ee-on) (Greek) lion of the woods. (Italian) from Naples. *Napoleone*
Narcissus (Nar-**siss**-us) (Greek) flower. In Greek mythology, the most beautiful youth in the world. Unfortunately, he caught sight of his own face while passing a pool and stayed for eternity staring back at himself, he was so enraptured by his own beauty. *Narciss, Narcisse, Nars*
Narrie (**Na**-ree) (Australian) bush fire.
Narve (**Naar**-vuh) (Scandinavian) strong and healthy.
Naseem (Na-**seem**) (Arabic) benevolent.
Natal (Na-**tal**) Spanish form of Noel, meaning born at Christmas.
Nathan (**Nay**-than) (Hebrew) God has given. A prophet who passed messages from God to King David. *Nat, Nate, Nathen, Nathin, Natthan, Natthen*
Nathaniel (Na-**than**-ee-el) (Hebrew) God has given. An Apostle who saw Jesus after the Resurrection. *Nat, Nate, Nathan, Nathaneal, Nathanial, Nathe*
Navarro (Na-**var**-oh) (Spanish) from the plains. *Navaro, Navarroh, Naverro*
Nayland (**Nay**-land) (English) one who lives on an island.
Neal/Neil (**Neel**) (Gaelic) derived from the Gaelic words for cloud and champion. *Neall, Neel, Nele, Niall*
Ned (**Ned**) (English) short form of Edward and Edwin.
Nehemiah (**Nay**-he-**my**-ah) (Hebrew) God's compassion. A Jewish leader in the Bible. *Nehemyah*
Nelek (**Nel**-ek) Polish form of Cornelius, meaning the colour of horn.
Nels (**Nels**) (Danish) a short form of Neil (cloud/champion) and Nelson (Neil's son).
Nelson (**Nel**-son) (Danish) Neil's son. *Nelsen*
Nemo (**Nee**-mo) (Hebrew) a short form of Nehemiah, meaning God's compassion. (Greek) from the glade.
Neptune (**Nep**-tyoon) (Latin) the Roman god of the sea.

Nestor (**Ness**-tor) (Greek) to come back safely from a journey. A figure from the Trojan War who had a string of adventures in his youth, but matured into a wise counsellor. *Nester, Nestir*
Neville (**Nev**-ill) (Norman) new place. *Nev, Nevil, Nevile, Niville*
Nevin/Nevan (**Nev**-in/**Nev**-an) (Irish) holy one.
Newell (**New**-el) (English) from the new hall. *Newall, Newel, Nywell*
Newlin (**New**-lin) (Welsh) from the new lake. *Newl, Newlynn, Nule*
Newman (**New**-man) (English) newcomer. *Neuman, Newmann*
Newton (**New**-ton) (Old English) from the new farm. *Newt*
Niall (**Nile**) (Gaelic) cloud or champion. Also a fourth-century king who kissed an ugly girl at a well, at which point she transformed into a beauty.
Nicholas (**Nick**-o-las) (Greek) victory over the people. Relates to the Greek goddess of victory, Nike. Saint Nicolas is the patron saint of Greece and Russia. Saint's day: 6 December. *Nick, Nickolas, Nicky, Nykolas*
Nicodemos (Nik-o-**deem**-os) (Greek) conqueror of the people.
Nicolai (**Nick**-o-lie) Russian form of Nicholas, which means victory over the people.
Nils (**Neels**) Scandinavian forms of Neil, meaning cloud or champion. *Neils*
Nigel (**Nye**-jel) (Latin) dark.
Niles (**Niles**) (English) son of Neil, which means cloud or champion.
Ninian (**Nin**-ee-an) (Latin) full of life. The Irish form is Ninnidh.
Noah (**No**-ah) (Hebrew) rest. A well-known figure from the Old Testament. *Noa*
Noble (**No**-bull) (Latin) noble. *Nobel*
Nolan (**No**-lan) (Irish) famous and noble. *Nolen, Nolun, Nolyn*
Norbert (**Nor**-bert) (Old German) northern brightness. Saint's day: 6 June.
Norman (**Nor**-man) (Old German) originally meant man from the north, but now usually associated with Normandy. *Norm, Normen, Normon, Normun*
Norris (**Nor**-iss) (English) Norman's horse.
Northcliff (**North**-cliff) (English) northern cliff.
Norththrop (**North**-rup) (English) from the northern farm.
Norton (**Nor**-ton) (Old English) from the northern town. *Nort, Nortan, Nortun*
Norvell (Nor-**vell**) (French) from the northern town. *Norvelle, Norville, Norvyl*
Norwin (**Nor**-win) (English) friend from the north. *Norvin, Norwen, Norwinn*
Norwood (**Nor**-wood) (English) from the northern wood.
Nye (**Nye**) (Welsh) short form of Aneurin, meaning gold. *Ni, Nie, Nyee*
Nyle (**Nyle**) (English) from the island. (Irish) a form of Neil, meaning cloud or champion. *Nyl, Nyles*

Oakes (**Oaks**) (English) from the oak trees.
Oakley (**Oak**-lee) (English) from the clearing of the oaks. *Oak, Oakly*
Obadiah (**Oh**-bad-**eye**-ah) (Hebrew) one who serves God. *Obadyah, Obediah, Oby*
Oberon (**Oh**-ber-on) (German) noble bear. In Shakespeare's *A Midsummer Night's Dream*, Oberon is the King of the Fairies. *Obaron, Oburon*
Obert (**Oh**-bert) (German) rich and clever.
Odhran (O-**ran**) (Irish) pale. The name of Saint Patrick's chariot driver. *Odran, Orran*
Odin (**Oh**-din) (Scandinavian) overlord. From the name of the Norse god of war.
Odysseus (Oh-**dee**-see-us) (Greek) wandering traveller. The name of a wily Greek hero who took ten years to return from the Trojan War because he faced myriad adversities along the way.
Ogden (**Og**-den) (Old English) from the valley of the oak trees. *Ogdan, Ogdun*
Oghe (**Ock**-ee) (Irish) horseman.
Ogilvy (**Oh**-gill-vee) (Welsh) born on a high hill.
Ogun (Oh-**goon**) (Yoruba) the name of the god of iron, war and travelling.
Oisin (Ush-**een**) (Irish) small deer. Also the name of a hero in Irish legend.
Oisten (**Ost**-in) the Irish form of Austin, which means venerable or consecrated.
Olaf/Olav (**Oh**-laf/**Oh**-lav) (Scandinavian) ancestor. Saint Olaf is the patron saint of Norway. *Olan, Olen*
Oldrich (**Old**-rich) (Czech) powerful and rich. A form of Ulrich, meaning leader of wolves.
Oleg (**Oh**-leg) (Russian) holy man. *Olag, Olig*
Oliver (**Ol**-iv-er) (Norse) ancestor. Also thought to be associated with the Mediterranean fruit and tree, the olive. *Ollie, Olly*
Omar (**Oh**-mar) (Arabic) from the highest. (Hebrew) one who reveres God. *Omarh*
Omri (**Om**-ree) (Hebrew) sheaf of grain. The name of a biblical King of Israel.
Oran (**Orr**-an) (Celtic) from the cold spring.
Orestes (Or-**est**-eez) (Greek) man from the hills. The son of Agamemnon, who led the Greeks in the Trojan War. *Oreste*
Orion (Or-**eye**-on) (Greek) son of fire. Also the name of the constellation depicting a hunter.
Orlando (Or-**land**-o) Italian form of Roland, meaning famous in the land. A lover of King Arthur's daughter. *Orl, Orland, Orlie, Orlondo, Orly*
Orman (**Or**-man) (German) rower, sailor.

Ormond (**Or**-mund) (English) from the mountain of the bear. *Ormand, Ormande, Orme, Ormund*
Ori (**Or**-ee) (Hebrew) my light. *Orrie, Ory*
Oro (**Or**-oh) (Spanish) golden.
Orrick (**Or**-ick) (English) from the old oak tree.
Orrin (**Or**-in) (English) from the river.
Orson (**Or**-son) (French) son of the bear. *Orsan, Orsen, Orsey, Orsun*
Orton (**Or**-ton) (Old English) from the town by the sea.
Orville (**Or**-vil) (French) from the golden town. *Orvalle*
Orvin (**Or**-vin) (English) friend of the vine.
Osbert (**Oz**-bert) (Old English) famous to God. *Osbart, Osburt, Ozbart, Ozburt*
Osborn/Osborne (**Oz**-born) (English) soldier of God. *Osbourn, Osbourne*
Oscar (**Oss**-car) (Irish/Scandinavian) the Irish derivation means friend of deer.; the Scandinavian means God's spear. *Oskar*
Osgood (**Oz**-good) (English) divinely good. *Ozgood*
Osmar (**Oz**-mar) (English) divinely beautiful. *Ozmar*
Osred (**Oz**-red) (English) advised by God. *Ozred*
Osric (**Oz**-rik) (English) divine ruler. *Ozric*
Osten (**Os**-ten) (English) from God's town.
Oswald (**Oz**-wald) (English) God's power. *Ozwald*
Oswin (**Oz**-win) (English) God's friend. *Ozwin*
Ota (**Oh**-ta) (Czech) rich.
Otaden (**Oh**-ta-den) (Native American) bountiful.
Otis (**Oh**-tiss) (Old German) son of Otto, which means rich. (Greek) one who hears well. *Otes*
Otto (**Ot**-oh) (German) rich.
Ottokar (**Ott**-a-kar) (German) one who loves war. Saint's day: 2 July.
Overton (**Ove**-er-ton) (English) from the high town.
Owen (**Oh**-wen) (Welsh) well-born. *Owan, Owain, Owin*
Oxford (**Ox**-ford) (English) from the ford where cattle cross. A place name from the English University town.
Oxley (**Ox**-lee) (English) from the cattle clearing.
Ozzy (**Oz**-ee) (English) short forms of Osborn (soldier of God) and Oswald (God's power). *Oz*

P

Pace/Pacey (**Pace/Pace**-ee) English form of Pascal, a French name meaning born at Easter.

Paco (**Pa**-co) (Spanish) a diminutive form of Francisco (see Francis). (Italian) pack. *Pako*

Paddy (**Pad**-ee) (Irish) a diminutive form of Patrick, meaning patrician or nobleman. *Paddan*

Padarn (Pad-**ern**) (Celtic) derived from the Latin word for father. Also a key figure in founding the Welsh church.

Padget (**Pad**-jet) (English) a form of Page, which means child.

Padraigh (**Pad**-rig) see Patrick. *Pawdy, Padrey, Padge*

Pagiel (Pa-**geel**) (Hebrew) one who worships God.

Pål (**Pol**) Scandinavian form of Paul, meaning small.

Palani (Pa-**lah**-ni) (Hawaiian) free man.

Palmer (**Pah**-mer) (English) one who has carried the palm, which means one who has made the pilgrimage to Jerusalem. In medieval times it was the custom for pilgrims to carry palm fronds on the last leg of the journey.

Panas (Pa-**nass**) (Russian) immortal.

Parker (**Park**-er) (English) one who looks after a park. *Park, Parks*

Parlan (**Par**-lan) Scottish form of Bartholomew, which means son of Tolmai.

Parnell (Par-**nel**) (French) little Peter. *Parnel*

Parr (**Par**) (English) from the barn or enclosed space.

Parrish (**Pa**-rish) English) from the area of the local church. *Parish*

Parry (**Pa**-ree) (Welsh) son of Harry.

Parthalan (**Parth**-lan) (Irish) son of the ploughman. Often shortened to Parth.

Patrick/Pat (**Pat**-rik/**Pat**) (Latin) patrician or nobleman. Saint Patrick was born in Britain. When he was about fourteen, he was kidnapped during a raid and taken to pagan Ireland to herd sheep. He learned the language and practices of the people and escaped from slavery. He later returned to convert the Irish to Christianity. The seventeenth of March is the feast day. Irish language forms include Padrig, Padraic and Padraigh.

Patrin (Pat-**rin**) (Romany) leader.

Patterson (**Pat**-er-sun) (Irish) son of Patrick.

Pattin (**Pat**-in) (Romany) leaf.

Patton (**Pat**-on) (Old English) from the town of warriors.

Paul (**Paul**) (Latin) little. Saint Paul was a key figure in the spread of early Christianity, and is famous for his conversion to Christianity while on the road to Damascus. Saint's day: 25 January.

Payne (**Pain**) (Latin) from the countryside.
Pax (**Pax**) (Latin) peace.
Paxton (**Pax**-ton) (Latin/English) from the peaceful town.
Peadar (**Pad**-ar) Irish form of Peter, meaning rock.
Pedat (Peh-**dat**) (Hebrew) atonement.
Peder (**Ped**-er) Scandinavian form of Peter, meaning rock.
Pello (**Pel**-oh) (Greek) rock.
Pelman (**Pel**-man) (English) one from beside the pool.
Pembroke (**Pem**-brook) (Welsh) from the headland. Also a town in southwest Wales. (English) from the broken border. *Brook, Brooke*
Pendle (**Pen**-dul) (English) from the hilltop.
Penley (**Pen**-lee) (English) from the enclosed clearing. *Penly*
Penn (**Pen**) (English) from the enclosure.
Pepe (**Pep**-pay) (Spanish) a nickname for the name José, which is the Spanish form of Joseph, which means God will add.
Pepin (**Pep**-in) (German) determined. A king of France in the eighth century. *Pepen*
Peppe (**Pep**-pay) (Italian) this is the Italian form of Joseph, meaning God will add.
Per (**Pair**) Swedish form of Peter, meaning rock.
Perceval (**Per**-siv-al) (Old French) piercing the valley. The Knight of the Round Table particularly associated with the quest for the holy grail. *Parsival, Percey, Percy, Perseval*
Percy (**Per**-see) (Norman) from a place name in Normandy.
Peregrine (**Per**-a-grin) (Latin) wanderer. The word pilgrim is derived from this. Also associated with the falcon of the same name.
Perth (**Perth**) (Scottish) from the thorn bush. The name of cities in Scotland and Western Australia.
Peter (**Peet**-er) (Greek) rock. One of the twelve Apostles and a key figure in the founding of the early Christian church. His original name was Simon. Saint's day: 22 February. *Per, Petar, Pete, Petur*
Peterson (**Peet**-er-son) (English) son of Peter.
Peverell (**Pev**-er-el) (French) piper. *Peverel, Peveril*
Pewlin (**Pew**-lin) (Welsh) small. *Pewlyn*
Peyton (**Pay**-ton) (Old English) from the town of the warriors. *Payton*
Phelan (**Fell**-an) (Irish) wolf. The origin of the word felon.
Philemon (**Fill**-a-mon) (Greek) loved as a brother.
Philip (**Fil**-ip) (Greek) lover of horses. One of the twelve Apostles. His saint's day is celebrated on 3 May. *Felip, Philippe, Phillip*

Philo (Fie-low) (Greek) loved as a brother.
Phineas (Finn-ee-ass) (Egyptian) dark-skinned. (Hebrew) oracle. *Fineas, Finny, Pheneas, Phineus*
Pierce (Pierce) (Irish/French) a form of Peter, meaning rock. *Pearce, Piercy*
Piers (Peers) French form of Peter, meaning rock.
Pinchas (Pinch-ass) (Hebrew) oracle.
Pippin (Pip-in) (German) father.
Piran (Pie-ron) (Irish) one who prays. Saint Piran is the patron saint of miners. *Pyran*
Pirrin (Pir-rin) (Australian) from the cave.
Pitney (Pit-nee) (English) stubborn.
Pitt (Pit) (English) from the pit or hollow.
Placido (Pla-see-doh) (Spanish) serene.
Platt (Plat) (French) from the flatland.
Pomeroy (Pom-roy) (French) from the orchard.
Pontus (Pont-us) (Latin) bridge. *Pontius*
Porter (Port-er) (Latin) keeper of the gate. (Norman) carrier. *Port*
Powell (Pow-ell) (Irish) watchful and alert. *Powel*
Prentice (Pren-tiss) (English) apprentice.
Presley (Prez-lee) (Old English) from the clearing of the priest. *Preslie*
Preston (Press-ton) English) from the town of the priest. *Prestyn*
Priam (Pry-am) (Greek) chief. He was the last King of Troy and father of the two princes, Hector and Paris.
Price (Price) (Welsh) ardent. *Pryce*
Prince (Prince) (Latin) prince.
Princeton (Prince-ton) (English) from the prince's town. Also an American Ivy League university.
Proctor (Proc-ter) Latin) official.
Prosper (Pross-per) (Latin) fortunate.

Quade (Kwade) (Latin) the fourth.
Quane (Kwane) (French) intelligent.
Quentin (Kwen-tin) (Latin) the fifth. *Quent, Qwentyn*
Quigley (Kwig-lee) (Irish) from the mother. *Quiggly*
Quillan (Kwill-an) (Irish) cub. *Quillian*
Quimby (Kwim-bee) (Scandinavian) from the mother's side.
Quinlan (Kwin-lan) (Irish) of a manly form.

R

Raamah (Ram-**ah**) (Hebrew) born in thunder.
Raanan (Rah-**nan**) (Hebrew) fresh.
Rabbie (**Rab**-ee) (Scottish) a pet form for Robert, meaning famous. *Rabi*
Racham (**Rack**-am) (Hebrew) full of compassion.
Rad (**Rad**) (Arabic) thunder. (English) adviser. Also short for Radbert, Radbourne and Radcliff.
Radbert (**Rad**-bert) (English) adviser.
Radbourne (**Rad**-born) (English) from the red brook or stream. *Radborne, Radburn*
Radcliff (**Rad**-cliff) (English) red cliff. *Radclyffe*
Radek (**Rad**-ek) (Czech) famous ruler. *Radec*
Radford (**Rad**-ford) (Old English) from the ford covered in reeds. *Radfurd*
Radimir (Rad-ee-**meer**) (Russian) from the happy peace. *Radymir*
Radley (**Rad**-lee) (English) from the red clearing. *Radleigh*
Radman (**Rad**-man) (Slavic) full of joy.
Radnor (**Rad**-nor) (Old English) from the shore of reeds, or from the red shore.
Radovan (Rad-oh-**van**) (Russian) happy. *Radyvan*
Radulf (**Rad**-ulf) (German) wise wolf.
Rafa (**Raf**-a) a form of Ralph (wolf counsel).
Rafael (Ra-fey-**el**/Ra-fie-**el**) (Spanish/Portuguese) God heals, or healed by God. *Raffaele, Raffaello*
Rafe (**Rafe**) (English) a variant of the Ralph (German) and Rafferty (Irish).
Rafferty (**Raf**-er-tee) (Irish) prosperous. *Raferty*
Raghnall (**Raw**-nall) (Irish) a wise and powerful ruler.
Ragnar (**Ran**-yar) Scandinavian form of the German Reginar (wise warrior).
Raguel (Ra-**gwel**) (Hebrew) friend of God. One of the Archangels.
Raibert (**Rye**-bert) (Gaelic) one whose fame shines brightly. The Scottish Gaelic form of Robert, meaning famous.
Raidon (**Rye-don**) (Japanese) the name of the Japanese thunder god.
Raigain (**Rye**-gan) (Gaelic) little king.
Raine (**Rain**) (English) wise ruler. Derived from the word reign. *Rayne*
Rainer (**Rye**-ner) (German) wise warrior. *Rayner, Raynier*
Rainier (**Rain**-ee-yay/**Rain**-ee-er) French form of the German name Rainer, which means wise warrior.
Raj (**Raj**) (Hindi) king. Another form with the same meaning is Rajan.
Rakesh (**Ra**-kesh) (Hindi) Lord of the Night.
Raleigh (**Rah**-lee) (Old English) from the clearing of the roe deer. Sir Walter Raleigh, Elizabethan explorer, founded the first English settlement in Virginia.

Ralph (**Ralf**) (German) wolf counsel, advised by wolves. *Ralf*
Ralston (**Ral**-stun) (English) from the town of Ralph.
Rambert (**Ram**-bert) (Teutonic) mighty and brilliant.
Rambures (**Ram**-boor-eez) a character from Shakespeare's *Henry V*.
Rameses (**Ram**-sees) (Egyptian) born of the sun.
Ramesh (**Ra**-mesh) (Sanskrit) at one with Rama (who was a legendary/historic Indian king who led an exemplary life).
Ramón (Ram-**on**) (Spanish) Spanish form of Raymond. *Rammon*
Ramiro (Ra-**mee**-ro) (Spanish) high judge.
Ramsey (**Ram**-zee) (Old English) from the island of rams. *Ramsay*
Ranald (**Ran**-ald) (Old English) wise and powerful ruler.
Rand (**Rand**) (Old English) shield. Also short for Randolph.
Randall (**Ran**-dal) (Old English) a person from a border area or a village edge. *Randal, Randell*
Randolph (**Ran**-dolf) (Old German) shield of the wolf. The name of Sir Winston Churchill's father. *Randolf*
Randy (**Ran**-dee) (English) a short form of Randall and Randolph.
Ranen (Ra-**nen**) (Hebrew) full of God's joy.
Ranger (**Range**-er) (French) the keeper of the forest.
Ranjit (**Ran**-jeet) (Hindi) victorious in battle. *Ranjeet*
Ransford (**Ranz**-ford) (Old English) from the ford of the raven.
Ransley (**Ranz**-lee) (Old English) from the meadow of the raven. *Ranslee, Ransly*
Raoul (Ra-**ool**) (French) a form of Ralph, meaning advised by wolves.
Raphael (**Ra**-fay-el) (Hebrew) God heals. The name of one of the seven Archangels. *Rafael*
Rasmus (**Raz**-muss) (Greek) a form of Erasmus, which means beloved.
Ranulf (**Ran**-ulf) (Norse) advised by wolves, or fearless advisor.
Rashid (Ra-**sheed**) (Arabic) the well-guided one.
Raul (**Rowl** – rhymes with 'growl') (Italian) a form of Ralph, meaning advised by wolves.
Rawdon (**Raw**-don) (English) from the rough hill. *Rawden, Rawdun*
Rawley (**Raw**-lee) (English) from the meadow of the roe deer. *Rawleigh*
Ray (**Ray**) (Anglo-French) the English derivation is based on roe deer; the French on the word for king (*roi*).
Rayburn (**Ray**-burn) (English) from the deer brook.
Rayfield (**Ray**-field) (English) from the field of deer.
Raymond (**Ray**-mond) (English) adviser and protector. Saint Raymond's mother suffered terribly to give birth to him, so he became patron saint of pregnancies. Saint's day: 31 August. *Ragimund, Ramond, Raymon, Raymund, Raymundo*

Raynard (**Ray**-nard) (English) wise and brave. *Reynard*
Rayner (**Ray**-ner) English form of the Germanic name Reginar, which means wise warrior. *Raynir*
Rearden (**Rear**-den) (Irish) royal poet.
Rebel (**Reb**-el) (American) rebel.
Red (**Red**) (American) from the colour. Also short for Redley, Redford, Redman and Redmond.
Redford (**Red**-ford) (English) means either from the red ford, or from the ford of reeds.
Redley (**Red**-lee) (English) from the clearing of reeds, or from the red clearing. *Redlee, Redly*
Redman (**Red**-man) (Old English) protector and adviser.
Redmond (**Red**-mund) (Irish) wise and mighty protector. *Redmund*
Reed (**Reed**) (English) red-haired. *Reid*
Rees (**Reece**) (Welsh) full of ardour. *Reece, Rhys*
Reeve (**Reev**) (English) steward.
Regin (**Regg**-in) (Norse) the name of a character in Norse mythology.
Reginald (**Rej**-in-ald) (Latin) a Latinized version of the German Reynold, which means adviser to the ruler. *Reg, Reggie*
Regis (**Ree**-jiss) (French) ruler or king.
Reidar (**Rye**-dar) (Scandinavian) cavalryman.
Reinhard (Rine-hart) (German) stern ruler.
Reilly (**Rye**-lee) (Irish) valiant. *Riley*
Remington (**Rem**-ing-ton) (Old English) from the town near the border. *Rem, Remmy*
Rémy (**Ray**-mee) (French) from the French town of Rheims. *Rémi*
Renaldo (Ren-**al**-doe) (Spanish) wise and powerful ruler.
Renaud (Ren-**oh**) (French) brave.
Renfred (**Ren**-fred) (English) mighty and peaceful. *Renfryd*
Renfrew (**Ren**-froo) (Celtic) from the still river.
Renshaw (**Ren**-shaw) (English) from the forest of ravens.
Renton (**Ren**-ton) (English) from the town of the roe deer.
Rexford (**Rex**-ford) (English) from the king's ford.
Reynard (**Ray**-nard) (German) adviser to the ruler. Reynold is an alternative spelling with the same meaning.
Rhett (**Rett**) (Dutch) advisor. Forever associated with the film *Gone with the Wind*.
Rhodes (**Roads**) (Greek) the place of roses. The name of an Aegean island.
Rhodri (**Rod**-ree) (Welsh) the ruler of the wheel.
Rhydderch (**Ruh**-therk) (Welsh) liberal, generous. It is the name of a sixth-century Welsh leader called Rhydderch Hael.
Rhydwyn (**Rud**-win) (Welsh) dweller by the white ford.
Rhys (**Reece**) (Welsh) full of ardour. *Rees*

Rian (**Ree**-an) (Irish) little king, *ri* being the Irish word for king. *Ryan*
Ric (**Rik**) (Norse) honourable ruler. Also a derivative of Eric and Richard. *Rik*
Ricardo (Ri-**car**-doe) (Spanish/Portuguese) form of Richard (brave ruler).
Richard (**Rich**-ard) (German) brave ruler. The name was introduced to Britain by the Normans. At that time, the English 'r' was pronounced as 'd', hence the shortened form, Dick. *Rich, Richey, Richie, Rickie, Ricky, Ritchie*
Richmond (**Rich**-mund) (German) powerful protector. *Rich, Richie, Ricky*
Rick (**Rick**) a short form of Richard, meaning brave ruler.
Riddock (**Rid**-ock) (Irish) from the smooth field.
Rider (**Rye**-der) (English) horseman. *Ryder*
Ridgeley (**Ridge**-lee) (English) from the clearing near the ridge.
Ridgeway (**Ridge**-way) (English) from the path along the ridge.
Ridley (**Rid**-lee) (English) from the clearing of the reeds. *Redley, Rid, Rydley*
Riley (**Rye**-lee) (Gaelic) courageous. (English) from the clearing of rye. *Reiley, Ryley*
Rimon (**Rim**-on) (Persian) from the name of the Persian god of storms.
Riordan (Ree-**ar**-dan) (Gaelic) poet to the king. *Reardon*
Risley (**Riz**-lee) (English) from the clearing of shrubs. *Rislee, Rizley*
Ritter (**Ritt**-er) (German) knight, cavalryman. *Ritt*
Roald (**Roe**-ald) (Scandinavian) famous ruler.
Robert (**Rob**-ert) (German) famous. Introduced by the Normans. The most famous bearer of the name was Scottish king, Robert the Bruce. *Bob, Bobbie, Bobby, Rob, Robbie, Robby, Roberto*
Rocco (**Rock**-oh) (Italian) rock. *Roc, Rocky*
Rock (**Rock**) (Latin) rock. *Rocky*
Rockley (**Rock**-lee) (Old English) from the rocky clearing. *Rock, Rocky*
Rockwell (**Rock**-well) (English) from the well by the rocks.
Rod (**Rod**) (English) a short form of Roderick and Rodney. *Rodd, Roddy*
Roddy (**Rod**-ee) (English) a short form of Roderick (famous and powerful).
Roden (**Roe**-den) (Irish) strong.
Roderick (**Rod**-er-ik) (German) famous and powerful. Saint's day: 13 March. *Roddy, Roderic, Rodrik*
Rodman (**Rod**-man) (German) famous hero. *Rodmin, Rodmun*
Rodney (**Rod**-nee) (English) Roda's Island. Originally a place in the marshes of Somerset. *Rod, Roddy, Rodnee*
Roe (**Roe**) (English) roe deer.
Rolf (**Rolf**) see Rudolf'.
Rogan (**Roe**-gan) (Gaelic) red-haired.
Roger (**Roj**-er) (German) famous spear. First introduced by the Normans. Saint's day: 5 January.

Roland (**Role**-and) (German) famous in the land. *Rowland*
Rollo (**Rol**-oh) Latinized form of Rolf.
Roman (**Rome**-an) (Latin) from Rome. The patron saint of those who drown and those who suffer from mental illness. Saint's day: 28 February. *Romy*
Romeo (**Rome**-ee-oh) (Latin) originally meant one from Rome, but being the name of the young lover in Shakespeare's *Romeo and Juliet* changed its connotations for all time.
Romney (**Rom**-nee) (Old English) from the broad river. *Rom, Romnie*
Ron (**Ron**) the short form of Ronald and Ronan. *Ronn*
Ronald (**Ron**-ald) (Norse) wise ruler. *Ron, Ronnie, Ronny*
Ronan (**Roe**-nan) (Irish) little seal. Irish legend has it that mermaids would take the form of seals to sleep with men; little seals being the result.
Rooney (**Roo**-nee) (Irish) red-haired. *Roony*
Roper (**Rope**-er) (English) rope-maker.
Rory (**Roar**-ee) (Celtic) means either red-haired or red king.
Roscoe (**Ross**-coe) (Scandinavian) red deer. *Rosco*
Ross (**Ross**) from the Scots Gaelic word for cape (headland in the sea, not cloak).
Rosswell (**Ross**-well) (English) from the red spring. *Roswell, Rozwell*
Rothwell (**Roth**-well) (Scandinavian) from the red spring.
Rourke (**Roo**-urk) (Irish) derived from the surname of the ruling household in tenth-century Ireland. *Roark, Rork, Rourke*
Rover (**Rove**-er) (English) one who journeys.
Rowan (**Roe**-an) (Irish) little red one. Also from the English tree name. *Rowen*
Rowley (**Roe**-lee) (English) from the rough clearing.
Roxbury (**Rox**-bree) (English) from the rook's castle.
Roy (**Roy**) (Scottish) red. (French) king.
Royal (**Roy**-ul) (French) of the king.
Royce (**Royce**) (English) son of Roy. *Roy, Royse*
Royden (**Roy**-den) (English) from the hill of rye. *Raydin, Royd*
Royston (**Roy**-ston) (Norman) Rohesia's cross (Rohesia is a Norman, artistocratic female name).
Ruardhan (**Roar**-den) (Irish) the meaning is unclear. Saint Ruardhan died in AD 584, having founded a monastery at Lorrha in Ireland. His saint's day is 5 April.
Rudd (**Rud**) (Old English) red-faced.
Rudolf (**Roo**-dolf) (German) famous wolf. Often shortened to Rolf. *Rudolph*
Rudy (**Roo**-dee) (English) the short form of Rudolf and Rudyard.
Rudyard (**Rud**-yard) (Old English) from the red enclosure. *Rud, Rudd, Ruddy*
Ruford (**Roo**-ford) (English) from the ford of reeds.

Rufus (**Roo**-fuss) (Latin) red or ruddy. King Rufus, son of William the Conqueror, was murdered in the New Forest by an arrow. The archer was never caught.
Rugby (**Rug**-bee) (English) from the rook's town. Also the name of a town in the English Midlands. *Rug, Ruggie*
Rumford (**Rum**-ford) (English) from the wide ford.
Rune (**Roon**) (Scandinavian) secret knowledge. *Roone, Runes*
Rupert (**Roo**-pert) (German) originally the German form of Robert (famous), it is now a name in its own right. *Ruprecht*
Rushford (**Rush**-ford) (English) from the ford of the rushes.
Ruskin (**Russ**-kin) (French) red head. *Ruske*
Russell (**Russ**-el) (Norman) red-haired. *Russ, Russel*
Rutherford (**Ruh**-ther-ford) (English) from the cattle ford.
Rutland (**Rut**-land) (Scandinavian) from the red land.
Rutley (**Rut**-lee) (English) from the red clearing.
Ruud (**Rood**) (Old German/Dutch) famous wolf.
Ryan (**Rye**-an) (Irish) follower of Riaghan, an Irish king. *Ryane, Ryann, Ryanne, Ryen*
Ryland (**Rye**-land) (English) from the land where rye grows. *Rylan*
Ryman (**Rye**-man) (English) seller of rye.

S

Saber (**Say**-ber) (French) sword. *Sabre*
Sadler (**Sad**-ler) (English) saddle-maker.
Salton (**Sol**-tun) (English) from the town of the willows.
Salvatore (Sal-va-**tor**-ee) (Italian) of the Saviour. Saint's day: 18 March. *Sal, Salvatori*
Samson (**Sam**-son) (Hebrew) sun. A strong man from the Bible, betrayed by Delilah. Just before his execution, his strength returned and he brought down a pagan temple, killing himself and all those in it. *Sam, Sampson*
Samuel (**Sam**-yoo-el) (Hebrew) heard by God. So-called because his mother longed for a child and her prayers were finally answered. *Sam, Sammuel, Sammy*
Sanborn (**San**-born) (English) from the sandy brook. *Sanbourn, Sanbourne, Sandy*
Sandon (**Sand**-on) (Old English) from the sandy hill.
Sancho (**San**-cho) (Latin) sanctified. *Sanchez*
Sanford (**San**-ford) (English) from the sandy ford. *Sandford, Sandy*
Santiago (San-ti-**ah**-go) (Spanish) Saint James. Disciple of Jesus and patron saint of Spain. He's reputedly buried at Santiago de Compostela in northwest Spain. *Santego, Tago*

Santo (San-toe) (Italian/Spanish) holy, saint.
Saul (Saul) (Hebrew) asked for. The King of Israel prior to David. Also Saint Paul's name before he converted to Christianity.
Sawyer (Soy-er) (English) carpenter. *Saw*
Saxon (Sax-on) (Old English) the people of the swords. *Seax* was the short sword used by the Saxons.
Sayer (Say-er) (Welsh) carpenter. *Saye, Sayers, Sayre*
Scanlon (Scan-lon) (Irish) little trapper. *Scan, Scanlin*
Schafer (Shay-fer) (German) shepherd.
Scott (Scot) (English) but it actually means man from Scotland. *Scot, Scotty*
Scully (Skull-ee) (Irish) town crier. *Scullee, Scullie*
Seabert (See-bert) (English) from the shining sea.
Seabrook (See-brook) (English) from the brook near the sea.
Seamus (Shay-mus) Irish form of James, a disciple of Jesus. *Shamey Shamus, Shay, Shea*
Sean (Shawn) Irish version of John, meaning favoured by God. Other forms are Shane, Shaun and Shawn.
Seanan (Shan-an) (Irish) wise one.
Seaton (Sea-ton) (Old English) from the town by the sea.
Sebastian (Seb-**ass**-tee-un) (Greek) revered. A third-century saint who became the patron saint of athletes. *Seb*
Sedgley (Sedj-lee) (English) from the clearing of the swords. *Sedge*
Sedgwick (Sedj-wik) (English) from the grass of the swords (a battlefield). *Sedge*
Seeley (See-lee) (English) blessed. *Seely*
Sef (Sef) the name of one of the two lions that guarded the gates of night and day in Egyptian mythology. *Seph*
Sefton (Sef-ton) (Norse) from the town surrounded by rushes. *Sef, Seph*
Seger (Say-ger) (Old English) sea spear. *Sedge*
Seibert (Sye-bert) (English) from the bright sea. Usually shortened to Sei.
Selby (Sell-bee) (Old German) from the manor farmhouse. *Sels*
Seldon (Sell-don) (English) from the valley of the willows. *Sel, Syldon*
Selwyn (Sell-win) (Latin) wood. (English) prosperous friend. *Celwyn, Selwin*
Sepp (Sep) German short form of Joseph, which means God will add.
Septimus (Sep-ti-mus) (Latin) the seventh son. *Sep, Sepp, Sept*
Seraphim (Sair-a-fim) (Hebrew) in the Bible, the Seraphim are the highest order of angels (the purest and most devout).
Sereno (Se-**ree**-no) (Latin) tranquil.
Serge (Sairje) (Latin) attendant.
Sergei (Sair-gay) Russian form of Serge, meaning attendant.
Seth (Seth) (Hebrew) appointed. The third son of Adam and Eve. He lived for 900 years.

Seton (See-ton) (Old English) from the agricultural town. *Sayton*
Seumas (Shem-mus) Scottish form of James, a disciple of Jesus.
Severin (Sev-rinn) (French) harsh and severe. *Sev, Sevvy*
Sewell (Soo-well) (English) from the sea wall. *Sywel*
Sexton (Sex-ton) (English) from the word sexton, a church official.
Sextus (Sex-tus) (Latin) sixth son.
Seymour (See-more) (Norman) from Saint Maur in Normandy. *Seamore, See, Seymore*
Shalom (Sha-**lom**) (Hebrew) peaceful.
Shanahan (Shan-a-han) (Irish) full of wisdom. *Shand*
Shane/Shayne (Shane) see Sean.
Shanley (Shan-lee) (Irish) small hero. *Shan, Shanlee, Shanly*
Shaw (Shaw) (Old English) from the wood. *Shawe*
Shay (Shay) (Irish) courteous. *Shai*
Sheehan (Shee-han) (Irish) small and tranquil. *Shehan, Shilan*
Sheldon (Shel-don) (Old English) from the shelter of the hill. *Shel, Shelden, Shelly*
Sherman (Sher-man) (Old English) shearman (literally, one who shears sheep).
Sherwin (Sher-win) (English) one who runs faster than the wind. Literally, wind-cutter.
Sherwood (Sher-wood) (English) from the bright forest. *Woodie, Woody*
Shimon (Shee-mon) (Hebrew) a form of Simon, which means God has heard.
Shiva (Shee-va) (Hindi) the name of the Hindu god of death and rebirth. *Shiv*
Sidney (Sid-nee) (English) land by the marsh. (Norman) from the place name Saint-Denis. *Sydney*
Sidwell (Sid-well) (English) from the wide stream.
Silas (Sye-lass) (Latin) a form of Silvan, meaning from the forest. *Sylas*
Silvan (Sil-van) (Latin) from the forest. *Sylvan*
Simon/Simeon (Sye-mon/**Sim**-ee-on) (Hebrew) God has heard. Name of several biblical figures, including one Apostle.
Simpson (Simp-son) (Hebrew) son of Simon.
Sinclair (Sin-**clair**) (Norman) originally meant from Saint-Clair in Normandy. The name is now strongly associated with Scotland. *Sinclare, Synclair*
Sinjon (Sin-jon) (Old English) Saint John. *Singe*
Skelly (Skel-ee) (Scottish) teller of stories.
Skelton (Skel-ton) (Dutch) shell town.
Skerry (Skeh-ree) (Scandinavian) from the stony island.
Skip (Skip) (Scandinavian) short form of Skipper, meaning captain of a boat.
Slane (Slane) (Czech) salt.
Smedley (Smed-lee) (English) from the flat clearing.
Snowden (Snow-den) (English) from the snowy mountain. *Snowy*

Sofian (So-**fee**-an) (Arabic) devout.
Solomon (**Sol**-o-mon) (Hebrew) peace. The son of King David and famous for his wisdom. *Sol, Solly*
Somerset (**Sum**-er-set) (Old English) from the summer land. The English county of this name was low-lying marshland which flooded in autumn, winter and spring, hence this name. *Somer, Somers*
Somerton (**Sum**-er-ton) (English) from the summer town. *Somer, Somers*
Somhairle (**Saw**-er-la) (Irish) summer traveller.
Sorrell (**Sor**-ell) (French) auburn. *Sorel*
Spear (**Speer**) (English) spear.
Spencer (**Spen**-ser) (Norman) literally, dispenser. Usually taken to be the name for someone whose job it was to dispense food from a kitchen. *Spence, Spenser*
Spiro (**Spy**-ro) (Greek) from the round basket. *Spi, Spiroh, Spiros, Spy, Spyro*
Stafford (**Staf**-ford) (Old English) from the landing place by the river. *Staff, Staffard*
Stamos (**Stam**-oss) Greek form of Stephen, which itself means crown or garland.
Stancliff (**Stan**-cliff) (English) from the stony cliff.
Standish (**Stand**-ish) (English) from the place of stones.
Stanford (**Stan**-ford) (Old English) from the rocky river crossing.
Stanislaus (**Stan**-iss-louse) (Latin) stand of glory. Saint Stanislaus was murdered while saying Mass and therefore went straight to heaven. Saint's day: 11 April. *Staneslaus, Stanis, Stanislus*
Stanley (**Stan**-lee) (English) from the stone clearing. *Stan, Stanlee, Stanly*
Stannard (**Stan**-ard) (English) hard as stone.
Starr (**Star**) (English) star. *Star*
Stavros (**Stav**-ross) A Greek form of Stephen, meaning crown or garland.
Steadman (**Sted**-man) (English) owner of a farmstead. *Stead, Steadmann*
Steinar (**Sty**-nar) (German) stone warrior. *Stein, Steiner*
Stephen (**Stee**-ven) (Greek) crown or garland. The first martyr in the Bible. *Stefan, Steve, Steven*
Sterling (**Ster**-ling) (English) little star. Now associated with the Scottish town.
Sterne (**Stern**) (German) star. (English) austere. *Stearne, Stern*
Steven (**Stee**-ven) see Stephen.
Stewart (**Stew**-art) (English) official of the royal household. *Stewert, Stu*
Stig (**Stig**) (Swedish) from the hill.
Sting (**Sting**) (English) spike of grain.
Stillman (**Still**-man) (English) quiet man. *Stilman*
Stockley (**Stock**-lee) (English) from the clearing of tree stumps. *Stock*
Stockton (**Stock**-ton) (English) from the town of tree stumps. Also the name of an English town. *Stock*

Stoddard (**Stod**-ard) (English) keeper of horses.
Stone (**Stone**) (English) stone.
Stratford (**Strat**-ford) (English) from the bridge over the river. Stratford-upon-Avon was the birthplace of William Shakespeare (1565–1616).
Strathan (**Stra**-han) (Irish) hidden.
Stratton (**Strat**-on) (Scottish) from the town in the river valley. *Straton*
Struthers (**Struth**-erz) (Irish) from the stream. *Strother, Strothers*
Stuart (**Stew**-art) French version of the name Stewart, which means official of the royal household. *Stu*
Sugden (**Sug**-den) (English) from the valley of sows. *Suggs*
Sullivan (**Sull**-iv-an) (Irish) black-eyed. Súill is Irish for eye.
Sutherland (**Suth**-er-land) (Scandinavian) southern land. The name of a county in northern Scotland.
Sven (**Sven**) (Scandinavian) youthful. *Svein, Svend, Swen*
Swain (**Swain**) (English) attendant to a knight. *Swaine, Swayne*
Swaley (**Sway**-lee) (English) from the clearing of the winding stream. *Swaly*
Sweeney (**Swee**-nee) (Irish) little hero.
Swinford (**Swin**-ford) (English) from the ford where the pigs cross the river.
Sylvester (Sill-**vest**-er) (Latin) from the woods. Saint's day: 31 December. *Silvester, Sly, Syl*

T

Tab (**Tab**) (English) a short form of Tabner, meaning drummer.
Tabner (**Tab**-ner) (English) drummer. (German/Old English) from the shining spring.
Tabor (Ta-**boar**) (Persian) drummer.
Tad (**Tad**) (Welsh) father. Also short for Thaddeus, meaning one who praises.
Tadan (Ta-**dan**) (Native American) bountiful.
Tadhg (**Tiyg** – sounds like 'tiger' without the 'er') Irish form of Tim, meaning he who honours God.
Tain (**Tay**-in) (Irish) from the stream. *Tayn*
Tadleigh (**Tad**-lee) (English) the poet from the clearing. *Tadlee, Tadly*
Tage (**Tah**-guh) (Scandinavian) day.
Taggart (**Tag**-art) (Irish) son of a priest.
Tal (**Tal**) (Hebrew) dew or light rain. (French) short for Talbot.
Talbot (**Tol**-bott) (French) shoemaker. *Tal, Talbott, Tally*
Talcott (**Tal**-cot) (English) from the cottage near the lake.
Talfryn (**Tal**-vrin) (Welsh) from the high hill.
Taliesin (Tal-**yess**-in) (Welsh) shining brow. A bard from Welsh legend with the gift of prophesy.

Tallon (**Ta**-lon) (Norman) claw or nail. *Talon*

Talmai (**Tal**-may) (Aramaic) from the small hill. *Tolmai*

Talman (**Tal**-man) (Aramaic) one who is beaten down.

Tam (**Tam**) (English) a short form of Thomas, meaning twin. (Hebrew) honest.

Taman (**Ta**-man) (Slavic) dark one.

Tamar (**Tay**-mar) (Hebrew) palm tree. Also the name of the river between Cornwall and Devon.

Tamir (Ta-**meer**) (Arabic) tall palm tree.

Tamson (**Tam**-son) (Scandinavian) son of Thomas.

Tane (Ta-**nay**) (Maori) one who husbands (i.e. farms the land).

Tanguy (**Ton**-ghee) (French) soldier.

Tanner (**Tan**-er) (English) one who works with leather. *Tan, Tann*

Tannin (**Tan**-in) (English) dark brown colour.

Tanton (**Tan**-ton) (English) from the town by the river.

Tarak (Ta-**rack**) (Sanskrit) protector.

Taran (Ta-**ran**) (Sanskrit) heavenly.

Taree (Ta-**ree**) (Australian) from the fig tree.

Tarleton (**Tarl**-ton) (English) from the town of Thor (the Norse god of thunder). *Tareton*

Tariq (Ta-**reek**) (Arabic) conqueror.

Taron (Ta-**ron**) (American) a combination of Tad and Ron.

Tarrant (**Ta**-rant) (Welsh) thunder.

Tarun (Ta-**run**) (Sanskrit) youthful.

Tate (**Tate**) (Scandinavian) of a cheerful character. *Tait, Tayt*

Tavish (**Tav**-ish) Scottish form of Thomas, which means twin. *Tavis*

Taz (**Taz**) (Arabic) from a small cup.

Teagan (Tee-**gan**) (Irish) a poet or bard. *Teague*

Teale (**Teel**) (English) small duck.

Tearlach (**Tar**-lack) Scottish form of Charles, meaning free man.

Tearle (**Turl**) (English) stern-minded, full of gravitas.

Ted/Teddy (**Ted**/**Ted**-ee) (English) short for Edward, Edwin and Theodore.

Telamon (**Tel**-a-mon) (Greek) bearing fruit. In mythology, the father of Ajax, a Greek hero who fought at Troy.

Telek (**Tel**-ek) Polish form of Telford, which means iron-worker.

Telem (**Tel**-em) (Hebrew) from the gentle hill.

Telford (**Tel**-ford) (French) iron-worker.

Teller (**Tel**-er) (English) counter or storyteller. *Telly*

Telly (**Tel**-ee) (Greek) short form of Theodore, meaning gift of God. (English) short form of Teller.

Teman (**Tem**-an) (Hebrew) from the right-hand side.

Templeton (**Temp**-ul-ton) (English) from the town of the temple. *Temple*

Tennant (**Ten**-ant) (English) one who rents land or property.

Tennessee (Ten-ess-ee) (American) originally the Cherokee word for mighty warrior, but now best know as the name of the US state.

Tennyson (Ten-iss-un) (English) a form of Dennison, meaning son of Dennis. Name of famous Victorian poet, Alfred Lord Tennyson.

Terach (Tair-ack) (Hebrew) ibex, wild goat. In the Bible, a descendent of Shem.

Terence (Tair-ence) (Latin) gracious. *Terance, Terrance, Terrence*

Terrick (Tair-ik) (American) Derrick with the Te– prefix.

Terry (Tair-ee) (English) the short form of Terence. *Terri*

Teva (Tay-va) (Hebrew) at one with nature. *Tevah*

Tevis (Tev-iss) a Scottish form of Thomas, meaning twin.

Thad (Thad) a short form of Thaddeus.

Thaddeus (Thad-ee-us) (Latin) one who praises. (Greek) courageous. Also one of the twelve Apostles. *Thaddius, Thadeus, Thadius*

Thady (Thay-dee) (Irish) one who gives praise. *Thad, Thaddy*

Thalmus (Thal-mus) (Greek) blossoming.

Thane (Thane) (Old English) noble warrior. In the Anglo-Saxon social hierarchy, a thane was one level above a freeman and one level below an earl. *Thain, Thayn*

Thanos (Tha-nos) (Greek) bear man, noble man.

Thatcher (Thatch-er) (English) builder of roofs. *Thatch*

Thaw (Thaw) (English) from the melting ice.

Thayer (Thay-er) (French) soldier of the army. *Thay, Thayar*

Theo (Thee-oh) based on the Greek word for God. Short for Theobald, Theodore, Theodoric and Theophilus.

Theobald (Thee-oh-bald) (Greek/German) an amalgam meaning God's brave people or God's brave ruler. *Theo*

Theodore (Thee-oh-dore) (Greek) gift of God. Saint Theodore was a monk and bishop who specialized in thwarting insect plagues by prayer. Saint's day: 22 April. *Theo*

Theodoric (Thee-**odd**-or-ic) (Greek/German) ruler of God's people. *Theo*

Theophilus (Thee-**off**-ill-us) (Greek) loved by God. *Theo*

Theron (Thair-on) (Greek) hunter. *Theryon*

Theseus (Thee-see-us) (Greek) in Greek mythology, the hero who killed the Minotaur. He was the lover of Ariadne, who helped him escape the Labyrinth.

Thierry (Tyair-**ee** – the first part rhymes with 'chair'). French form of Theodoric, meaning ruler of God's people.

Thomas/Tom (Tom-as/**Tom**) (Aramaic) twin. An Apostle famous for doubting the resurrection, and patron saint of doubters. Saint's day: 3 July. *Thom, Thomes, Thomus, Tom, Tommy*

Thor (**Thaw**/**Thaw**-rin) (Norse) named after the Scandinavian god of thunder. *Thorin, Thorr, Thors, Tor*

Thorald (**Thaw**-rald) (Scandinavian) follower of Thor. *Thor*

Thorbert (**Thaw**-bert) (Scandinavian) Thor bright. *Thor*

Thorburn (**Thaw**-burn) (Scandinavian) Thor's bear. *Thor*

Thorleif (**Thaw**-leaf) (Scandinavian) loved by Thor. *Thor*

Thorley (**Thaw**-lee) (Scandinavian/ English) from Thor's clearing. *Thor*

Thormond (**Thaw**-mond) (Scandinavian) protected by Thor. *Thor*

Thorn (**Thorn**) (English) thorn. *Thor, Thorne*

Thornley (**Thorn**-lee) (English) from the clearing of the thorns. *Thor, Thorne*

Thornton (**Thorn**-ton) (English) from the town of the thorns. *Thor, Thorne*

Thurlow (**Thur**-low) (Scandinavian/ English) from Thor's hill.

Thurman (**Thur**-man) (Scandinavian/ English) servant of Thor.

Thurston (**Thur**-ston) (Scandinavian) Thor's stone. *Torsten, Torston*

Tiarnach (**Teer**-nack) Irish spelling of Tiernan, which means lord.

Tibbot (**Tib**-bot) (Irish) courageous. *Tib*

Tibor (**Tee**-bor) (Hungarian) from a spiritual place. *Tib*

Tiernan (**Tier**-nan) (Irish) lord. (Tierney is the gender-neutral form of this name – see the gender-neutral list.)

Tiger (**Tie**-ger) (American) tiger.

Tilden (**Til**-den) (English) from the tilled valley. *Til, Till*

Tiford (**Tif**-ford) (English) from the rich ford. *Tyford*

Tilon (**Till**-on) (Hebrew) murmuring. *Til, Till*

Tilton (**Til**-tun) (English) from the rich town. *Til, Till*

Timon (**Tie**-mon) (Greek) honourable. *Timon of Athens* was an early play by Shakespeare. *Tymon*

Timothy (**Tim**-oth-ee) (Greek) he who honours God. His saint's day is 26 January. *Tim*

Timur (Tim-**oor**) (Russian) conqueror. Also a version of the Hebrew name Tamar, meaning palm tree. *Tim*

Titus (**Tie**-tuss) (Latin) hero. (Greek) giant. The name of a Roman Emperor (reigned AD 79–81). Titus was best known for crushing the Jewish revolt in AD 70 when he was Governor of Judea. Saint's day: 26 January.

Toal (**Too**-ul) English form of the Gaelic Tuathal, which means ruler of the people.

Tobias (Toe-**by**-as) (Hebrew) God is good. *Tobi, Tobin, Toby, Tobyas*

Todd (**Tod**) (Old English) fox-like. *Tod, Toddy*

Togar (**Toe**-gar) (Australian) smoke.

Toland (**Tol**-and) (English) owner of taxed land. *Tolland*

Toller (**Tol**-er) (English) one who collects taxes. *Toll*

Tomer (**Toe**-mer) (Hebrew) tall. *Tome*
Tomlin (**Tom**-lin) (English) little Tom.
Tony (**Toe**-nee) shortened form of Anthony, which means praiseworthy and priceless.
Topper (**Top**-er) (English) from the top of the hill. *Top, Topp, Topps*
Tor (**Tor**) (Scandinavian) thunder.
Torgar (**Tor**-gar) (Scandinavian/English) spear of thunder. *Tor, Torr*
Torin (Tor-**in**) (Gaelic) chief. *Tor, Torr, Toryn*
Torkel (**Tor**-kel) (Scandinavian) from Thor's cauldron. *Tork*
Tormod (**Tor**-mod) (Scottish) from the north. *Tor, Tormynd, Torr*
Torr (**Tor**) (English) from the hill or tower.
Torsten (**Tor**-sten) (Scandinavian) from Thor's stone. *Tor, Tors, Torstyn*
Townsend (**Towns**-end) (English) from the edge of town.
Trahern (Tra-**hern**) (Welsh) strong as iron.
Travis (**Tra**-viss) (French) meaning to cross, or crossroads. *Travers*
Trayton (**Tray**-ton) (Latin) torrent. (English) from the town of trees.
Tremain (Tre-**main**) (Cornish) from the house of stone. *Tremayne, Tramaine, Tremane, Tremen*
Trent (**Trent**) (Latin) fast-flowing stream, or torrent. Name of a river in the English East Midlandsand, and of the cricket ground Trent Bridge. *Trente*
Treston (**Tress**-ton) Welsh form of Tristan, which means riotous and noisy. *Trestyn*
Trevor (**Tre**-vor) (Irish) cautious. (Welsh) from the big village. The Welsh version is spelled Trefor, but pronounced the same.
Trey (**Tray**) (English) the third son (trey is an old word for three).
Tristan (**Triss**-tan) (Welsh) riotous and noisy. One of the Knights of the Round Table who fell passionately in love with his father's new young wife. They eloped together and ended up buried side by side. *Trestan, Trestyn, Trist, Tristen, Tristyn*
Tristram (**Triss**-tram) (French) sorrowful.
Troy (**Troy**) (French) from the French city of Troyes, itself named after the ancient city of Troy. *Troye*
Truman (**True**-man) (Old English) honest man.
Tucker (**Tuck**-er) (Old English) a fuller of cloth.
Tudor (**Tyoo**-der) Welsh form of Theodore, meaning gift of God. Also the name of the royal dynasty that ruled England and Wales from 1485 to 1603.
Tullis (**Tull**-iss) (Latin) one who bears a title. *Tull, Tullice, Tully*
Tully (**Tull**-ee) (Latin) a form of Tullis. (Irish) at peace with God.
Twain (**Twain**) (English) of two parts. *Twaine, Twayn*

Twyford (**Twy**-ford) (English) from the double river-crossing.
Tycho (**Tie**-ko) (Greek) one who hits the mark.
Ty/Tye (**Tie**) (English) short forms of Tyler, Tyrone and Tyrus.
Tyler (**Tie**-ler) (English) one who makes tiles.
Tymon (**Ti**-mon) the Polish form of Timothy, which means he who honours God.
Tynan (**Tie**-nan) (Celtic) dark one.
Tyree (**Tye**-ree) (Scottish) place name. From the island off the west coast of Scotland.
Tyrell (**Ti**-rel) (German) thunder ruler.
Tyrone (**Tye**-rone) (Irish) from the land of Owen. (Greek) monarch. *Tyrus*
Tzuriel (**Tzur**-ee-el) (Hebrew) God is my rock.

U

Uaine (**You**-an) Irish form of Owen, meaning well-born.
Ualtar (**Ul**-tar) Irish form of Walter, which means leader of an army.
Udell (**Oo**-dell) (English) from the valley of the yew trees. *Eudall, Udall, Udel*
Ugo (**Oo**-go) Italian form of Hugo, from the German name Hughbert, which means bright of mind.
Ulbrecht (**Ull**-brekt) a German form of Albert, which means noble knight.
Ulric (**Ull**-rik) (German) ruler of the wolves. *Ulrich*
Ultan (**Ull**-tan) (Irish) Ulsterman. (German) noble stone. *Ulten*
Ulysses (**You**-liss-eez) (Latin) wanderer. A wily Greek hero who took ten years to return from the Trojan War because he faced myriad adversities along the way. The Greek form of his name is Odysseus.
Umar (**Oo**-mar) (Arabic) flourishing. *Umarh, Umarr*
Umberto (Um-**bear**-toe) Italian form of Hubert or the German Hughbert, meaning bright of mind. Saint Hubert saw a crucifix between the horns of a stag when he was hunting and thereby became the patron saint of hunters. Later he was famous for performing miracles. Saint's day: 3 November.
Upton (**Up**-ton) (English) from the upper town.
Uriah (Yoo-**rye**-a) (Hebrew) God is my light. Uriah was a soldier of King David, who slept with Uriah's wife and then had Uriah killed.
Urian (**You**-ree-an) (Greek) from heaven. *Urien*
Uziel (**You**-zeel) (Hebrew) God is my strength.

V

Vaclav (**Vats**-lav) (Czech) crowned in glory.
Vadin (**Va**-din) (Hindi) good with words.
Valdemar (**Vall**-de-mar) (Swedish) powerful ruler.
Valentine (**Val**-en-tine) (Latin) healthy and strong. Strongly associated with the famous third-century saint who died for his love. His saint's day is 14 February which, by coincidence, was also the pagan day for lovers. *Valentin, Valentyne*
Valerian (Val-**air**-ee-an) (Latin) strong and healthy.
Vallis (**Val**-iss) (French) from Wales.
Van (**Van**) (Dutch) literally, from (a place), although the name also implies nobility. *Vann*
Vance (**Vance**) (Old English) man from the marsh. *Vanse*
Vanda (**Van**-da) (Dutch) he belongs. *Vander*
Varden (**Var**-den) (Old English) from the verdant hill. *Vardyn*
Vartan (**Var**-tan) (Armenian) rose grower.
Vaughn (**Vorn**) (Welsh) small. *Vaughan*
Verlin (**Ver**-lin) (Latin) blooming. *Verl*
Verney (**Ver**-nee) (French) from the alder grove.
Vernon (**Ver**-non) (French) from the place where alders grow. (French) springtime. *Vern, Vernen, Verney*
Victor (**Vic**-tor) (Latin) yes, it means victorious. *Viktor*
Viking (**Vye**-king) (Scandinavian) sea traveller.
Vincent (**Vin**-sent) (Latin) to be victorious. *Vin, Vincente, Vinn*
Virgil (**Verge**-ill) (Latin) bearer of the staff. *Vergil*
Vitus (**Vye**-tuss) (Latin) full of vitality.
Vladimir (Vlad-ee-**meer**) (Russian) famous prince. *Vlad, Vlada, Vladamir*
Volney (**Vol**-nee) (German) spirit of the nation.

Wade (**Wade**) (Old English) crosser of the river. *Wayde*

Wagner (**Wag**-ner) (German) wagoner. *Waggner, Wagnar*

Wainwright (**Wain**-rite) (English) maker of wagons.

Wake (**Wake**) (English) awake. Hereward the Wake was a famous English resister of the Norman Conquest. He was leader of a rebellion in the Fenlands of East Anglia.

Wakeley (**Wake**-lee) (English) from the wet meadow.

Wakeman (**Wake**-man) (English) watchman.

Walcott (**Wall**-cot) (English) from the cottage by the wall.

Waldemar (**Vall**-de-mar) (German) powerful ruler. *Valdemar*

Walden (**Wall**-den) (English) from the wooded valley. *Wald, Waldo, Waldy*

Waldron (**Wall**-dron) (English) ruler. *Wald, Waldo, Waldy*

Walford (**Wall**-ford) (English) from the ford of the Welsh. *Wald, Waldo, Waldy*

Walker (**Walk**-er) (English) cloth worker. *Walk, Wally*

Wallace (**Woll**-iss) (English) foreigner. Popular in Scotland, thanks to the national hero, William Wallace.

Waller (**Vall**-er) (German) powerful.

Walter (**Wall**-ter) (German) leader of an army. The name was introduced by the Normans and is often shortened to Walt. Saint Walter was made an abbot against his will, so he kept running away from the abbey. Each time they got him back, until one day he escaped to Rome to give his resignation directly to the Pope. The Pope asked him to stay as abbot and Walter agreed, thereby becoming a saint. Saint's day: 8 April. *Walder, Wally, Walt, Waltur, Wat*

Walton (**Wall**-ton) (English) from the walled town. *Walt*

Walworth (**Wall**-worth) (English) from the fenced farm.

Walwyn (**Wall**-win) (English) friend from Wales.

Wanbi (**Wan**-bee) (Australian) dingo.

Ward (**Ward**) (English) guardian.

Wardell (**War**-dell) (English) watchman from the hill.

Warden (**War**-den) (English) guardian of the valley.

Wardley (**Ward**-lee) (English) guardian of the clearing. *Wardly*

Warford (**War**-ford) (English) guardian of the crossing.

Warner (**War**-ner) (German) defender of the town. *Warne*

Warren (**Wor**-en) (German) guard or warden. (Norman) gamepark.

Warwick (**Wor**-ick) (English) watcher of the weir.

Watson (**Wot**-son) (English) son of Walter. *Watsen*
Wayman (**Way**-man) (English) traveller.
Wayne (**Wain**) (English) one who works with wagons. *Wain, Waine, Wayn*
Webley (**Web**-lee) (English) from the weaver's meadow. *Webb*
Webster (**Web**-ster) (English) one who weaves. *Webb*
Weddel (**Wed**-ul) (English) from the valley of the ford. *Weddyl*
Welborne (**Well**-born) (English) from the brook sourced from a spring.
Wellington (**Well**-ing-ton) (English) originally from a town in Somerset. Now associated with the Duke who won the Battle of Waterloo. He took this title despite no member of his family having lived in Wellington for 600 years.
Wen (**Wen**) (Romany) born in winter.
Wendell (**Wen**-dell) (German) wanderer. (English) from the good valley. *Wendel, Wendyl, Wendyll*
Wenlock (**Wen**-lock) (Welsh) from the monastery by the lake.
Wesley (**Wez**-lee) (Old English) from the clearing in the west. It was the surname of the founder of the Methodist Church. *Wes*
Weston (**West**-on) (Old English) from the town in the west. *Wes*
Wharton (**War**-ton) (English) from the town by the lake.
Wheatley (**Weet**-lee) (English) from the wheat field.
Wheaton (**Weet**-on) (English) from the wheat town.
Wickham (**Wick**-am) (English) from the village enclosure.
Whistler (**Wiss**-ler) (English) whistler or piper.
Whitley (**Wit**-lee) (English) from the white clearing. *Wit*
Whitlock (**Wit**-lock) (English) white-haired. *Wit*
Whitman (**Wit**-man) (English) white-haired man. *Wit*
Whitmore (**Wit**-more) (English) from the white moor. *Wit*
Wickley (**Wick**-lee) (English) from the village green.
Wilbur (**Wil**-burr) (English) from the walled town. Also, from the bright willows. *Wilbyr, Will*
Wilder (**Wilde**-er) (English) wild and free. *Will, Wild*
Wildon (**Will**-don) (English) from the wooded hill. *Will*
Willard (**Will**-ard) (German) determined. *Will*
William (**Will**-ee-am) (German) strong protector. Often shortened to Bill or Billy. Saint's day: 6 April. *Bill, Billy, Will, Willie, Wills, Willy*
Willoughby (**Will**-o-bee) (English) from the farm of willows. *Will*
Wilstan (**Will**-stan) (German) from the wolf's stone. *Will*
Wilton (**Will**-ton) (English) from the farm of the well. *Will*

Windell (**Win**-dell) (English) from the windy valley. *Wyndell*
Winfield (**Win**-field) (English) from the friendly field.
Winston (**Win**-ston) (English) from the friendly town of victory. *Win, Winnie, Winny*
Winthrop (**Win**-thrup) (English) victory at the crossroads. *Win, Winnie, Winny*
Winward (**Win**-ward) (English) friend from the wood. *Win, Winnie, Winny*
Wit (**Wit**) (English) full of life and humour.
Wolfe (**Wolf**) (German) a diminutive of Wolfgang, meaning one who walks with the wolves. (English) wolf. Saint Wolfgang gained his sainthood by forcing Satan to build a church. *Wolf*
Woodley (**Wood**-lee) (English) from the clearing in the wood. *Wood, Woody*
Woodrow (**Wood**-roe) (Old English) from a row of cottages in the wood. *Wood, Woody*
Wyatt (**Wye**-at) (French) small soldier.
Wyborn (**Wye**-born) (Scandinavian) war bear. *Wybourn, Wybourne*
Wyman (**Wye**-man) (Old English) soldier.
Wymer (**Wye**-mer) (Old English) famous warrior. *Weimar, Wymar*
Wyndham (**Wind**-am) (Scottish) from the village near the winding stream. *Win, Winn, Winny*
Wystan (**Wiss**-tan) (Old English) battle stone.

Xanthus (**Zan**-thus) (Latin) golden-haired. *Zanthus*
Xavier (**Za**-vee-yay) (Basque) boy from the new house. Francis Xavier was the founder of the Jesuits.
Xenos (**Zen**-os) (Greek) foreigner. Short form of Xenophon.
Xylon (**Zy**-lon) (Greek) from the forest.

Yabarak (**Ya**-ba-rak) (Australian) from the sea.
Yadid (Ya-**deed**) (Hebrew) loving friend.
Yale (**Yale**) (Scottish) vigorous. Now associated with the American University. Yale means old in medieval English.
Yan (**Yan**) Russian form of John, meaning favoured by God. *Yann*
Yana (**Yon**-uh) (Native American) bear.
Yanni (**Yan**-ee) Greek form of John, meaning favoured by God.
Yanto (**Yan**-toe) a Welsh form of John, meaning favoured by God.

Yardley (**Yard**-lee) (English) from the enclosed meadow. *Yard, Yardly*
Yates (**Yates**) (English) gates. *Yeats*
Yehudi (Yeh-**hoo**-dee) (Hebrew) a form of Judah, which means praised.
Yestin (**Yes**-tin) (Welsh) form of Justin, meaning just.
Yeoman (**Yo**-man) (English) retainer.
Yitzchak (**Yits**-zhack) (Hebrew) a form of Isaac, which means he who laughs.
Yorick (**Yor**-ik) (English) farmer. The Scandinavian form of George and the name of the skull in *Hamlet*.
Yosef (**Yo**-sef) (Hebrew) a form of Joseph, meaning God will add. Now most common in Slavic countries.
Yosu (**Yo**-soo) (Hebrew) a form of Jesus.
Yule (**Yool**) (English) born at Christmas. *Yul*
Yves (**Eve**) The French form of Ivor, meaning army of archers. *Eve, Ives*

Z

Zac (**Zak**) (Hebrew) a short form of Zachariah, meaning God has remembered.
Zachariah (Zak-a-**rye**-a) (Hebrew) God has remembered. The father of John the Baptist. Usually shortened to Zac.
Zahir (Za-**here**) (Arabic) shining bright.
Zale (**Zale**) (Greek) strength from the sea.
Zarek (**Za**-rek) (Polish) God save the king. *Zarec*
Zebadiah (Ze-ba-**die**-a) (Hebrew) God's gift. Usually shortened to Zeb.
Zebedee (**Zeb**-ed-ee) (Hebrew) God has given. Father of James and John, two of the Apostles.
Zebulon (**Zeb**-yoo-lon) (Hebrew) honoured and exalted.
Zedekiah (Zed-a-**kye**-a) (Hebrew) God is strong and just.
Zephyr (**Zef**-er) (Greek) west wind. Often shortened to Zeph.
Zeus (**Zyoos**) (Greek) ruler of the Greek gods. Associated with power and good luck.

A–Z of Gender-neutral names

Aidan (**Aid**-an) (Irish) fire. It is an ncreasingly popular name in recent years. Saint Aidan founded a monastery on Lindisfarne in the seventh century. His saint's day is 31 August. *Adan, Adin, Aiden, Ayden*

Ainsley (**Ainz**-lee) (English) from the meadow. *Ainslee, Ainslie*

Albany (**All**-ban-ee) (English/Latin) an anglicized version of Alban, meaning white. Also means a resident of the ancient city of Alba Longa southeast of Rome. Saint Alban was Britain's first martyr to be executed for his faith.

Angel (**Ain**-jel) (Greek) messenger of God. Gender neutral in North America, but a girl's name in most other English-speaking countries.

Arden (**Are**-den) (Latin) ardent. (English) from the forest of Arden. The maiden name of Shakespeare's mother and the name of a forest near Stratford-upon-Avon, which was the setting for his play *As You Like It*. *Ard, Arda, Ardie, Ardin, Ardon, Arrden*

Ari (**Ah**-ree) (Hebrew) a short form of Ariel, meaning lion of God.

Ariel (**Ah**-ree-el) (Hebrew) lion of God. Also the name of a spirit in Shakespeare's play, *The Tempest*.

Asa (**Ace**-a) (Hebrew) healer or doctor. Particularly common in the English West Midlands. *Ase, Aza*

Ash (**Ash**) (English) from the ash tree. Also a short form of Ashley.

Ashley (**Ash**-lee) (English) from the clearing of ash trees. In the top ten most popular names in Canada and the USA.

Aspen (**Asp**-en) (English) from the name of the aspen tree.

Aubrey (**Awe**-bree) (Old English) elf counsel.

Audrey (**Awe**-dree) (Old English) noble strength. In use since the seventh century, and a Shakespearian character in *As you Like It*. Actress Audrey Hepburn caused a great increase in its popularity.

Austin (**Ost**-in) (Latin) venerable or consecrated. Originally derived from Augustine (see boys' names), the name is becoming increasingly associated with the Texan city of the same name.

Avery (**Ave**-er-ee) based on an Old English word meaning ruler of the elves. This is actually the Norman pronunciation of that word. *Averey, Avry*

Avon (**Ave**-on) (Celtic) river. In Welsh, *afon*, in Gaelic, *abhainn*.

B

Bailey (**Bay**-lee) (English) from the berry clearing. (Norman) bailiff or fortification. (Irish) home. *Baile, Bailee, Bailly, Baily, Baleigh, Baley, Bali, Bayla, Baylee, Baylie*

Bailon (**Bay**-lon) American version of Bailey.

Barrie (**Ba**-ree) (Celtic) spear. (Canadian) named after a city in southern Ontario. Also a feminine version of Barry. *Bari, Barri*

Bentley (**Bent**-lee) (Old English) from the clearing overgrown with bent grass. *Ben, Bentlea, Bentlee, Bentlie, Bently, Lee*

Bevin (**Bev**-in) (Irish) an anglicized form of the Gaelic name Béibhinn, meaning good-looking one.

Billie (**Bill**-ee) (English) a short form of William, meaning strong protector. (German) a short form of Wilhelmina (the feminine version of Wilhelm, which is the German form of William). *Billa, Billee, Billi, Billie-Jean, Billie-Jo, Billie-Sue, Billina, Billy, Billye, Willa*

Blaine (**Blain**) (Gaelic) yellow.

Blair (**Blare**) (Gaelic) battleground.

Blaise (**Blaze**) (Latin) stuttering. (English) flame. Saint Blaise was a fourth-century bishop and martyr. His feast day is 3 February.

Blake (**Blake**) (English) dark and handsome. *Blakely*

Blyth (**Blithe**) (English) merry. Also the name of rivers in Northumberland and Suffolk. *Blythe*

Bo (**Bo**) (Chinese) precious. Also a short form for names beginning with Bo, such as Boris and Bonnie.

Bobbie (**Bob**-ee) (German) bright fame. (English) a diminutive of Barbara and Robert.

Brayden (**Bray**-den) (Irish/Gaelic) descendant of Bradán, which is Irish for salmon, and he's also a figure in Irish folklore. *Bradden, Braddon, Bradin, Bradon, Braeden, Braedon*

Brice (**Brice**) (French) dappled or freckled. (Welsh) alert and ambitious. *Bryce*

Brook (**Brook**) (English) from the brook or stream. *Brooke*

C

Caley (**Kay**-lee) (Irish) slender, lean. *Cailey, Cale, Coley, Kaley, Kayley*

Cameron (**Cam**-er-un) (Scottish) crooked nose. A Scottish clan name and surname, now used as a first name for both sexes. *Cam, Camaron, Cami, Cammy, Camron*

Campbell (**Cam**-bull) (Scottish) crooked mouth. *Cambell, Cammie, Camp, Campie, Campy*

Caolan (**Kay**-lan) (Gaelic) slender. *Caelan, Cailey*

Carmel (**Car**-mel) (Hebrew) garden. Also a town in California.

Caroll (**Ca**-rol) (Old German) a form of Charles, meaning free man. *Caroll, Cary, Caryl, Caryll*

Carey (**Care**-ee) (Irish) castle. (Welsh) from the river. (Cornish) loved one. *Care, Cari, Cary, Karey*

Carlin (**Car**-lin) (Cornish) from the fort by the pool. (Irish) little champion. *Carlan, Carle, Carlen, Carlie, Carly*

Carson (**Car**-sun) (Scottish) son of Carr, meaning one who dwells by the marsh. *Carsyn, Karsen, Karson*

Casey (**Case**-ee) (Irish) observant. The name of an American train driver hero, Casey Jones, who tried to prevent a crash with a freight train and save the lives of those on board, but died himself in the attempt. Kasey is the American spelling. (There's no K in the Irish language.)

Cassidy (**Cass**-id-ee) (Gaelic) clever. *Cass, Cassady, Cassedy*

Cedar (**See**-der) (Latin) from the name of the tree.

Chance (**Chance**) (Old English) blessed by fortune. (French) a form of Chauncey, which means chancellor. *Chanse, Chantz, Chanze, Chaunce, Chauncey, Chauncy*

Chaney (**Chain**-ee) (French) from the oak tree.

Charlie (**Char**-lee) Nickname for Charles, which means free man.

Cherokee (**Cher**-oh-kee) (Native American) the tribal name of the native American Cherokee.

Chris (**Kris**) diminutive of Christopher, Christine and Christian.

Christian (**Kris**-tee-un) (Greek) anointed. The name of ten Danish kings. *Kristian, Kristien*

Chrysander (Kris-**an**-der) (Greek) golden.

Clancy (**Clan**-see) (Irish) son of Flannchadh. Flannchadh is an ancient Irish name, meaning red warrior. *Clancey, Claney*

Clarry (**Cla**-ree) (Latin) from the girl's name Clara, meaning clear and bright. (Irish) from the boy's name Clarence, meaning from Clare, the Irish county.

Cody (**Coe**-dee) (English) cushion. (Gaelic) descendant of Cuidightheach, which means one who helps. *Code, Codey, Codie, Cuddy, Kodey, Kodi, Kody*

Colby (**Coll**-bee) (English/ Scandinavian) from the coal village. *Colbee, Colbey, Colbie, Collby, Kolby*

Connor (**Conn**-er) (Irish) lofty desires. Also the name of a legendary Irish king. *Con, Conn, Conner, Kon, Konner*

Corey (**Core**-ee) (Irish) from the hollow. *Correy, Corrianne, Corrie, Corry, Cory*

Courtney (**Court**-nee) (Norman) one who waits at court. *Cortenay, Corteney, Cortnee, Cortney, Cortny, Courtenay*

Crisiant (**Kris**-ee-ant) (Welsh) crystal. *Cris, Crissie, Kristy*

Cymry (**Kum**-ree) (Welsh) derived from the word *Cymru*, the Welsh for Wales.

D

Dacey (**Dace**-ee) (Gaelic) from the south.

Dai (**Die**) (Welsh) beloved and adored one. (Japanese) great.

Dakota (Da-**coe**-ta) (Native American) trusted friend. Also the name of a US state.

Daley (**Daily**) (English) from the clearing in the valley. *Dailey, Daily*

Dallas (**Dal**-ass) place name of a Scottish town and a Texan city.

Dani (**Dan**-ee) (English) nickname for Daniel or Danielle.

Dana (**Dan**-a) (Old English/ Scandinavian) from Denmark. (Czech) God is my judge.

Dara (**Da**-ra) (Irish) son of oak. (Hebrew) compassionate and wise.

Darby (**Dar**-bee) (Irish) free from envy. (Old English) deer settlement.

Darcy (**Dar**-see) (French) originally brought to England by Norman D'Arcy, a companion of William the Conqueror. Immortalized by Jane Austen in *Pride and Prejudice*. *Darcey, Darsey, Darsy*

Darnell (**Dar**-nl) (Old English) from the hidden place. *Darnall, Darneil, Darnel, Darnyl*

Dayton (**Day**-ton) (Old English) from the sunny town. Also the name of a city in Ohio, USA. *Daytan, Dayten*

Dee (**Dee**) (Old English) dark. Also a short form of names beginning with the letter D.

Del (**Dell**) (English) the short-form of Delphine and Delaney.

Dell (**Dell**) (English) from the small hollow. Also short for Udell, meaning from the valley of the yew trees.

Delaney (De-**lane**-ee) (Irish) descended from the challenger.

Derry (**Derry**) (Irish) oak grove. Also a place name, surname and original name of the Irish city of Londonderry. *Derrie*

Deryn (**Dair**-in) (Welsh) bird. *Deren, Derhyn, Deron, Derran, Derrin*
Devan (**Dev**-un) (French) the female version is derived from the name Divine. (English) the male derivation is from the county name Devon. *Devane, Devaun, Deven, Devin, Devyn*
Devin (**Dev**-in) (Irish) bard or poet. (French) divine. *Dev, Deven, Devine, Devinn*
Devon (**Dev**-un) (Old English) a county in England noted for its cream teas! *Devan, Devana, Devanna, Deven, Devin*
Dexter (**Dex**-ter) (Latin) right-handed, good with the hands. *Dex, Dexton, Dexy*
Diamond (**Die**-a-mund) (Latin) from the name of the precious stone.
Dillon (**Dill**-un) (Irish) faithful. *Dylon*
Dion (**Dee**-on) (Greek) a short form of Dionysus, the god of wine, celebrations and excess.
Donnelly (**Don**-el-ee) (Celtic) brown and dark. The Irish for brown is *donn*.
Dorian (**Dor**-ee-un) (Greek) of the sea. In *The Picture of Dorian Gray*, by Oscar Wilde, Dorian is granted a wish that his portrait in the attic ages while he remains young and handsome. *Dorean, Dorien*
Drew (**Droo**) (French) favourite. (Celtic) druid. Also a short form of Andrew, meaning strong man.
Dusty (**Dust**-ee) English) the gender-neutral form of Dustin, meaning warrior. Usually used for boys in North America and for girls in other countries.
Dylan (**Dill**-un) (Welsh) son of the sea. Also the name of a legendary Welsh hero. *Dillan, Dillon, Dyllon*

Eddie (**Ed**-ee) (English) rich guard. Often used as a short form of names beginning with Ed, such as Edward, Eden, Edsel, Edgar and Edmund. *Ed, Eddy*
Eden (**Ee**-dun) (Hebrew) an idyllic place. (Old English) bear cub.
Edsel (**Ed**-sel) English) from a rich home.
Elan (Eh-**lan**) (French) dashing and spirited.
Ellery (**Ell**-er-ee) (Old English) from the alder tree. (Latin) a form of Hilary, which means cheerful. *Ellary, Ellerey*
Ellis (**Ell**-iss) (English) an anglicization of Elias, which is a form of the Hebrew name Elijah, meaning the Lord is my God. *Eliss, Elliston*
Elton (**Ell**-tun) (Old English) from the old town. *Alton, Elden, Eldon*
Emer (**Ee**-mer) (Celtic) ready and swift. The name of a mythical character who fell in love with the hero Cuchullainn. The Scottish spelling is usually Eimhear, the Irish usually Eimear.

Emmanuel (Em-**an**-you-el) (Hebrew) literally, God is with us. *Emanual, Emanuel, Emanuele, Emmanual, Imanuel, Immanuel, Immanuele*

Emmet (**Em**-it) (Old English) truth. *Emmit, Emmitt, Emmot, Emmott*

Enda (**En**-da) (Irish) bird-like. Saint Enda was a sixth-century monk associated with the Aran Islands off the west coast of Ireland.

Ennis (**En**-iss) (Irish) one and only chance. Place name of a town in western Ireland.

Ennor (**En**-or) (Cornish) from the boundary.

Erin (**Air**-in) (Irish) peace. Also the name of an Irish goddess and the original name for Ireland before the Romans called it Hibernia. *Erinne, Errin, Eryn, Erynn, Erinna, Erynna*

Eryl (**Air**-ill) (Welsh) one who watches. *Eril, Erol, Errell, Erroll, Erryl*

Esme (**Ez**-mee) (Old French) one who is esteemed and loved. *Esmee*

Evan (**Ev**-an) (Celtic) young warrior. (Welsh) a form of John, meaning favoured by God. Also a short form of Evangelos, which means bringer of good news. *Evyn*

Evelyn (**Eve**-lin/**Ev**-a-lin) (Norman) from the place name Aveline in northern France. (Old German) hazelnut. *Eveline*

Everild (**Ev**-er-ild) (Old English) slayer.

Fallon/Faren (**Fa**-lon/**Fa**-ren) (Irish) grandchild of the ruler. (Old English) traveller. Generally, the boy's name is spelled Fallon, and the girl's Faren. *Falyn*

Fernley (**Fern**-lee) (English) from the field of ferns. *Fern, Fernly*

Flynn (**Flin**) (Irish) of a ruddy complexion. *Flin, Flinn, Flyn*

Fortune (**For**-tune) (Latin) lucky. *Fortino*

Frankie/Franky (**Frank**-ee) (Latin) a person from France. A pet name for Frances (for girls) and Frank (for boys).

Gabby (**Gab**-ee) (English) an anglicized version of the Hebrew name Gabriel. *Gabe, Gabi,*

Gabriel (**Gabe**-ree-el) (Hebrew) God is my strength. One of the seven Archangels, celebrated on 29 September. *Gabe, Gabi, Gabreal, Gabrel, Gabriele*

Gale (**Gale**) (Celtic) stranger. The Irish word for foreigner is *gall*. (Greek) healer. Named after the famous Greek physician Galen (AD 129–200). *Gael*

Gavin (**Gav**-in) (Welsh) small, white falcon. A form of the medieval name Gawain. *Gavan, Gaven, Gavino Gavyn, Gavynn*

Gay (**Gay**) (French) merry and cheerful. *Gaye*

Gene (**Jeen**) (Greek) noble, well-born. Originally a short form of Eugene, meaning noble, but now a name in its own right. *Jeno*

Germain(e) (Jer-**main**) (Anglo-Saxon) cousin. (from which the word German derives). The female version is usually spelt with an 'e'. (French) from Germany.

Gerry/Jerry (Jair-ee) (English) spear warrior. A name in its own right and also a short form of Gerald, Geraldine, Jeremy and Jerome.

Ghislain(e) (**Giss**-laine) Old English) pledge, or hostage. Also the name of a seventh-century Belgian saint.

Glen (**Glen**) (Welsh) from the valley. A name in its own right and also a short form of Glenys and Glenda. *Gleann, Glendale, Glendon, Glendyn, Glenn, Glin*

Gervaise (Jer-**vaice**) (Norman) the patron saint of haymaking and those trying to discover thieves. Saint's day: 19 June. *Jervaise*

Gladwin (**Glad**-win) (English) happy friend. *Gladwyn*

Gryffyn (**Griff**-in) Welsh spelling of the mythological beast with the body of a lion and the head and wings of an eagle. *Griffen, Griffon, Griffyn, Gryffin*

Gwyn (**Gwin**) (Welsh) blessed or fortunate. A name in its own right and a short form of names beginning with Gwyn, such as Gwyneth.

Hadley (**Had**-lee) (English) from the field of heather.

Hali (**Hal**-ee) (Greek) from the sea. (English) holy.

Harley (**Har**-lee) (Old English) from the clearing of the hares, or from the clearing of the army. *Arlea, Arleigh, Arley, Harlea, Harlee, Harleigh, Harly*

Harper (**Harp**-er) (Old English) harpist or minstrel.

Hilary (**Hill**-a-ree) (Latin) cheerful. Saint Hilary was a key figure in defending the divinity of Christ in the early church. Saint's day: 13 January.

Hollis (**Hol**-iss) (English) from the holly bushes. *Holliss, Hollister, Hillice*

I

Idris (**Id**-riss) (Welsh) fiery, ardent and impulsive. Also the name of a Welsh mountain.

Isidore (**Iz**-i-dore) (Greek) gift of Isis, a river goddess. Isis was also a key deity in Ancient Egypt. Isadora is the usual feminine form. There were several saint Isidores, one of the best-known being Saint Isidore of Seville, who wrote the first encyclopaedia. *Isador, Isadore, Isidor, Issy, Izidor, Izydor, Izzy*

J

Jackie (**Jack**-ee) (English) a pet form of both Jack and Jacqueline. Also used as a name in its own right. *Jackee, Jackey, Jacki, Jacky, Jacqui, Jacquie*

Jade (**Jayd**) (Spanish) from the name of the precious stone. Also the name for a shade of green.

Jael (**Jail**) (Hebrew) meaning either wild goat or to ascend.

Jaime (**Jay**-mee) (French) meaning I love. Also a form of James.

Jamal (Ja-**mal**) (Arabic) handsome one.

Jamie (**Jay**-mee) (English) originally a pet form of James (one of Jesus' disciples), it is now used by both sexes. *Jaimi, Jamee, Jamey, Jami, Jaymee, Jaymie*

Jan (**Jan**) (Hebrew) favoured by God. A form of John, Janet and Janice. Also a Scandinavian and Slavic form of John, which is pronounced Yan. *Jana, Janah, Janina, Janine, Jann*

Jarrah (**Ja**-rah) (Australian) a type of eucalyptus tree.

Jay (**Jay**) (French) a bird that's mainly pinkish-brown, with bright blue on its wings. A name in its own right, but also used as a short form of many names beginning with J. Also the name of several Hindu gods. *Jae, Jai, Jaye*

Jayden (**Jay**-den) (English) an elaborated form of Jade and a variation of Jadon. *Jaden, Jaiden, Jayde, Jaydon*

Jersey (**Jer**-zee) (English) from the grass island. Place name from the Channel Island and the US state, and another name for jumper or pullover.

Jessie (**Jess**-ee) (Hebrew) God sees. *Jess, Jessa, Jessalyn, Jesse*

Jett (**Jet**) (English) from the hard, shiny, black mineral used to make jewellery.

Jocelyn (**Joss**-a-lin) (Latin) the merry one. *Jocelin, Joceline, Joscelin*

Jodene (**Jo**-deen) (English) an elaborated form of Jody. *Jodi, Jodie*

Jody (**Jo**-dee) (Hebrew) a short form of Joseph, meaning God will add, and Josephine, the feminine version.

Jo/Joe (Jo) (English) Joe is the male form, and short for Joseph. Jo is the female form and short for Josephine.
Jonesey (Jone-see) (English) child of someone called Jones.
Jordan (Jor-dan) (Hebrew) literally, to flow down. The name of the major river in the holy land. *Jordaan, Jordain, Jorden, Jordi, Jordon, Jordy*
Jude (Jood) (Hebrew) a boy's name meaning praise to the Lord. One of the twelve Apostles and the patron saint of desperate situations and lost causes. (Hebrew) for girls, a short form of Judith, meaning woman of Judea.
Jules (Jools) (French) the French form of Julius (youthful). Also an American pet name for Julia, Julie or Julian. *Jools, Jule*

K

Kai (Kye) (Welsh) keeper of the keys. (Hawaiian) of the sea. *Keh, Kye*
Keaton (Kee-ton) (English) from the town of the hunting birds. *Keaten, Kearns, Kerney, Kirney*
Keegan (Kee-gan) (Irish) little and fiery.
Keelan (Kee-lan) (Irish) small and slight. *Kaelan, Kealan, Keallan, Keallin, Kellan*
Keeley (Kee-lee) (Irish) good-looking. *Kealey, Kealy, Keelie, Keely*
Kelly (Kell-ee) (Irish) based on the Irish word for church, or the word for fighter – they are very similar in the Irish language.
Kelsey (Kell-see) (Scandinavian) from the island of ships. *Kells, Kelly, Kels, Kelsie, Kelzy*
Kenya (Ken-ya) (Hebrew) animal horn. Also the name of the east African country.
Kerry (Keh-ree) (Irish) dark-haired. Also the name of an Irish county. *Kearie, Keary, Kerr, Kerrey, Kerrie, Kerrigan, Korry*
Kersen (Ker-sen) (Indonesian) cherry. *Kiersen, Kierson, Kiersyn*
Kim (Kim) (English) a short form of Kimberley (after the South African town) and Kimball (warrior chief). *Kym*
Kinsey (Kin-zee) (Old English) from the king's island. The name of the heroine in Sue Grafton's series of murder mysteries. *Kinsee, Kinsie, Kinzee, Kinzie, Kinzy*
Kit (Kit) (English) a short form of either Christopher or Katherine. The Caribbean island of Saint Kitts is named after Saint Christopher, the patron saint of travellers. *Kitt*
Kris (Kris) means a follower of Christ. Short for (girls) Kristine (see Christine), and (boys) Kristian (see Christian).

L

Lacy (**Lacy**) Greek) full of cheer. *Lacey*
Lamar (La-**mar**) (French) from the lake.
Laurel (**Law**-rell) (Latin) from the name of the plant. A form of Laura (girls) and Laurie (gender-neutral). *Lauralle, Laurell, Laurelle, Lauriel, Loralle, Lorel, Lorelle*
Laurie (**Law**-ree) (Latin) crowned with laurels. Originally a short form of Laurence, but used for both sexes. *Laurian, Lauren, Lawrie, Lorrie*
Lee (**Lee**) (English) a person who lives in a clearing in a wood. *Leigh*
Lesley/Leslie (**Lez**-lee) (Scottish) from the grey castle. A place name in Scotland and the name of a prominent Scottish clan. Used mainly for boys in Britain and mainly for girls in the USA. In Britain, Leslie is usually for boys and Lesley for girls. *Leslea, Leslee, Lesleigh, Lesley, Lesli, Lesly, Lezlee, Lezley and Lezlie*
Linden (**Lin**-den) (Old English) from the name of the tree now called linden in North America and lime elsewhere. (It's actually the same tree, but the Americans kept the Old English name.) *Lindon, Lynden, Lyndon*
Lindsey (**Lind**-zee) (English) from the island of linden (or lime) trees. Also, from the marsh of Lincoln. *Linsay, Linsey, Lindsay, Lyndsay, Lyndsey, Lyndsie, Lynsey*
Logan (**Low**-gan) (Irish) from the meadow. A popular name for boys in North America. *Logen, Logun*
Loren (**Law**-ren) (English) a variant of Lorenzo/Laurence for boys, and Lauren for girls. *Loran, Lorin, Loron, Lorren, Loryn*
Lorne (**Lorn**) (Latin) a form of Laurence (laurel) and Lorna (invented by the author of *Lorna Doone*).

Macaulay (Ma-**call**-lay) (Scottish) the actual meaning is son of righteousness, but it is now used for both sexes.
Mackenzie (Ma-**ken**-zee) (Gaelic) means child of the wise ruler, but there is also an influence of the Gaelic word *cainnech*, which means good-looking. *Makensie, Mackenzey, Makenzie, M'Kenzie*
Macy (**Mace**-ee) (French) iron club or mace. The second meaning is from the estate of Matthew. *Macee, Macey, Maci, Macie, Maicey, Maicy*
Maddox (**Mad**-ucks) (Welsh) child of the benefactor.
Madison (**Mad**-iss-un) (Old English) good son, or son of Maud or Maddie. The name of the fourth American president. *Maddie, Maddison, Maddy*

Mallory (**Mal**-or-ee) (Old German) counsellor of the army.
Marlin (**Mar**-lin) (English) a form of Merlin, the Welsh name meaning sea fort. Also a blend of Mary (Latin), meaning bitter, and Lynn (Spanish), meaning pretty. *Marlen, Marlenn, Marlinn, Marrlen, Marrlin, Marlyn*
Marlow (**Mar**-low) (English) driftwood – the literal translation is lake leavings. It became the name of a town in Buckinghamshire, and was then used as a surname for people from that area. Marlowe and Marley are the more common girl's forms. *Marlea, Marloe, Marlowe, Marly*
Marden (**Mar**-den) (English) from the hill near the lake.
Maresha (Ma-**resh**-a) (Hebrew) leader, or from the capital city. It is the name of two men and one city in the Old Testament.
Melbourne (**Mel**-born) (Old English) from the mill stream. The name of the city in Australia, which was named after the Prime Minister of England in 1837, Lord Melbourne. *Mel, Melborn, Melburn, Milborne, Milbourn, Milbourne, Milburn, Millburn, Millburne*
Melrose (**Mel**-rose) (Old English) the male form means from the bare moor; the female form is a condensed form of Melissa Rose.
Mercer (**Mer**-ser) (English) storekeeper. *Merce, Merser*
Meredith (**Mare**-a-dith) (Welsh) great lord or sea lord. *Meradith, Meredithe, Meredyth, Merridie, Meridith, Merry*
Merrill (**Mare**-ill) (Old English/German) the English meaning is sparkling sea. The German form means famous. *Mere, Merell, Merill, Merrell, Merril, Meryll*
Mickey (**Mick**-ee) a diminutive form of Michael (male) and Michelle (female).
Monroe (Mun-**roe**) (Gaelic) its Irish derivation means a person from the mouth of the River Rotha. Its Scottish derivation is from a clan name. The name of the fifth US president, James Monroe. *Monro, Munro*
Monserrat (Mon-**ser**-rat) (Latin) from the jagged mountain. The name of a mountain in Spain, a monastery and a celebrated image of the Virgin Mary. *Montserrat*
Montague (**Mont**-a-gyoo) (French) from the pointed mountain. *Montagu, Monte, Monty*
Morgan (**More**-gan) (Welsh/Old English) dweller by the bright sea. Morgan le Fay was King Arthur's jealous half-sister. *Morgaine, Morgana, Morgance, Morgane, Morganica, Morgann, Morganne, Morgayne, Morgen, Morgin*
Murphy (**Mur**-fee) (Irish) warrior from the sea. *Murphey*
Myrddin (**Mirth**-in) (Welsh) the Welsh form of Merlin, meaning sea fort.

N

Nat (**Nat**) (English) a short form of Nathan, Nathaniel and Natalie. *Nata, Nate, Natty*

Nick/Nicky (**Nick/Nick**-ee) short forms of Dominic, Nicola and Nicholas. The name Nicholas refers to Nike, the Greek goddess of victory. Nikki and Nikko are also Japanese surnames, respectively meaning two trees and daylight. *Nicco, Nickey, Nico, Nikki*

Noel/Noelle (**Nole**/No-**ell**) (French) born at Christmas. *Noela, Noele, Noeleen, Noelene, Noeline, Noell, Noella, Noelleen, Noelynn, Nowel*

Ocean (**O**-shun) from the Greek word for ocean. Sometimes feminized to Oceana, or Latinized for a boy to Oceanus.

Odell (**O**-dell) (Greek) song, ode. (Irish) otter. *Dell, Odall, Odie, Udell*

P

Padgett (**Padj**-ett) (French) attendant or page.

Page (**Page**) (Greek) child. *Pageant, Paige*

Paisley (**Payz**-lee) (Scottish) from the church. Also the name of the patterned fabric first made in the Scottish town of Paisley.

Paris (**Pa**-riss) (Greek) a Trojan prince who eloped with Helen of Sparta and started the Trojan war. The French capital is named after him.

Pascal(e) (Pas-**cal**) (French) one born at Easter. Derived from the French word for Easter (Pâques). Used as a name in English-speaking countries only since the 1960s. Pasquale is the Italian form and Pascual the Spanish.

Pasha (**Pash**-a) (Russian/Greek) the Russian meaning is small, and the Greek form means of the sea.

Payton (**Pay**-ton) (Old English/Irish) the English form means from the warrior's town; the Irish form is a variant of Patricia (female) and Patrick (male). *Paiton, Pathina, Payten, Peyton*

Pelham (**Pell**-am) (Old English) the name originally means one from Pelham, Hertfordshire (there are three towns with Pelham in their name here). *Pellam*

Perry (**Pe**-ree) (Old English) from the pear tree. (Latin) a short form of Peregrine, from which the word pilgrim derives. *Parry, Parr, Parrey, Peer, Per, Perrie*

Phoenix (**Fee**-nix) (Latin) mythical bird, which is reborn in fire; also a city in Arizona, USA.

Piper (**Pie**-per) (English) one who plays the pipes.

Precious (**Presh**-us) (Latin) of great value.

Q

Quincy (**Kwin**-see) (Latin) originally a Roman family name, it means estate of the fifth son. Also the surname of a prominent American family from Massachusetts, whose name is borne by a town and by the sixth US president, John Quincy Adams. *Quin, Quincey, Quinsy*

Quinn (**Kwin**) (Gaelic/English) the Gaelic meaning is one who counsels. A Scottish and Irish surname used as a given name from very ancient times. The English form actually means queen, but is used for both sexes. *Quin, Quinlan*

Quennell(e) (**Kwen**-ell) (French) from the small oak. (English) queen.

R

Randall (**Ran**-dal) (Old English) protected all around. *Randa, Randelle*

Raphael (**Ra**-fay-el) (Hebrew) God has healed. The name of one of the seven Archangels who stand before the throne of God. He is the patron saint of the blind, of happy meetings, and of nurses and doctors. His feast day is 29 September. *Rafaela, Rafaele, Rafaella, Rafela*

Razi (**Raz**-ee) Hebrew) secret. *Raz, Razia, Razzi, Rezi*

Raven (**Ray**-ven) (English) the short form of Ravenel, which means... raven.

Ravenel (**Rav**-en-ell) (Old English) raven. A bird that had special associations with wisdom and death in the Dark Ages.

Rebel (**Reb**-el) (Latin) rebellious one. A popular American celebrity name.

Regan (**Ree**-gan) (Irish) queen. Used by Shakespeare for one of the three daughters of King Lear. In the play, she acts in exactly the manner her name suggests. Now used for both sexes and based on the Irish surname. For this reason, it is sometimes spelled Reagan.

Reece (**Reese**) (Welsh) enthusiastic. Rhys is the native Welsh form. *Rees, Reese, Rice*

René(e) (Ren-**nay**) (French) re-born.

Reuben (**Roo**-ben) (Hebrew) the son who sees. The oldest of Jacob's twelve sons. He persuaded his brothers not to kill Joseph (of the coat), but instead to sell him into slavery. *Reubin, Reubyn*
Rex (**Rex**) (Latin) the Roman word for king or ruler. Also short for Rexford, meaning from the king's ford.
Reynold (**Ren**-old) (English) a wise and powerful ruler. Ray, Raynold
Ricky (**Rick**-ee) (English) a short form of Richard and Frederick, but also a name in its own right. *Ricci, Rickey, Ricki, Rikky*
Riley (**Rye**-lee) (Irish) courageous. (English) from the rye meadow. *Reilly, Rylee, Ryley*
Rio (**Ree**-o) (Spanish) river. A place name, a short form of names ending in -rio, and a name in its own right. Rio de Janeiro means January River in Portuguese; the Rio Grande is the border river between Texas and Mexico. *Reo*
Ripley (**Rip**-lee) (Old English) from the long clearing. *Riplee*
River (**Riv**-er) (English) from the river, or riverbank.
Robin (**Rob**-in) (German) famous. A short form of either Robert or Roberta. Often spelled Robyn for girls.
Rohan (**Roe**-an) (Hindi) sandalwood.
Ronny/Roni (**Ron**-ee) Hebrew) my joy. (English) strong counsel. *Ronni*
Rudy (**Roo**-dee) (English) a familiar form of Rudolf. Most commonly used as a girl's name in North America.
Rusty (**Russ**-tee) (English) a short form of Russell, meaning red-haired.
Rowan (**Roe**-an) (English) from the rowan tree.

S

Sander/Sandy (**San**-der/**San**-dee) (English) a short form of Alexander, Alexandra and Sandra, meaning defender of mankind; and of Lysander (liberator of men).
Sasha (**Sash**-a) (Russian) a shortened version of Alexander or Alexandra, meaning defender of mankind.
Seraiah (Se-**rye**-a) (Hebrew) warrior of God.
Shelby (**Shell**-bee) (English) from the farm on the ledge. *Shel, Shelbey, Shell, Shelly*
Shelley (**Shell**-ee) (English) from the farm on the ledge. (French) a short form of Michelle. *Shellie, Shelly*
Sheridan (**Share**-i-dan) (Old English) derived from the words for eternal and treasure. *Sherida*
Sky (**Sky**) (English) sky.
Stacey/Stacy (**Stay**-see) a short form of Eustace for boys and Anastasia for girls. Increasingly, it is becoming a girl's name only.

T

Tallis (**Tal**-iss) (Persian) wise.
Tally (**Tal**-ee) (Arabic) young lamb.
Tammy (**Tam**-ee) (English) a short form of Thomas (twin) and Tamara (date tree).
Tatum (**Tay**-tum) (Anglo-American) cheerful.
Taylor (**Tay**-ler) (French) to cut. An occupational name for tailors. *Tayla*
Terry (**Teh**-ree) (German/Greek) originally the shortened version of Derek, it is now more commonly short for Terence or Theresa. The female version is usually spelled Teri.
Tierney (**Teer**-nee) (Irish) noble, or lord. Also an Irish surname.
Tobi/Toby (**Toe**-bee) (Hebrew) a short form of Tobias, meaning God is good.
Toni (**Toe**-nee) (Greek) flourishing. (Latin) worthy of praise. *Tonia, Tonie*
Tory/Tori (**Tore**-ee) Short forms of Terence and Victoria.
Trinity (**Trin**-it-ee) (Latin) the holy trinity.

U

Uri (**Oo**-ree) (Hebrew) a short form of Uriah, which means my light.

V

Valery (**Val**-er-ee) (Latin) strong. *Valeria, Valerie*
Vidal (**Vee**-dal) (Latin) full of life.
Vivian(e)/Vivien/Vivienne (**Viv**-ee-an) derived from the Latin word for life and so implies a spirited child who is full of life. The female version is usually spelled Vivienne. Also the name of the magician Merlin's mistress.

Wallis (**Wol**-iss) the Old English word for a person from Wales.
Waverley (**Wave**-er-lee) (English) from the aspen meadow.
Whitley (**Wit**-lee) (English) from the white field.
Whitney (**Wit**-nee) (English) from the white island.
Winnie (**Win**-ee) (English) a short form of Edwina, Gwyneth, Winifred, Winona, Winston, and Wynne.
Wynn (**Win**) (Welsh) fair. The female version is usually spelled Wynne.

Namesakes

In this section you'll find names ranging from the bizarre to the banal. If you're considering naming a child after a celebrity or a fictional character, you'll find the Top Hundreds of these categories, and more, below.

Celebrity choices

There may have been times when your intuition told you that some celebrities had rather let things go to their head, but you lacked the evidence to be absolutely sure. For many people, the following list of baby names for celebrity children will be all the evidence they need.

Parent	**Child/ren**
Bob Geldof, campaigner	Fifi Trixibelle, Peaches Honeyblossom
Bono, U2 singer	Elijah Bob Patricius Guggi Q
Cher, singer	Chastity Sun, Elijah Blue
Christie Brinkley, model	Sailor
David Bowie, singer	Zowie
Elle MacPherson, model	Aurelius
Helena Christensen, model	Mingus
Jackson Lee, film director	Satchel
Jamie Oliver, celebrity cook	Daisy Boo, Poppy Honey
Jason Lee, actor	Pilot Inspektor
Jermaine Jackson, singer	Jermajesty
John Travolta, actor	Jett
Jonathan Davis, singer	Pirate

Jonathan Ross, TV presenter	Honey Kinney, Harvey Kirby, Betty Kitten
Julia Roberts, actress	Phinnaeus
Keith Richard, Rolling Stone	Dandelion
Larry King, TV presenter	Chance
Marcia Gay Harden, actress	Eulala
Marisa Berenson, actress	Starlite Melody
Michael Jackson, singer	Prince Michael, Paris, Blanket
Nicholas Cage, actor	Kal-el (*Superman's name in Krypton*)
Penn Jillette, comedian	Moxie Crimefighter
Rachael Griffiths, actress	Banjo
Richard Gere, actor	Homer James Jigme
Shannyn Sossamon, actress	Audio Science
Sylvester Stallone, actor	Sage Moon Blood
Woody Allen, film director	Moses, Amadeus, Satchel, Lark
Paula Yates, celebrity	Heavenly Hiraani Tiger Lily

The prize, however, must surely go to Frank Zappa, father of five named: Dweezil, Diva Muffin, Ahmed Emuukha, Rodan and Moon Unit. What *was* he thinking?

'If evolution really works, how come mothers only have two hands?'

Milton Berle, 1908–2002, actor.

Pure Puritan

The Puritans had a particular flair for naming. On occasion they would even close their eyes and point a pin randomly at a page in the Bible to find a name. Records in Britain and America show this method produced the following results:

Be-Courteous
Be-Faithful
Be-Thankful
Consider
Faint-Not
Faith-My-Joy
Fear-God
Fear-Not
Fear-The-Lord
Fight-The-Good-Fight-Of-Faith
Fly-Debate
Fly-Fornication
Freegift
From-Above
God-Reward
Hate-Evil
Help-On-High
Jesus-Came-Into-The-World-To-Save
Job-Raked-Out-Of-The-Ashes
Kill-Sin

Mercy-Me
Misericordia-Adulterina
More-Fruit
No-Merit
Pardon
Praise-God
Recompense
Rejoice
Safely-On-High
Search-The-Scriptures
Sin-Deny
Small-Hope
Sorry-For-Sin
Stand-Fast-On-High
The-Lord-Is-Near
Wrestling-With-The-Devil
Zeal-For-The-Lord

And the ever-zippy:
If-Christ-Had-Not-Died-For-Thee-Thou-Hadst-Been-Damned.

Alberts (sic) Ottilie arrived, finally, on August 13th. Tallulah, Xayla-Rae, Inigo and Affrika are enchanted and delighted.

Birth announcement from *The Times*, August 2006.

Real people, real names

Mr B. Careful was Head of Risk Management at Lloyds TSB Bank.

Winner Lane and Loser Lane are two brothers. Winner has been arrested over twenty times by the police. Loser became a sergeant in the New York Police force.

The senior Catholic figure in the Philippines is called Cardinal Sin.

The *Commissaire de Police* of Paris in the 1930s was Charles Adolphe Faux-pas Bidet.

Justin Tune sang for Westminster College Choir in Princeton.

In 1636, Nicholas Bone and Priscilla Skin were married. Charles Swine and Jane Ham went to the altar in 1711. John Mutton and Ann Veale followed in 1791, and Richard Dinner and Mary Cook followed them in 1802.

100 best characters in fiction since 1900

Compiled by *Book Magazine* through a poll of their readers.

Literature can show the songs and sorrows of our souls and so is an ideal source of inspiration for names. Just remember that while the name James may seem attractive to you, it's best avoided if your surname is Bond. And especially if your child is a girl.

1. Jay Gatsby, *The Great Gatsby*. F. Scott Fitzgerald, 1925
2. Holden Caulfield, *The Catcher in the Rye*. J. D. Salinger, 1952
3. Humbert Humbert, *Lolita*. Vladimir Nabokov, 1955
4. Leopold Bloom, *Ulysses*. James Joyce, 1922
5. Rabbit Angstrom, *Rabbit Run*. John Updike, 1960
6. Sherlock Holmes, various titles, Sir Arthur Conan Doyle
7. Atticus Finch, *To Kill a Mockingbird*. Harper Lee, 1960
8. Molly Bloom, *Ulysses*. James Joyce, 1922
9. Stephen Dedalus, *Portrait of the Artist as a Young Man*. James Joyce, 1916
10. Lily Bart, *The House of Mirth*. Edith Wharton, 1905
11. Holly Golightly, *Breakfast at Tiffany's*. Truman Capote, 1958
12. Gregor Samsa, *The Metamorphosis*. Franz Kafka, 1915
13. The Invisible Man, *The Invisible Man*. Ralph Ellison, 1952
14. Lolita, *Lolita*. Vladimir Nabokov, 1955
15. Aureliano Buendia, *One Hundred Years of Solitude*. Gabriel Garcia Marquez, 1967
16. Clarissa Dalloway, *Mrs Dalloway*. Virginia Wolfe, 1925

17. Ignatius Reilly, *A Confederacy of Dunces*. John Kennedy Toole, 1980
18. George Smiley, *Tinker, Tailor, Soldier, Spy*. John le Carré, 1974
19. Mrs Ramsay, *To the Lighthouse*. Virginia Wolfe, 1927
20. Bigger Thomas, *Native Son*. Richard Wright, 1940
21. Nick Adams, *In Our Time*. Ernest Hemingway, 1925
22. Yossarian, *Catch-22*. Joseph Heller, 1961
23. Scarlett O'Hara, *Gone with the Wind*. Margaret Mitchell, 1936
24. Scout Finch, *To Kill a Mockingbird*. Harper Lee, 1960
25. Philip Marlow, *The Big Sleep*. Raymond Chandler, 1939
26. Kurtz, *Heart of Darkness*. Joseph Conrad, 1902
27. Stevens, *The Remains of the Day*. Kazuo Ishiguro, 1989
28. Cosimo Piovasco di Ronda, *The Baron in the Trees*. Italo Calvino, 1957
29. Winnie the Pooh, *Winnie the Pooh*. A. A. Milne, 1926
30. Oskar Matzerath, *The Tin Drum*. Günter Grass, 1959
31. Hazel Motes, *Wise Blood*. Flannery O'Connor, 1952
32. Alex Portnoy, *Portnoy's Complaint*. Philip Roth, 1969
33. Binx Bolling, *The Moviegoer*. Walker Percy, 1961
34. Sebastian Flyte, *Brideshead Revisited*. Evelyn Waugh, 1945
35. Jeeves, *My Man Jeeves*. P. G. Wodehouse, 1919
36. Eugene Henderson, *Henderson the Rain King*. Saul Bellow, 1959
37. Marcel, *Remembrance of Things Past*. Marcel Proust, 1922
38. Toad, *The Wind in The Willows*. Kenneth Grahame, 1908
39. The Cat in the Hat, *The Cat in the Hat*. Dr Seuss, 1955
40. Peter Pan, *The Little White Bird*. J. M. Barrie, 1902
41. Augustus McCrae, *Lonesome Dove*. Larry McMurtry, 1985

42. Sam Spade, *The Maltese Falcon*. Dashiell Hammett, 1930
43. Judge Holden, *Blood Meridian*. Cormac McCarthy, 1985
44. Willie Stark, *All the King's Men*. Robert Penn Warren, 1946
45. Stephen Maturin, *Master and Commander*. Patrick O'Brian, 1969
46. The Little Prince, *The Little Prince*. Antoine de Saint-Exupéry, 1943
47. Santiago, *The Old Man and the Sea*. Ernest Hemingway, 1952
48. Jean Brodie, *The Prime of Miss Jean Brodie*. Muriel Spark, 1961
49. The Whiskey Priest, *The Power and the Glory*, Graham Greene, 1940
50. Neddy Merrill, *The Swimmer*. John Cheever, 1964
51. Sula Peace, *Sula*. Toni Morrison, 1973
52. Meursault, *The Stranger*. Albert Camus, 1942
53. Jake Barnes, *The Sun Also Rises*. Ernest Hemingway, 1926
54. Phoebe Caulfield, *The Catcher in the Rye*. J. D. Salinger, 1951
55. Janie Crawford, *Their Eyes Were Watching God*. Zora Neale Hurston, 1937
56. Antonia Shimerda, *My Antonia*. Willa Cather, 1918
57. Grendel, *Grendel*. John Gardner, 1971
58. Gulley Jimson, *The Horse's Mouth*. Joyce Cary, 1944
59. Big Brother, *1984*. George Orwell, 1949
60. Tom Ripley, *The Talented Mr Ripley*. Patricia Highsmith, 1955
61. Seymour Glass, *Nine Stories*. J. D. Salinger, 1953
62. Dean Moriarty, *On the Road*. Jack Kerouac, 1957
63. Charlotte, *Charlotte's Web*. E. B. White, 1952
64. T. S. Garp, *The World According to Garp*. John Irving, 1978
65. Nick and Nora Charles, *The Thin Man*. Dashiell Hammett, 1934
66. James Bond, various titles. Ian Fleming

67. Mr Bridge, *Mrs Bridge*. Evan S. Connell, 1959
68. Geoffrey Firmin, *Under the Volcano*. Malcolm Lowry, 1947
69. Benjy, *The Sound and the Fury*. William Faulkner, 1929
70. Charles Kinbote, *Pale Fire*. Vladimir Nabokov, 1962
71. Mary Katherine Blackwood, *We Have Always Lived in the Castle*. Shirley Jackson, 1962
72. Charles Ryder, *Brideshead Revisited*. Evelyn Waugh, 1945
73. Claudine, *Claudine at School*. Collette, 1900
74. Florentino Ariza, *Love in the Time of Cholera*. Gabriel Garcia Márquez, 1985
75. George Follandbee Babbitt, *Babbitt*. Sinclair Lewis, 1922
76. Christopher Tietjens, *Parade's End*. Ford Maddox-Ford, 1924–8
77. Frankie Adams, *The Member of the Wedding*. Carson McCullers, 1946
78. The Dog of Tears, *Blindness*. José Saramago, 1995
79. Tarzan, *Tarzan of the Apes*. Edgar Rice Burroughs, 1914
80. Nathan Zuckerman, *My Life as a Man*. Philip Roth, 1979
81. Arthur 'Boo' Radley, *To Kill a Mockingbird*. Harper Lee, 1960
82. Henry Chinaski, *Post Office*. Charles Bukowski, 1971
83. Joseph K. *The Trial*. Frank Kafka, 1925
84. Yuri Zhivago, *Dr Zhivago*. Boris Pasternak, 1957
85. Harry Potter, various titles. J. K. Rowling
86. Hana, *The English Patient*. Michael Ondaatje, 1992
87. Margaret Schlegel, *Howards End*. E. M. Forster, 1910
88. Jim Dixon, *Lucky Jim*. Kingsley Amis, 1954
89. Maurice Bendrix, *The End of the Affair*. Graham Greene, 1951
90. Lennie Small, *Of Mice and Men*. John Steinbeck, 1937

91. Mr Biswas, *A House for Mr Biswas*. V. S. Naipaul, 1961
92. Alden Pyle, *The Quiet American*. Graham Greene, 1955
93. Kimball 'Kim' O'Hara, *Kim*. Rudyard Kipling, 1901
94. Newland Archer, *The Age of Innocence*. Edith Wharton, 1920
95. Clyde Griffiths, *An American Tragedy*. Theodore Dreiser, 1925
96. Eeyore, *Winnie the Pooh*. A. A. Milne, 1926
97. Quentin Compson, *The Sound and the Fury*. William Faulkner, 1929
98. Charlie Marlow, *Heart of Darkness*. Joseph Conrad, 1902
99. Celie, *The Colour Purple*. Alice Walker, 1982
100. Augie March, *The Adventures of Augie March*. Saul Bellow, 1953

Antarctica has the lowest birth rate of any continent (one child, born in 1978.)

The 100 greatest movie characters of all time

As voted for by readers of *Premiere* magazine.

Much of what we see on the silver screen is fantasy and a little of that does us all good. And so does a little borrowing from it.

1. Vito Corleone from *The Godfather*
2. Fred C. Dobbs from *The Treasure of the Sierra Madre*
3. Scarlett O'Hara from *Gone with the Wind*
4. Norman Bates from *Psycho*
5. James Bond from *Dr No*
6. Annie Hall from *Annie Hall*
7. Indiana Jones from *Raiders of the Lost Ark*
8. Ellen Ripley from *Alien*
9. Jeff Spicoli from *Fast Times at Ridgemont High*
10. Gollum from *Lord of the Rings*
11. Margo Channing from *All About Eve*
12. Charles Foster Kane from *Citizen Kane*
13. Atticus Finch from *To Kill a Mockingbird*
14. Randle McMurphy from *One Flew over the Cuckoo's Nest*
15. Hannibal Lecter from *The Silence of the Lambs*
16. Robin Hood from *The Adventures of Robin Hood*
17. Dorothy Gale from *The Wizard of Oz*
18. Carl Spackler from *Caddyshack*
19. Rick Blaine from *Casablanca*

20. Virgil Tibbs from *In the Heat of the Night*
21. Susan Vance from *Bringing up Baby*
22. Travis Bickle from *Taxi Driver*
23. Ethan Edwards from *The Searchers*
24. The Little Tramp from *Mabel's Strange Predicament*
25. Gordon Gekko from *Wall Street*
26. ET from *ET the Extra-Terrestial*
27. Marge Gunderson from *Fargo*
28. Captain Quint from *Jaws*
29. Daphne/Jerry from *Some Like It Hot*
30. King Kong from *King Kong*
31. Norma Desmond from *Sunset Boulevard*
32. Holly Golightly from *Breakfast at Tiffany's*
33. Ratso Rizzo from *Midnight Cowboy*
34. Bonnie Parker from *Bonnie and Clyde*
35. Dr Evil from *Austin Powers*
36. Alex Forrest from *Fatal Attraction*
37. Jake Gittes from *Chinatown*
38. Willy Wonka form *Willy Wonka & the Chocolate Factory*
39. Michael Dorsey/Dorothy Michaels from *Tootsie*
40. The Terminator from *The Terminator*
41. Jane Craig from *Broadcast News*
42. 'Dirty' Harry Callahan from *Dirty Harry*
43. Forrest Gump from *Forrest Gump*
44. Jules Winnfield from *Pulp Fiction*
45. Mary Poppins from *Mary Poppins*
46. John McClane from *Die Hard*

47. Mrs Robinson from *The Graduate*
48. John 'Bluto' Blutarsky from *Animal House*
49. Chance the gardener from *Being There*
50. Blondie from *The Good, The Bad and The Ugly*
51. Freddy Krueger from *A Nightmare on Elm Street*
52. Howard Beale from *Network*
53. Ninotchka from *Ninotchka*
54. Frank Booth from *Blue Velvet*
55. The Dude from *The Big Lebowski*
56. Alan Swann from *My Favourite Year*
57. Tom Powers from *The Public Enemy*
58. Phyliss Dietrichson from *Double Indemnity*
59. Lt Kilgore from *Apocalypse Now*
60. George Bailey from *It's a Wonderful Life*
61. J. J. Hunsecker from *Sweet Smell of Success*
62. John Shaft from *Shaft*
63. Carrie White from *Carrie*
64. Rocky Balboa from *Rocky*
65. Edward Scissorhands from *Edward Scissorhands*
66. Navin Johnson from *The Jerk*
67. Inspector Clouseau from *The Pink Panther*
68. Alex DeLarge from *A Clockwork Orange*
69. Terry Malloy from *On the Waterfront*
70. Judy Benjamin from *Private Benjamin*
71. Revd Harry Powell from *The Night of the Hunter*
72. Lloyd Dobler from *Say Anything*
73. Norma Rae from *Norma Rae*

74. Tony Montana from *Scarface*
75. Dr Strangelove from *Dr Strangelove*
76. Tony Manero from *Saturday Night Fever*
77. Annie Wilkes from *Misery*
78. 'Mad' Max Rockatansky from *Mad Max*
79. Hans Beckert from *M*
80. Sam Spade from *The Maltese Falcon*
81. Aurora Greenway from *Terms of Endearment*
82. Jack Torrance from *The Shining*
83. William Cutting from *Gangs of New York*
84. Darth Vader from *Star Wars*
85. Stanley Kowalski from *A Streetcar Named Desire*
86. Melanie Daniels from *The Birds*
87. Captain Jack Sparrow from *Pirates of the Caribbean*
88. Raymond Babbit from *Rain Man*
89. Sandy Ollson from *Grease*
90. John Malkovich from *Being John Malkovich*
91. Mrs Iselin from *The Manchurian Candidate*
92. Dil from *The Crying Game*
93. Harry Lime from *The Third Man*
94. Rose Sayer from *The African Queen*
95. Oda Mae Brown from *Ghost*
96. Tommy DeVito from *Goodfellas*
97. Ace Ventura from *Ace Ventura: Pet Detective*
98. Antoine Doinel from *The 400 Blows*
99. Kevin McCallister from *Home Alone*
100. Roger 'Verbal' Kint from *The Usual Suspects*

Top 100 singers of all time

Compiled from a poll of *MOJO* readers.

If you both have a musical hero, it might well make a good basis for choosing a name – just be aware of the usual pitfalls.

1. John Lennon
2. Elvis Presley
3. Aretha Franklin
4. Frank Sinatra
5. Bob Dylan
6. Roy Orbison
7. Paul McCartney
8. Otis Redding
9. Robert Plant
10. Ray Charles
11. Van Morrison
12. Marvin Gaye
13. David Bowie
14. Dusty Springfield
15. Sandy Denny
16. Mick Jagger
17. Sam Cooke
18. Brian Wilson
19. Joni Mitchell
20. Captain Beefheart
21. Eric Burdon
22. Freddie Mercury
23. Howlin' Wolf
24. Ella Fitzgerald
25. Tom Waits
26. Roger Daltry
27. Nina Simone
28. John Fogerty
29. Steve Marriott
30. Jim Morrison
31. Richard Manuel
32. Morrissey
33. Michael Stipe
34. Billie Holiday
35. Smokey Robinson
36. Jeff Buckley
37. Ray Davis
38. James Taylor
39. Neil Young
40. Tim Buckley

41. Buddy Holly
42. Stevie Wonder
43. Emmylou Harris
44. Little Richard
45. Johnny Cash
46. k. d. lang
47. Willie Nelson
48. Kate Bush
49. Peter Green
50. Thom Yorke
51. Barbra Streisand
52. Nat King Cole
53. Bessie Smith
54. Lowell George
55. Patsy Cline
56. Rod Stewart
57. Jerry Lee Lewis
58. Joe Cocker
59. Lou Reed
60. Karen Carpenter
61. Paul Rogers
62. Scott Walker
63. Elvis Costello
64. Bonnie Raitt
65. Art Garfunkel
66. Bobby Darin
67. Bob Marley
68. John Martyn
69. Harry Nilsson
70. Charlie Rich
71. James Brown
72. Gram Parsons
73. Janis Joplin
74. Robert Wyatt
75. Tori Amos
76. Nick Drake
77. Beth Gibbons
78. Joan Baez
79. Ian Curtis
80. Donald Fagen
81. Patti Smith
82. Paul Buchanan
83. Prince
84. Roger Chapman
85. Liam Gallagher
86. Tracy Thorn
87. Paul Weller
88. Al Green
89. Levi Stubbs
90. Robert Johnson
91. Hank Williams
92. Aaron Neville
93. Dionne Warwick
94. Curtis Mayfield

95. June Tabor
96. Big Joe Turner
97. Diana Ross
98. Kurt Cobain
99. Solomon Burke
100. Tina Turner

A guide to the laws for **registering births**

Please note: the following is meant as a guide for each country rather than a definitive statement of the law.

United Kingdom

If your baby was born in England, Wales or Northern Ireland you should register the birth within 42 days. Usually this is done at the local registry office, but in some hospitals they can even do it at the bedside.

In Scotland you only have 21 days to register the birth.

Who can register the birth?

It largely depends on whether you are married. If you are, then either of you can register the birth on your own. If you are not, then the mother can still register the birth on her own and, in certain circumstances, so can other people. These are:

- the father, but only if he has a Form 16. This is available from the registry office and is basically a statutory declaration by mother and father that both parties believe him to be the natural father. If the father can't make it to the registry office, but wants to be acknowledged as the father, then this form, handed in by someone else at the time of registration, will do that.

Provided there are reasonable grounds for doing so, other people who can register the birth are:

- the occupier of the house or hospital where the child was born;
- someone who was present at the birth;
- someone who is responsible for the child.

Changing names later in life

People can apply to change their own names once they reach 18 (16 in Scotland).

Some parents want to change their child's name prior to their reaching 16 or 18. The most common reason for this is in order for a child to be confirmed into a particular church. Only the mother, father or guardian of a child can apply to change a child's forename. And if the child is given the new forenames by baptism, the minister with custody of the baptismal register needs to complete a form as well.

If your reasons for changing the child's name are based on 'regular use', you need to provide documentary evidence that the new forenames have indeed been used within 12 months of registration.

Other restrictions include:

- forename changes can only be made once in the birth register – any later forename changes cannot be recorded;
- if your child has been baptized within twelve months of the birth registration, only the baptismal names may be added to the register.

The new forenames are written in the space at the end of the birth record and you need to arrange for this to be done by the registry office where the birth was registered. If you no longer live in that area, you can post the paperwork to them.

What details are required to register a birth?

In all UK countries you should take the document given to you by the hospital, your marriage certificate and, ideally, some other form of ID.

What will the registrar give you?

Once the registration is completed, the registrar will give you one free, short birth certificate and an infant registration card to register with the family doctor.

Further certified copies – either short or full – may be purchased from the registrar at the time of registration. There is a charge for the full version and you'll need this to get a passport for your child.

In case you were wondering, there's no law in Britain restricting what you can call your child. Parents are free to choose any name they want, although as Alison Cathcart, superintendent registrar at Westminster Registrars' Office commented, 'if someone is from a different culture and wants to register a name that sounds like a swear word in English, then we do advise them of that.'

Eire

A birth notification form will usually be completed with the parent(s) by hospital staff (in the case of hospital births); or by a doctor or midwife (for home births).

The law says you must register a child's name within three months of birth, but it also says you do not have to give the child an actual name at that point. Possibly, the law was designed to accommodate parents who can't agree on a name, but feel they'd like a naming ceremony anyway.

Recent changes mean the birth no longer needs to be registered in the district where the birth occurred. Rather, you can choose whichever registry office is easiest for you.

In the case of a birth where the parents are married to each other, either parent can register the child. The position with unmarried couples is more complicated, so the General Registrar of Ireland has produced a 'simplified guide' that reads that a birth can be registered:

> 'At the written joint request of the father and mother (Form CRA 9). In this case, both parents will be required to attend together at the Office of the Registrar to sign the Register of Births.
>
> At the written request of the mother on production of a declaration by her naming the father. This form (CRA 1) must be accompanied by a Statutory Declaration by the father acknowledging paternity (Form CRA 3). In this case, the mother will be required to attend at the Office of the Registrar to sign the Register of Births.
>
> At the written request of the father on production of a declaration by him acknowledging paternity. This form (CRA 2) must be accompanied by a Statutory Declaration by the mother naming the father (Form CRA 4). In this case, the father will be required to attend at the Office of the Registrar to sign the register of Births.

> At the written request of the mother (Form CRA 5 completed), or the father (Form CRA 6 completed), on production of a certified copy of any court order issued by the District, or Circuit Court regarding guardianship of infants or maintenance, or under the Social Welfare (Consolidation) Act 1993 naming him as the father of the child. In this case, the mother (if CRA 5 used), or father (if CRA 6 used) will be required to attend at the Office of the Registrar to sign the Register of Births. Please ensure all parties are named fully and correctly on the court order.'

There is also a form – CRA 7 – that men can fill in to state they are not the father of a particular child. There is no upper limit to how many of these forms a man may fill in.

New Zealand

In New Zealand you are meant to register a child 'as soon as is reasonably practicable after the birth'. In practice, this means within two months.

How to do it

A 'Notification of Birth for Registration' form is generally provided to the parent(s) shortly after the birth. You just fill it in and post it to:
Births, Deaths and Marriages
PO Box 31203
Lower Hutt
New Zealand

(Of the major English-speaking countries, New Zealand is the only one with a single, central place for registering births, deaths and marriages.)

One power of the New Zealand Registry is that, as in Sweden, Brazil, France and Germany, parents can be barred from giving silly names to their offspring.

South Africa

In South Africa, basically you are asked to register your child within 30 days of birth and all you need to do is fill out the BI-24 form and submit it to your nearest Home Affairs office. You will need to bring your ID books and the child's hospital certificate or clinic card, but that's about it. There are no fees for registering.

If you cannot register within the 30 days, it doesn't seem to be much of a problem. There are forms for registering between 30 days and one year, between one year and 15 years, and for over 15 years. It seems they are just happy that you registered.

Australia, Canada and America

It is very difficult to provide detailed advice for registering births in these three countries because, in each case, everything happens at state level. The nearest things to general rules are that Australians should register a birth within 60 days and Canadians within 30. Apart from that, there are different fees, forms and procedures depending on where you live.

Bibliography

Periodicals

Doyle, Brian. 'Naming: A Name Is a Thing of Immense Power.' *America* 170, No. 16 (7 May 1994), pp. 10–12.

Sagert, Kelly. 'Angela Barbara, Cheri'. *Hopscotch* 8, No. 2 (August-September 1996), pp. 20–2.

'Top 5 Baby Names'. *Time for Kids* 1, no. 16 (February 16, 1996).

Books

7,000 Baby Names. (Cippenham, Berkshire: Foulsham, 2001).

Anderson, Christopher P. *The Name Game.* (New York: Simon and Schuster, 1977).

Baby Names Day by Day (London. Hamlyn: 2005).

Cresswell, Julia. *Bloomsbury Dictionary of First Names* (London: Bloomsbury, 1991).

Delaforce, Gillian. *The Little Book of Baby Names* (London: Vermillion, 2004).

Dictionary of First Names (New Lanark, Scotland: Geddes & Grosset, 2000).

Dunkling, Leslie Alan. *The Guinness Book of Names* (Enfield, Middlesex. Guinness Publishing, 1993).

Fergusson, Rosalind. *Choose Your Baby's Name* (London: Penguin, 1987).

Hanks, P., & Hodges, F. *A Concise Dictionary of First Names* (Oxford. OUP: 2001).

Mehrabian, Albert. *The Name Game: The Decision that Lasts a Lifetime* (Bethesda, Maryland: National Press Books, 1990).

Osborn, Susan. *What's in a name?* (New York: Simon and Schuster, 1999).

Rose, Margaret *Baby Names for Dummies* (Indianapolis: Wiley, 2005).

Rosenkrantz, Linda. *Last Word on First Names* (New York: St Martin's Press, 1997).

Satran, P., & Rosencrantz, L. *Cool Names for Babies.* (London: HarperCollins, 2004).

Shaw, Lisa. *Everything you need to know about Baby Names.* (Newton Abbott, Devon. David & Charles, 2005).

Spence, Hilary. *The Modern book of Babies' Names* (London: Foulsham, 1999).

Spence, Hilary. *The Complete Book of Baby Names* (Cippenham, Berkshire: Foulsham, 2001).

Stafford, Diane. *40,001 Best Baby Names* (London: Vermilion, 2004).
Wilson, Stuart. *Simply the Best Baby Name Book* (London: Pan, 2001).
Wood, Emily. *The Virgin Book of Baby Names* (London: Virgin Books, 2006).

Internet sites

African

namesite.com/namesite/mainpage.html
swagga.com/name.htm

Biblical

ballina.net/babynames/
biblical-baby-names.com
http://en.wikipedia.org/wiki/List_of_Biblical_names

Chinese

mandarintools.com/chinesename.html

English

www.s-gabriel.org/names/english.shtml

General

20000-names.com/index.htm
babycenter.com/babyname/index.html
babyhold.com
babynameaddicts.com
babynamegenie.com
babynamenetwork.com/
BabyNamesGarden.com
babynamesheaven.com
babynology.com/
behindthename.com
bellaonline.com/subjects/2070.asp
cool-baby-names.com/

geocities.com/edgarbook/names/welcome.html
kabalarians.com/gkh/your.htm ummah.org.uk/family.html
last-names.net/
name-meanings.com/
nameyobaby.com
parenthoodweb.com/parent_cfmfiles/babynames.cfm
ruf.rice.edu/~pound/
thenamemachine.com/
thenamesite.com
thinkbabynames.com
vornamen-liste.de/index_eng.html
zoope.com/about/about_names.html

Hungarian
geocities.com/Athens/1336/magfem.html
geocities.com/Athens/1336/magyar16.html
geocities.com/Athens/1336/magyarnames101.html

Indian
babynamesindia.com
indiaexpress.com/specials/babynames
sikhs.org/names.htm

Medieval
s-gabriel.org/names/

Pacific and Asia
heptune.com/ocnames.html

Saints
catholic.org/saints

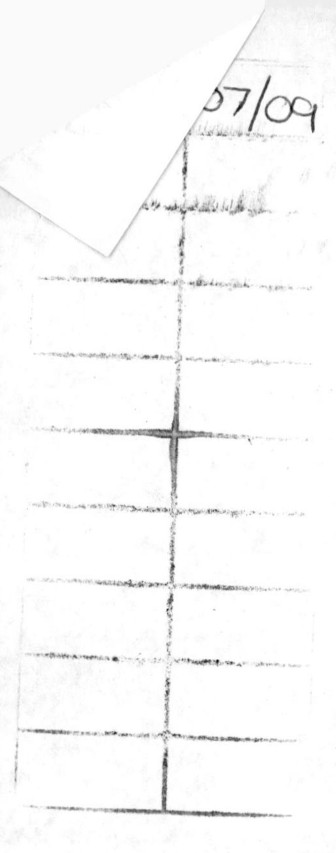
07/09